Workshop on Biomedical Natural Language Processing

(BioNLP 2013)

Sofia, Bulgaria
8 August 2013

ISBN: 978-1-62748-980-5

Printed from e-media with permission by:

Curran Associates, Inc.
57 Morehouse Lane
Red Hook, NY 12571

Some format issues inherent in the e-media version may also appear in this print version.

Printed by Curran Associates, Inc. (2013)

Association for Computational Linguistics
209 N. Eighth Street
Stroudsburg, Pennsylvania 18360

Phone: 1-570-476-8006
Fax: 1-570-476-0860

acl@aclweb.org

Additional copies of this publication are available from:

Curran Associates, Inc.
57 Morehouse Lane
Red Hook, NY 12571 USA
Phone: 845-758-0400
Fax: 845-758-2634
Email: curran@proceedings.com
Web: www.proceedings.com

ACL 2013

BioNLP 2013

2013 Workshop on Biomedical Natural Language Processing

Proceedings of the Workshop

August 8, 2013
Sofia, Bulgaria

Introduction

BioNLP 2013 has accepted 11 outstanding full papers and five posters. The themes in this year's papers and posters are divided equally between clinical and biomedical text processing. In addition to the customary research in practical and theoretical issues, such as domain adaptation, question answering, temporal relations extraction, and evaluation of text mining methods, this year, we see a growing body of research in languages other than English. The issues with clinical text processing in resource-poor languages are also discussed in the keynote presentation.

Keynote: Processing clinical narratives in less-resourced languages: the challenge to start from scratch

Galia Angelova, Ph.D. Linguistic Modeling Department, Institute of Information and Communication Technologies, Bulgarian Academy of Sciences

Dr. Angelova presents automatic analysis of free texts in Bulgarian hospital discharge letters of patients with endocrine and metabolic diseases. Processing Bulgarian clinical texts is challenging due to some specific reasons: the notes contain about 37% Latin terms that might occur in Latin alphabet characters as well as transliterated to Cyrillic alphabet (34% of all tokens); the lack of important medical nomenclatures in Bulgarian: for example, the ATC classification is supported in Latin only and requires manual augmentation with Bulgarian drug names in Cyrillic alphabet; no electronic resource with medical terminology is available so the collection of terms and important phrases involves analysis of documents, such as manuals for coding to ICD-10 terms, or collection of collocations directly from the corpus of discharge letters, among others. Currently available resources and methods include automatic recognition of ICD-10 diagnoses; drugs, especially those taken during hospitalization; patient status; values of laboratory tests; and the temporal structure of diabetic case histories. Dr. Angelova discusses scenarios for application of the extraction components in practical settings when cleaning and validation of patient data is required.

Dr. Claire Nedellec presents an overview of the BioNLP Shared Task 2013.

Acknowledgments

We are profoundly grateful to the authors who chose BioNLP as venue for presenting their innovative research. The authors' willingness to share their work through BioNLP consistently makes the workshop noteworthy among the increasing numbers of available venues. We are equally indebted to the program committee members (listed elsewhere in this volume) who produced at least three thorough reviews per paper on a tight review schedule and with an admirable level of insight. Finally, we acknowledge the gracious sponsorship of the Computational Medicine Center and Division of Biomedical Informatics, Cincinnati Children's Hospital Medical Center.

Organizers:

Kevin Bretonnel Cohen, University of Colorado School of Medicine
Dina Demner-Fushman, US National Library of Medicine
Sophia Ananiadou, University of Manchester and National Centre for Text Mining, UK
John Pestian, Computational Medical Center, University of Cincinnati,
Cincinnati Children's Hospital Medical Center
Jun'ichi Tsujii, Microsoft Research Asia
and National Centre for Text Mining, UK

Program Committee:

Emilia Apostolova, DePaul University, USA
Eiji Aramaki, University of Tokyo, Japan
Alan Aronson, US National Library of Medicine
Sabine Bergler, Concordia University, Canada
Olivier Bodenreider, US National Library of Medicine
Kevin Cohen, University of Colorado, USA
Nigel Collier, National Institute of Informatics, Japan
Dina Demner-Fushman, US National Library of Medicine
Noemie Elhadad, Columbia University, USA
Marcelo Fiszman, US National Library of Medicine
Filip Ginter, University of Turku, Finland
Graciela Gonzalez, Arizona State University, USA
Antonio Jimeno Yepes, NICTA, Australia
Halil Kilicoglu, US National Library of Medicine
Jin-Dong Kim, University of Tokyo, Japan
Robert Leaman, US National Library of Medicine
Ulf Leser, Humboldt University of Berlin, Germany
Zhiyong Lu, US National Library of Medicine
Makoto Miwa, National Centre for Text Mining, UK
Naoaki Okazaki, Tohoku University, Japan
Jong Park, KAIST, South Korea
Rashmi Prasad, University of Wisconsin-Milwaukee, USA
Sampo Pyysalo, National Centre for Text Mining, UK
Bastien Rance, Georges Pompidou European Hospital, France
Andrey Rzhetsky, University of Chicago, USA
Matthew Simpson, US National Library of Medicine
Pontus Stenetorp, University of Tokyo, Japan
Yoshimasa Tsuruoka, University of Tokyo, Japan
Karin Verspoor, NICTA, Australia
W. John Wilbur, US National Library of Medicine
Pierre Zweigenbaum, LIMSI, France

Invited Speakers:

Galia Angelova, Bulgarian Academy of Sciences
Processing clinical narratives in less-resourced languages: the challenge to start from scratch
Claire Nedellec, INRA
Overview of the BioNLP Shared Task 2013

Table of Contents

Conference Program

Thursday, August 8, 2013

8:40–8:50 Opening Remarks

Session 1: Clinical text processing

8:50–9:10 *Earlier Identification of Epilepsy Surgery Candidates Using Natural Language Processing*
Pawel Matykiewicz, Kevin Cohen, Katherine D. Holland, Tracy A. Glauser, Shannon M. Standridge, Karen M. Verspoor and John Pestian

9:10–9:30 *Identification of Patients with Acute Lung Injury from Free-Text Chest X-Ray Reports*
Meliha Yetisgen-Yildiz, Cosmin Bejan and Mark Wurfel

9:30–9:50 *Discovering Temporal Narrative Containers in Clinical Text*
Timothy Miller, Steven Bethard, Dmitriy Dligach, Sameer Pradhan, Chen Lin and Guergana Savova

9:50–10:10 *Identifying Pathological Findings in German Radiology Reports Using a Syntacto-semantic Parsing Approach*
Claudia Bretschneider, Sonja Zillner and Matthias Hammon

10:10–10:30 *Corpus-Driven Terminology Development: Populating Swedish SNOMED CT with Synonyms Extracted from Electronic Health Records*
Aron Henriksson, Maria Skeppstedt, Maria Kvist, Martin Duneld and Mike Conway

10:30–11:00 Morning coffee break

11:00–12:00 Invited Talk by Galia Angelova

12:00–12:30 BioNLP Shared Task overview by Claire Nedellec

12:30–14:00 Lunch break

Thursday, August 8, 2013 (continued)

Session 2: Biomedical language processing

14:00–14:20 *Unsupervised Linguistically-Driven Reliable Dependency Parses Detection and Self-Training for Adaptation to the Biomedical Domain*
Felice Dell'Orletta, Giulia Venturi and Simonetta Montemagni

14:20–14:40 *Interpreting Consumer Health Questions: The Role of Anaphora and Ellipsis*
Halil Kilicoglu, Marcelo Fiszman and Dina Demner-Fushman

14:40–15:00 *Evaluating Large-scale Text Mining Applications Beyond the Traditional Numeric Performance Measures*
Sofie Van Landeghem, Suwisa Kaewphan, Filip Ginter and Yves Van de Peer

15:00–15:20 *Recognizing Sublanguages in Scientific Journal Articles through Closure Properties*
Irina Temnikova and Kevin Cohen

15:30–16:00 Afternoon coffee break

16:00–16:20 *BEL Networks Derived from Qualitative Translations of BioNLP Shared Task Annotations*
Juliane Fluck, Alexander Klenner, Sumit Madan, Sam Ansari, Tamara Bobic, Julia Hoeng, Martin Hofmann-Apitius and Manuel Peitsch

16:20–16:40 *Exploring Word Class N-grams to Measure Language Development in Children*
Gabriela Ramirez-de-la-Rosa, Thamar Solorio, Manuel Montes, Yang Liu, Lisa Bedore, Elizabeth Pena and Aquiles Iglesias

Poster Session (16:40–17:30)

Adapting a Parser to Clinical Text by Simple Pre-processing Rules
Maria Skeppstedt

Using the Argumentative Structure of Scientific Literature to Improve Information Access
Antonio Jimeno Yepes, James Mork and Alan Aronson

Using Latent Dirichlet Allocation for Child Narrative Analysis
Khairun-nisa Hassanali, Yang Liu and Thamar Solorio

Effect of Out Of Vocabulary Terms on Inferring Eligibility Criteria for a Retrospective Study in Hebrew EHR
Raphael Cohen and Michael Elhadad

Thursday, August 8, 2013 (continued)

Earlier Identification of Epilepsy Surgery Candidates Using Natural Language Processing

Pawel Matykiewicz[1], Kevin Bretonnel Cohen[2], Katherine D. Holland[1], Tracy A. Glauser[1], Shannon M. Standridge[1], Karin M. Verspoor[3,4], and John Pestian[1]§
[1] Cincinnati Children's Hospital Medical Center, Cincinnati OH USA
[2] University of Colorado, Denver, CO
[3] National ICT Australia and [4]The University of Melbourne, Melbourne, Australia
§corresponding author: john.pestian@cchmc.org

Abstract

This research analyzed the clinical notes of epilepsy patients using techniques from corpus linguistics and machine learning and predicted which patients are candidates for neurosurgery, i.e. have intractable epilepsy, and which are not. Information-theoretic and machine learning techniques are used to determine whether and how sets of clinic notes from patients with intractable and non-intractable epilepsy are different. The results show that it is possible to predict from an early stage of treatment which patients will fall into one of these two categories based only on text data. These results have broad implications for developing clinical decision support systems.

1 Introduction and Significance

Epilepsy is a disease characterized by recurrent seizures that may cause irreversible brain damage. While there are no national registries, epidemiologists have shown that roughly three million Americans require $17.6 billion USD in care annually to treat their epilepsy (Epilepsy Foundation, 2012; Begley et al., 2000). Epilepsy is defined by the occurrence of two or more unprovoked seizures in a year. Approximately 30% of those individuals with epilepsy will have seizures that do not respond to anti-epileptic drugs (Kwan and Brodie, 2000). This population of individuals is said to have intractable or drug-resistant epilepsy (Kwan et al., 2010).

Select intractable epilepsy patients are candidates for a variety of neurosurgical procedures that ablate the portion of the brain known to cause the seizure. On average, the gap between the initial clinical visit when the diagnosis of epilepsy is made and surgery is six years. If it were possible to predict which patients should be considered candidates for referral to surgery earlier in the course of treatment, years of damaging seizures, under-employment, and psychosocial distress may be avoided. It is this gap that motivates this research.

In this study, we examine the differences between the clinical notes of patients early in their treatment course with the intent of predicting which patients will eventually be diagnosed as intractable versus which will be amenable to drug-based treatment. The null hypothesis is that there will be no detectable differences between the clinic notes of patients who go on to a diagnosis of intractable epilepsy and patients who do not progress to the diagnosis of intractable epilepsy (figure 1). To further elucidate the phenomenon, we look at both the patient's earliest clinical notes and notes from a progression of time points. Here we expect to gain insight into how the linguistic characteristics (and natural language processing-based classification performance) evolve over treatment course. We also study the linguistic features that characterize the differences between the document sets from the two groups of patients. We anticipate that this approach will ultimately be adapted for various clinical decision support systems.

2 Background

2.1 Related work

Although there has been extensive work on building predictive models of disease progression and of mortality risk, few models take advantage of natural language processing in addressing this task.

(Abhyankar et al., 2012) used univariate analysis, multivariate logistic regression, sensitivity analyses, and Cox proportional hazards models to predict 30-day and 1-year survival of overweight and obese Intensive Care Unit patients. As one of the features in their system, they used smoking status extracted from patient records by natural language processing techniques.

(Himes et al., 2009) used a Bayesian network model to predict which asthma patients would go on to develop chronic obstructive pulmonary disease. As one of their features, they also used smoking status extracted from patient records by natural language processing techniques.

(Huang et al., under review) is the work most similar to our own. They evaluated the ability of a Naive Bayesian classifier to predict future diagnoses of depression six months prior and twelve months prior to the actual diagnoses. They used a number of feature types, including fielded data such as billing codes, ICD-9 CM diagnoses, and others, as well as data drawn from natural language processing.

In particular, they used an optimized version of the NCBO Annotator (Jonquet et al., 2009) to recognize terms from 22 clinically relevant ontologies and classify them additionally as to whether they were negated or related to the patient's family history. Their system demonstrated an ability to predict diagnoses of depression both six months and one year prior to the actual diagnoses at a rate that exceeds the success of primary care practitioners in diagnosing active depression.

Considering this body of work overall, natural language processing techniques have played a minor role, providing only a fraction of a much larger set of features—just one feature, in the first two studies discussed. In contrast, in our work natural language processing is the central aspect of the solution.

2.2 Theoretical background to the approaches used in this work

In comparing the document sets from the two patient populations, we make use of two lines of inquiry. In the first, we use information-theoretic methods to determine whether or not the contents of the data sets are different, and if they are different, to characterize the differences. In the second, we make use of a practical method from applied machine learning. In particular, we determine whether it is possible to train a classifier to distinguish between documents from the two sets of patients, given an appropriate classification algorithm and a reasonable set of features.

From information-theoretic methods, we take Kullback-Leibler divergence as a way to determine whether the contents of the two sets of documents are the same or different. Kullback-Leibler divergence is the relative entropy of two probability mass functions—"a measure of how different two probability distributions (over the same event space) are" (Manning and Schuetze, 1999). This measure has been previously used to assess the similarity of corpora (Verspoor et al., 2009). Details of the calculation of Kullback-Leibler divergence are given in the Methods section. Kullback-Leibler divergence has a lower bound of zero; with a value of zero, the two document sets would be identical. A value of 0.005 is assumed to correspond to near-identity.

From practical applications of machine learning, we test whether or not it is possible to train a classifier to distinguish between documents from the two document sets. The line of thought here is that provided that we have an appropriate classification algorithm and a reasonable feature set, then if clinic notes from the two document sets are indeed different, it should be possible to train a classifier to distinguish between them with reasonable accuracy.

3 Materials and methods

3.1 Materials

The experimental protocol was approved by our local Institutional Review Board (#2012-1646). Neurology clinic notes were extracted from the electronic medical record system. Records were sampled from two groups of patients: 1) those with intractable epilepsy referred for and eventually undergoing epilepsy surgery and 2) those with epilepsy who were responsive to medications and never referred for surgical evaluation. They were also sampled at three time periods before the "zero point", the date at which patients were either referred for surgery or the date of last seizure for the non-intractable group. Table 1 shows the distribution of patients and clinic notes.

3.2 Methods

As described in the introduction, we applied information-theoretic and machine learning techniques to determine whether the two document collections were different (or differentiable).

	Non-Intractable	Intractable
-12 to 0	355 (127)	641 (155)
-6 to +6	453 (128)	898 (155)
0 to +12 months	454 (132)	882 (149)

Table 1: Progress note and patient counts (in parentheses) for each time period. A minus sign indicates the period before surgery referral date for intractable epilepsy patients and before last seizure for non-intractable patients. A plus sign indicates the period after surgery referral for intractable epilepsy patients and after last seizure for non-intractable patients. Zero is the surgery referral date or date of last seizure for the two populations, respectively.

3.2.1 Feature extraction

Features for both the calculation of Kullback-Leibler divergence and the machine learning experiment were unigrams, bigrams, trigrams, and quadrigrams. We applied the National Library of Medicine stopword list `http://mbr.nlm.nih.gov/Download/2009/WordCounts/wrd_stop`. All words were lower-cased, all numerals were substituted with the string *NUMB* for abstraction, and all non-ASCII characters were removed.

3.3 Information-theoretic approach

Kullback-Leibler divergence compares probability distribution of words or n-grams between different datasets $D_{KL}(P||Q)$. In particular, it measures how much information is lost if distribution Q is used to approximate distribution P. This method, however, gives an asymmetric dissimilarity measure. **Jensen-Shannon divergence** is probably the most popular symmetrization of D_{KL} and is defined as follows:

$$D_{JS} = \frac{1}{2}D_{KL}(P||Q) + \frac{1}{2}D_{KL}(Q||P) \quad (1)$$

where

$$D_{KL}(P||Q) = \sum_{w \in P \cup Q} \left(p(w|c_P) \log \frac{p(w|c_P)}{p(w|c_Q)}\right) \quad (2)$$

By Zipf's law any corpus of natural language will have a very long tail of infrequent words. To account for this effect we use D_{JS} for the top N most frequent words/n-grams. We use Laplace smoothing to account for words or n-grams that did not appear in one of the corpora.

We also aim to uncover terms that distinguish one corpus from another. We use a metamorphic D_{JS} test, log-likelihood ratios, and weighted SVM features. Log-likelihood score will help us understand where precisely the two corpora differ.

$$n_{ij} = \frac{k_{ij}}{k_{iP} + k_{iA}} \quad (3)$$

$$m_{ij} = \frac{k_{Pj} + k_{Qj}}{k_{QP} + k_{PP} + k_{QA} + k_{PA}} \quad (4)$$

$$LL(w) = 2\sum_{i,j} k_{ij} \log \frac{n_{ij}}{m_{ij}} \quad (5)$$

3.4 Machine learning

For the classification experiment, we used an implementation of the libsvm support vector machine package that was ported to R (Dimitriadou et al., 2011). Features were extracted as described above in Section 3.2.1. We used a cosine kernel. The optimal C regularization parameter was estimated on a scale from 2^{-1} to 2^{15}.

3.5 Characterizing differences between the document sets

We used a variety of methods to characterize differences between the document sets: log-likelihood ratio, SVM normal vector components, and a technique adapted from metamorphic testing.

3.5.1 Applying metamorphic testing to Kullback-Leibler divergence

As one of our methods for characterizing differences between the two document sets, we used an adaptation of metamorphic testing, inspired by the work of (Murphy and Kaiser, 2008) on applying metamorphic testing to machine learning applications. The intuition behind metamorphic testing is that given some output for a given input, it should be possible to predict in general terms what the effect of some alternation in the input should be on the output. For example, given some Kullback-Leibler divergence for some set of features, it is possible to predict how Kullback-Leibler divergence will change if a feature is added to or subtracted from the feature vector. We adapted this observation by iteratively subtracting all features one by one and ranking them according to how much of an effect on the Kullback-Leibler divergence its removal had.

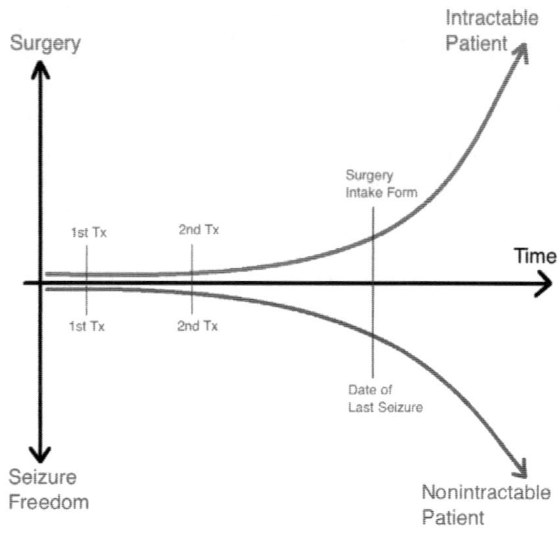

Figure 1: Two major paths in epilepsy care. At the begining of epilepsy care two groups of patients are indistinguishable. Subsequently, the two groups diverge.

4 Results

4.1 Kullback-Leibler (Jensen-Shannon) divergence

Table 2 shows the Kullback-Leibler divergence, calculated as Jensen-Shannon divergence, for three overlapping time periods—the year preceding surgery referral, the period from 6 months before surgery referral to six months after surgery referral, and the year following surgery referral, for the intractable epilepsy patients; and, for the non-intractable epilepsy patients, the same time periods with reference to the last seizure date.

As can be seen in the left-most column (-12 to 0), at one year prior, the clinic notes of patients who will require surgery and patients who will not require surgery cannot easily be discriminated by Kullback-Leibler divergence—the divergence is only just above the .005 near-identity threshold even when 8000 unique n-grams are considered. If the -6 to +6 and 0 to +12 time periods are examined, we see that the divergence increases as we reach and then pass the period of surgery (or move into the year following the last seizure, for the non-intractable patients), indicating that the difference between the two collections becomes more pronounced as treatment progresses. The divergence for these time periods does pass the assumed near-identity threshold for larger numbers of n-grams, largely accounted for by terms that are unique to one notes set or the other.

n-grams	-12 to 0 months	-6 to +6 months	0 to +12 months
125	0.00125	0.00193	0.00244
250	0.00167	0.00229	0.00286
500	0.00266	0.00326	0.00389
1000	0.00404	0.00494	0.00585
2000	0.00504	0.00618	0.00718
4000	0.00535	0.00657	0.00770
8000	0.00555	0.00681	0.00796

Table 2: Kullback-Leibler divergence (calculated as Jensen-Shannon divergence) for difference between progress notes of the two groups of patients. Results are shown for the period 1 year before, 6 months before and 6 months after, and one year after surgery referral for the intractable epilepsy patients and the last seizure for non-intractable patients. 0 represents the date of surgery referral for the intractable epilepsy patients and date of last seizure for the non-intractable patients.

4.2 Classification with support vector machines

Table 3 shows the results of building support vector machines to classify individual notes as belonging to the intractable epilepsy or the non-intractable epilepsy patient population. Three time periods are evaluated, as described above. The number of features is varied by row. For each cell, the average F-measure from 20-fold cross-validation is shown.

As can be seen in the left-most column (-12 to 0), at one year prior to referral to surgery referral date or last seizure, the patients who will become intractable epilepsy patients can be distinguished from the patients who will become non-intractable epilepsy patients *purely on the basis of natural language processing-based classification* with an F-measure as high as 0.95. This supports the conclusion that the two document sets are indeed different, and furthermore illustrates that this difference can be used to predict which patients will require surgical intervention.

4.3 Characterizing the differences between clinic notes from the two patient populations

Tables 4 and 5 show the results of three methods for differentiating between the document col-

n-grams	-12 to 0 months	-6 to +6 months	0 to +12 months
125	0.8885	0.9217	0.9476
250	0.8928	0.9297	0.9572
500	0.9107	0.9367	0.9667
1000	0.9245	0.9496	0.9692
2000	0.9417	0.9595	0.9789
4000	0.9469	0.9661	0.9800
8000	0.9510	0.9681	0.9810

Table 3: Average F_1 for the three time periods described above, with increasing numbers of features. Values are the average of 20-fold cross-validation. See Figure 2 for an explanation of the time periods.

lections representing the two patient populations. The methodology for each is described above. The most strongly distinguishing features when just the 125 most frequent features are used are shown in Table 4, and the most strongly distinguishing features when the 8,000 most frequent features are used are shown in Table 5. Impressionistically, two trends emerge. One is that more clearly clinically significant features are shown to have strong discriminatory power when the 8,000 most frequent features are used than when the 125 most frequent features are used. This result is supported by the Kullback-Leibler divergence results, which demonstrated the most divergent vocabularies with larger numbers of n-grams. The other trend is that the SVM classifier does a better job of picking out clinically relevant features. This has implications for the design of clinical decision support systems that utilize our approach.

5 Discussion

5.1 Behavior of Kullback-Leibler divergence

Kullback-Leibler divergence varies with the number of words considered. When the vocabularies of two document sets are merged and the words are ordered by overall frequency, the further down the list we go, the higher the Kullback-Leibler divergence can be expected to be. This is because the highest-frequency words in the combined set will generally be frequent in both source corpora, and therefore carry similar probability mass. As we progress further down the list of frequency-ranked words, we include progressively less-common words, with diverse usage patterns, which are likely to reflect the differences between the two document sets, if there are any. Thus, the Kullback-Leibler divergence will rise.

To understand the intuition here, imagine looking at the Kullback-Leibler divergence when just the 50 most-common words are considered. These will be primarily function words, and their distributions are unlikely to differ much between the two document sets unless the syntax of the two corpora is radically different. Beyond this set of very frequent common words will be words that may be relatively frequent in one set as compared to the other, contributing to divergence between the sets.

In Table 2, the observed behavior for our two document collections follows this expected pattern. However, the divergence between the vocabularies remains close to the assumed near-identity threshold of 0.005, even when larger numbers of n-grams are considered. The divergence never exceeds 0.01; this level of divergence for larger numbers of n-grams is consistent with prior analyses of highly similar corpora (Verspoor et al., 2009).

We attribute this similarity to two factors. The first is that both document sets derive from a single department within a single hospital; a relatively small number of doctors are responsible for authoring the notes and there may exist specific hospital protocols related to their content. The second is that the clinical contexts from which our two document sets are derived are highly related, in that all the patients are epilepsy patients. While we have demonstrated that there are clear differences between the two sets, it is also to be expected that they would have many words in common. The nature of clinical notes combined with the shared disease context results in generally consistent vocabulary and hence low overall divergence.

5.2 Behavior of classifier

Table 3 demonstrates that classifier performance increases as the number of features increases. This indicates that as more terms are considered, the basis for differentiating between the two different document collections is stronger.

Examining the SVM normal vector components (SVMW) in Tables 4 and 5, we find that unigrams, bigrams and trigrams are useful in differentiation between the two patient populations. While no quadrigrams appear in this table, they may in fact contribute to classifier performance. We will perform an ablation study in future work to quantify

JS metamorphic test (JSMT)	**Log-likelihood ratio (LLR)**	**SVM normal vector components (SVMW)**
family = -0.000114	none = 623.702323	bilaterally = -19.009380
normal = -0.000106	family = -445.117177	age.NUMB = 17.981459
seizure = -0.000053	NUMB.NUMB.NUMB.NUMB = 422.953816	review = 17.250652
problems = -0.000053	normal = -244.603033	based = -14.846495
none = 0.000043	problems = -207.021130	family.history = -14.659653
detailed = -0.000037	left = 176.434519	NUMB = -14.422525
including = -0.000036	bid = 142.105691	lower = -13.553434
risks = -0.000033	NUMB = 136.255678	mother = -13.436694
NUMB = 0.000032	detailed = -133.012908	first = -13.001744
concerns = -0.000032	right = 120.453596	including = -12.800433
NUMB.NUMB.NUMB.NUMB = 0.000031	seizure = -120.047686	extremities = 11.709199
additional = -0.000029	including = -119.061518	documented = -11.441394
brain = -0.000026	risks = -116.543250	awake = -11.418535
NUMB.NUMB = 0.000022	concerns = -101.366110	hpi = 11.121019
minutes = -0.000021	additional = -95.880792	follow = -10.550802
NUMB.minutes = -0.000020	clear = 83.848170	neurology = -10.533895
reviewed = -0.000018	brain = -74.267220	call = -10.422606
history = -0.000017	seizures = 71.937757	effects = 10.298221
noted = -0.000017	one = 65.203819	brain = -9.900864
upper = -0.000017	epilepsy = 46.383564	weight = 9.819712
well = -0.000015	hpi = 45.932630	patient.s = -9.603531
side = -0.000015	minutes = -45.278770	discussed = -9.473544
bilaterally = -0.000014	NUMB.NUMB.NUMB = 43.320354	today = 9.390896
motor.normal = -0.000014	negative = 42.914770	allergies = -9.346146
notes = -0.000014	NUMB.minutes = -42.909968	NUMB.NUMB.NUMB.NUMB = 9.342800
Spearman correlation between JSMT and LLR = 0.912454	Spearman correlation between LLR and SVMW = 0.086784	Spearman correlation between SVMW and JSMT = 0.101965

Table 4: Comparison of three different methods for finding the strongest differentiating features. This table shows features for the -12 to 0 periods with the 125 most frequent features. The JSMT and LLR statistics give values greater than zero. We add sign to indicate which corpus has higher relative frequency of the feature: a positive value indicates that the relative frequency of the feature is greater in the intractable group, while a negative value indicates that the relative frequency of the feature is greater in the non-intractable group. The last row shows the correlation between two different ranking statistics.

JS metamorphic test (JSMT)	**Log-likelihood ratio (LLR)**	**SVM normal vector components (SVMW)**
family = -0.000118	family = -830.329965	john = -4.645071
normal = -0.000109	normal = -745.882086	lamotrigine = 4.320412
seizure = -0.000057	problems = -386.238711	surgery = 4.299546
problems = -0.000057	seizure = -369.342334	jane = 4.091609
none = 0.000047	none = 337.461504	epilepsy.surgery = 4.035633
including = -0.000040	detailed = -262.240496	janet = -3.970101
detailed = -0.000040	including = -255.076808	excellent.control = -3.946283
additional.concerns = -0.000038	additional.concerns.noted = -246.603655	excellent = -3.920620
additional.concerns.noted = -0.000038	concerns.noted = -246.603655	NUMB.seizure = -3.886997
concerns.noted = -0.000038	additional.concerns = -243.353912	mother = -3.801364
NUMB = -0.000036	NUMB.NUMB.NUMB.NUMB = 238.065700	jen = 3.568809
concerns = -0.000036	risks = -232.741511	back = -3.319477
risks = -0.000036	concerns = -228.805299	visit = -3.264600
NUMB.NUMB.NUMB.NUMB = 0.000035	additional = -204.462411	james = 3.174763
additional = -0.000033	brain = -182.413340	NUMB.NUMB.NUMB.normal = -3.024471
brain = -0.000030	NUMB = -162.992065	continue = -3.011293
NUMB.NUMB = -0.000026	surgery = 153.646067	idiopathic.localization = -2.998177
minutes = -0.000025	minutes = -142.761961	idiopathic.localization.related = -2.998177
surgery = 0.000024	NUMB.minutes = -134.048116	increase = 2.948187
NUMB.minutes = -0.000023	diff = -131.388230	diastat = -2.937431
diff = -0.000023	NUMB.NUMB = -125.067347	taking = -2.902673
history = -0.000021	reviewed = -116.013417	lamictal = 2.898987
reviewed = -0.000021	noted = -114.241532	going = 2.862764
noted = -0.000021	idiopathic = -112.331060	described = 2.844830
upper = -0.000020	shaking = -112.186858	epilepsy = 2.745872
Spearman correlation between JSMT and LLR = 0.782918	Spearman correlation between LLR and SVMW = 0.039860	Spearman correlation between SVMW and JSMT = 0.165159

Table 5: Comparison of three different methods for finding the strongest differentiating features. This table shows features for the -12 to 0 periods with the 8,000 most frequent features. The JSMT and LLR statistics give values greater than zero. We add sign to indicate which corpus has higher relative frequency of the feature: a positive value indicates that the relative frequency of the feature is greater in the intractable group, while a negative value indicates that the relative frequency of the feature is greater in the non-intractable group. The last row shows the correlation between two different ranking statistics.

the contribution of the different feature sets. In addition, we find that table 5 shows many clinically relevant terms, such as seizure frequency ("excellent [seizure] control"), epilepsy type ("localization related [epilepsy]"), etiology classification ("idiopathic [epilepsy]"), and drug names ("lamotrigine", "diastat", "lamictal"), giving nearly complete history of the present illness.

6 Conclusion

The classification results from our machine learning experiments support rejection of the null hypothesis of no detectable differences between the clinic notes of patients who will progress to the diagnosis of intractable epilepsy and patients who do not progress to the diagnosis of intractable epilepsy. The results show that we can predict from an early stage of treatment which patients will fall into these two classes based only on textual data from the neurology clinic notes. As intuition would suggest, we find that the notes become more divergent and the ability to predict outcome improves as time progresses, but the most important point is that the outcome can be predicted from the earliest time period.

SVM classification demonstrates a stronger result than the information-theoretic measures, uses less data, and needs just a single run. However, it is important to note that we cannot entirely rely on the argument from classification as the sole methodology in testing whether or not two document sets are similar or different. If the finding is positive, i.e., it is possible to train a classifier to distinguish between documents drawn from the two document sets, then interpreting the results is straightforward. However, if documents drawn from the two document sets are not found to be distinguishable by a classifier, one must consider the possibility of multiple possible confounds, such as selection of an inappropriate classification algorithm, extraction of the wrong features, bugs in the feature extraction software, etc. Having established that the two sets of clinical notes differ, we noted some identifying features of clinic notes from the two populations, particularly when more terms were considered.

The Institute of Medicine explains that "...to accommodate the reality that although professional judgment will always be vital to shaping care, the amount of information required for any given decision is moving beyond unassisted human capacity (Olsen et al., 2007)." This is surely the case for those who care for the epileptic patient. Technology like natural language processing will ultimately serve as a basis for stable clinical decision support tools. It, however, is not a decision making tool. Decision making is the responsibility of professional judgement. That judgement will labor over such questions as: what is the efficacy of neurosurgery, what will be the long term outcome, will there be any lasting damage, are we sure that all the medications have been tested, and how the family will adjust to a poor outcome. In the end, it is that judgement that will decide what is best; that decision will be supported by research like what is presented here.

7 Acknowledgements

This work was supported in part by the National Institutes of Health, Grants #1R01LM011124-01,and 1R01NS045911-01; the Cincinnati Children's Hospital Medical Center's: Research Foundation, Department of Pediatric Surgery and the Department of Paediatrics's divisions of Neurology and Biomedical Informatics. We also wish to acknowledge the clinical and surgical wisdom provided by Drs. John J. Hutton & Hansel M. Greiner, MD. K. Bretonnel Cohen was supported by grants XXX YYY ZZZ. Karin Verspoor was supported by NICTA, which is funded by the Australian Government as represented by the Department of Broadband, Communications and the Digital Economy and the Australian Research Council.

References

[Abhyankar et al.2012] Swapna Abhyankar, Kira Leishear, Fiona M. Callaghan, Dina Demner-Fushman, and Clement J. McDonald. 2012. Lower short- and long-term mortality associated with overweight and obesity in a large cohort study of adult intensive care unit patients. *Critical Care*, 16.

[Begley et al.2000] Charles E Begley, Melissa Famulari, John F Annegers, David R Lairson, Thomas F Reynolds, Sharon Coan, Stephanie Dubinsky, Michael E Newmark, Cynthia Leibson, EL So, et al. 2000. The cost of epilepsy in the united states: An estimate from population-based clinical and survey data. *Epilepsia*, 41(3):342–351.

[Dimitriadou et al.2011] Evgenia Dimitriadou, Kurt Hornik, Friedrich Leisch, David Meyer, and Andreas Weingessel, 2011. *e1071: Misc Functions of the Department of Statistics (e1071), TU*

Wien. http://CRAN.R-project.org/package=e1071. R package version 1.5.

[Epilepsy Foundation2012] Epilepsy Foundation, 2012. *What is Epilepsy: Incidence and Prevalence*. http://www.epilepsyfoundation.org/ aboutepilepsy /whatisepilepsy/ statistics.cfm.

[Himes et al.2009] Blanca E. Himes, Yi Dai, Isaac S. Kohane, Scott T. Weiss, and Marco F. Ramoni. 2009. Prediction of chronic obstructive pulmonary disease (copd) in asthma patients using electronic medical records. *Journal of the American Medical Informatics Association*, 16(3):371–379.

[Huang et al.under review] Sandy H. Huang, Paea LePendu, Srinivasan V Iyer, Anna Bauer-Mehren, Cliff Olson, and Nigam H. Shah. under review. Developing computational models for predicting diagnoses of depression. In *American Medical Informatics Association*.

[Jonquet et al.2009] Clement Jonquet, Nigam H. Shah, Cherie H. Youn, Mark A. Musen, Chris Callendar, and Margaret-Anne Storey. 2009. NCBO Annotator: Semantic annotation of biomedical data. In *8th International Semantic Web Conference*.

[Kwan and Brodie2000] Patrick Kwan and Martin J Brodie. 2000. Early identification of refractory epilepsy. *New England Journal of Medicine*, 342(5):314–319.

[Kwan et al.2010] Patrick Kwan, Alexis Arzimanoglou, Anne T Berg, Martin J Brodie, W Allen Hauser, Gary Mathern, Solomon L Moshé, Emilio Perucca, Samuel Wiebe, and Jacqueline French. 2010. Definition of drug resistant epilepsy: consensus proposal by the ad hoc task force of the ilae commission on therapeutic strategies. *Epilepsia*, 51(6):1069–1077.

[Manning and Schuetze1999] Christopher Manning and Hinrich Schuetze. 1999. *Foundations of statistical natural language processing*. MIT Press.

[Murphy and Kaiser2008] Christian Murphy and Gail Kaiser. 2008. Improving the dependability of machine learning applications.

[Olsen et al.2007] LeighAnne Olsen, Dara Aisner, and J Michael McGinnis. 2007. The learning healthcare system.

[Verspoor et al.2009] K. Verspoor, K.B. Cohen, and L. Hunter. 2009. The textual characteristics of traditional and open access scientific journals are similar. *BMC Bioinformatics*, 10(1):183.

Identification of Patients with Acute Lung Injury from Free-Text Chest X-Ray Reports

Meliha Yetisgen-Yildiz
University of Washington
Seattle, WA 98195
melihay@uw.edu

Cosmin Adrian Bejan
University of Washington
Seattle, WA 98195
bejan@uw.edu

Mark M. Wurfel
University of Washington
Seattle, WA 98195
mwurfel@uw.edu

Abstract

Identification of complex clinical phenotypes among critically ill patients is a major challenge in clinical research. The overall research goal of our work is to develop automated approaches that accurately identify critical illness phenotypes to prevent the resource intensive manual abstraction approach. In this paper, we describe a text processing method that uses Natural Language Processing (NLP) and supervised text classification methods to identify patients who are positive for Acute Lung Injury (ALI) based on the information available in free-text chest x-ray reports. To increase the classification performance we enhanced the baseline unigram representation with bigram and trigram features, enriched the n-gram features with assertion analysis, and applied statistical feature selection. We used 10-fold cross validation for evaluation and our best performing classifier achieved 81.70% precision (positive predictive value), 75.59% recall (sensitivity), 78.53% f-score, 74.61% negative predictive value, 76.80% specificity in identifying patients with ALI.

1 Introduction

Acute lung injury (ALI) is a critical illness consisting of acute hypoxemic respiratory failure with bilateral pulmonary infiltrates that is associated with pulmonary and non-pulmonary risk factors. ALI and its more severe form, acute respiratory distress syndrome (ARDS), represent a major health problem with an estimated prevalence of 7% of intensive care unit admissions (Rubenfeld et al., 2005) for which the appropriate treatment is often instituted too late or not at all (Ferguson et al., 2005; Rubenfeld et al., 2004). Early detection of ALI syndrome is essential for appropriate application of the only therapeutic intervention demonstrated to improve mortality in ALI, lung protective ventilation (LPV).

The identification of ALI requires recognition of a precipitating cause, either due to direct lung injury from trauma or pneumonia or secondary to another insult such as sepsis, transfusion, or pancreatitis. The consensus criteria for ALI include the presence of bilateral pulmonary infiltrates on chest radiograph, representing non-cardiac pulmonary edema as evidenced by the absence of left atrial hypertension (Pulmonary Capillary Wedge Pressure < 18 mmHg (2.4 kPa)) or absence of clinical evidence of congestive heart failure, and oxygenation impairment as defined by an arterial vs. inspired oxygen level ratio (PaO_2/FiO_2) <300 mmHg (40 kPa)) (Argitas et al., 1998; Dushianthan et al., 2011; Ranieri et al., 2012).

In this paper, we describe a text processing approach to identify patients who are positive for ALI based only on the free-text chest x-ray reports.

2 Related Work

Several studies demonstrated the value of Natural Language Processing (NLP) in a variety of health care applications including phenotype extraction from electronic medical records (EMR) (Demner-Dushman et al., 2009). Within this domain, chest x-ray reports have been widely studied to extract different types of pneumonia (Tepper et al., 2013; Elkin et al., 2008; Aronsky et al., 2001; Fiszman et al., 2000). Chest x-ray reports have also been studied for ALI surveillance by other researchers. Two of the prior studies relied on rule-based keyword search approaches. Herasevich et al. (2009) included a free text Boolean query containing trigger words *bilateral*, *infiltrate*, and *edema*. Azzam et al. (2009) used a more extensive list of trigger words and phrases to identify the presence of bilateral infiltrates and

ALI. In another study, Solti et al. (2009) represented the content of chest x-ray reports using character n-grams and applied supervised classification to identify chest x-ray reports consistent with ALI. In our work, different from prior research, we proposed a fully statistical approach where (1) the content of chest x-ray reports was represented by token n-grams, (2) statistical feature selection was applied to select the most informative features, and (3) assertion analysis was used to enrich the n-gram features. We also implemented Azzam et al.'s approach based on the information available in their paper and used it as a baseline to compare performance results of our approach to theirs.

3 Methods

The overall architecture of our text processing approach for ALI identification is illustrated in Figure 1. In the following sections, we will describe the main steps of the text processing approach as well as the annotated chest x-ray corpus used in training and test.

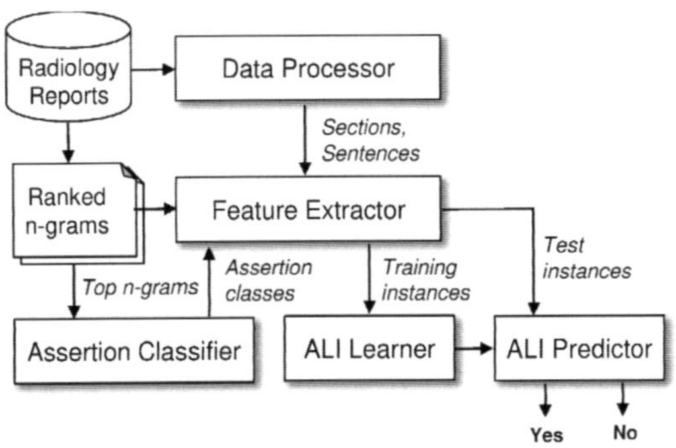

Figure 1 Overall system architecture of ALI extractor.

3.1 Chest X-ray Corpora

To develop the ALI extractor, we created a corpus composed of 1748 chest x-ray reports generated for 629 patients (avg number of reports=2.78, min=1, max=3). Subjects for this corpus were derived from a cohort of intensive care unit (ICU) patients at Harborview Medical Center that has been described previously (Glavan et al., 2011). We selected 629 subjects who met the oxygenation criteria for ALI (**PaO2/FiO2<300 mmHg**) and then three consecutive chest radiographs were pulled from the radiology database. Three Critical Care Medicine specialists reviewed the chest radiograph images for each patient and annotated the radiographs as consistent (positive) or not-consistent (negative) with ALI. We assigned ALI status for each subject based on the number of physician raters calling the chest radiographs consistent or not consistent with ALI. Table 1 shows the number of physicians with agreement on the radiograph interpretation. There were 254 patients in the positive set (2 or more physicians agreeing on ALI positive) and 375 patients in the negative set (2 or more physicians agreeing on ALI negative). Table 1 includes the distribution of patients over the positive and negative classes at different agreement levels. We will refer to this annotated corpus as the development set in the remaining of the paper.

Annotation	Agreement	Patient Count
ALI positive	3	147
patients	2	107
ALI negative	3	205
patients	2	170

Table 1 Agreement levels

For validation, we used a second dataset generated in a similar fashion to the development set. We obtained chest radiographs for 55 subjects that were admitted to ICU and who met oxygenation criteria for ALI (1 radiograph and report per patient). A specialized chest radiologist annotated each report for the presence of ALI. There were 21 patients in the positive set and 34 in the negative set. We will refer to this corpus as the validation set in the remaining of the paper.

The retrospective review of the reports in both corpora was approved by the University of Washington Human Subjects Committee of Institutional Review Board who waived the need for informed consent.

3.2 Pre-processing – Section and Sentence Segmentation

Although radiology reports are in free text format, they are somewhat structured in terms of sections. We used a statistical section segmentation approach we previously built to identify the boundaries of the sections and their types in our corpus of chest x-ray reports (Tepper et al., 2012). The section segmenter was trained and tested with a corpus of 100 annotated radiology reports and produced 93% precision, 91% recall and 92% f-score (5-fold cross validation).

After identifying the report sections, we used the OpenNLP [1] sentence chunker to identify the boundaries of sentences in the section bodies.

This pre-processing step identified 8,659 sections and 15,890 sentences in 1,748 reports of the development set and 206 sections and 414 sentences in 55 reports of the validation set. We used the section information to filter out the sections with clinician signatures (e.g., *Interpreted By*, *Contributing Physicians*, *Signed By*). We used the sentences to extract the assertion values associated with n-gram features as will be explained in a later section.

3.3 Feature Selection

Representing the information available in the free-text chest x-ray reports as features is critical in identifying patients with ALI. In our representation, we created one feature vector for each patient. We used unigrams as the baseline representation. In addition, we used bigrams and trigrams as features. We observed that the chest x-ray reports in our corpus are short and not rich in terms of medical vocabulary usage. Based on this observation, we decided not to include any medical knowledge-based features such as UMLS concepts or semantic types. Table 2 summarizes the number of distinct features for each feature type used to represent the 1,748 radiology reports for 629 patients.

Feature Type	# of Distinct Features
Unigram (baseline)	1,926
Bigram	10,190
Trigram	17,798

Table 2 Feature set sizes of the development set.

As can be seen from the table, for bigrams and trigrams, the feature set sizes is quite high. Feature selection algorithms have been successfully applied in text classification in order to improve the classification accuracy (Wenqian et al., 2007). In previous work, we applied statistical feature selection to the problem of pneumonia detection from ICU reports (Bejan et al., 2012). By significantly reducing the dimensionality of the feature space, they improved the efficiency of the pneumonia classifiers and provided a better understanding of the data.

We used statistical hypothesis testing to determine whether there is an association between a given feature and the two categories of our problem (i.e, positive and negative ALI). Specifically, we computed the χ^2 statistics (Manning and Schutze, 1999) which generated an ordering of features in the training set. We used 10-fold cross validation (development set) in our overall performance evaluation. Table 3 lists the top 15 unigrams, bigrams, and trigrams ranked by χ^2 statistics in one of ten training sets we used in evaluation. As can be observed from the table, many of the features are closely linked to ALI.

Unigram	Bigram	Trigram
Diffuse	diffuse lung	opacities consistent with
Atelectasis	lung opacities	diffuse lung opacities
Pulmonary	pulmonary edema	change in diffuse
Consistent	consistent with	lung opacities consistent
Edema	opacities consistent	in diffuse lung
Alveolar	in diffuse	with pulmonary edema
Opacities	diffuse bilateral	consistent with pulmonary
Damage	with pulmonary	low lung volumes
Worsening	alveolar damage	or alveolar damage
Disease	edema or	pulmonary edema pneumonia
Bilateral	low lung	diffuse lung disease
Clear	edema pneumonia	edema pneumonia no
Severe	or alveolar	diffuse bilateral opacities
Injury	lung disease	lungs are clear
Bibasilar	pulmonary opacities	lung volumes with

Table 3 Top 15 most informative unigrams, bigrams, and trigrams for ALI classification according to $\chi 2$ statistics.

Once the features were ranked and their corresponding threshold values (*N*) were established, we built a feature vector for each patient. Specifically, given the subset of *N* relevant features extracted from the ranked list of features, we considered in the representation of a given patient's feature vector only the features from the subset of relevant features that were also found in the chest x-ray reports of the patient. Therefore, the size of the feature space is equal to the size of relevant features subset (*N*) whereas the length of each feature vector will be at most this value.

3.4 Assertion Analysis

We extended our n-gram representation with assertion analysis. We built an assertion classifier (Bejan et al., 2013) based on the annotated corpus of 2010 Integrating Biology and the Beside (i2b2) / Veteran's Affairs (VA) NLP challenge (Uzuner et al., 2011). The 2010 i2b2/VA challenge introduced assertion classification as a

[1] OpenNLP. Available at: http://opennlp.apache.org/

shared task, formulated such that each medical concept mentioned in a clinical report (e.g., asthma) is associated with a specific assertion category (present, absent, conditional, hypothetical, possible, and not associated with the patient). We defined a set of novel features that uses the syntactic information encoded in dependency trees in relation to special cue words for these categories. We also defined features to capture the semantics of the assertion keywords found in the corpus and trained an SVM multi-class classifier with default parameter settings. Our assertion classifier outperformed the state-of-the-art results and achieved 79.96% macro-averaged F-measure and 94.23% micro-averaged F-measure on the i2b2/VA challenge test data.

For each n-gram feature (e.g., *pneumonia*), we used the assertion classifier to determine whether it is present or absent based on contextual information available in the sentence the feature appeared in (e.g., <u>*Feature*</u>: pneumonia, <u>*Sentence*</u>: There is no evidence of *pneumonia*, congestive heart failure, or other acute process., <u>*Assertion*</u>: absent). We added the identified assertion value to the feature (e.g., *pneumonia_absent*). The frequencies of each assertion type in our corpus are presented in Table 4. Because chest x-rays do not include family history, there were no instances of not associated with the patient. We treated the three assertion categories that express hedging (conditional, hypothetical, possible) as the present category.

Assertion Class	Frequency
Present	206,863
Absent	13,961
Conditional	4
Hypothetical	330
Possible	3,980

Table 4 Assertion class frequencies.

3.5 Classification

For our task of classifying ALI patients, we picked the Maximum Entropy (MaxEnt) algorithm due to its good performance in text classification tasks (Berger et al., 1996). In our experiments, we used the MaxEnt implementation in a machine learning package called Mallet[2].

4 Results

4.1 Metrics

We evaluated the performance by using precision (positive predictive value), recall (sensitivity), negative predictive value, specificity, f-score, and accuracy. We used 10-fold cross validation to measure the performance of our classifiers on the development set. We evaluated the best performing classifier on the validation set.

4.2 Experiments with Development Set

We designed three groups of experiments to explore the effects of (1) different n-gram features, (2) feature selection, (3) assertion analysis of features on the classification of ALI patients. We defined two baselines to compare the performance of our approaches. In the first baseline, we implemented the Azzam et. al.'s rule-based approach (2009). In the second baseline, we only represented the content of chest x-ray reports with unigrams.

4.3 N-gram Experiments

Table 5 summarizes the performance of n-gram features. When compared to the baseline *unigram* representation, gradually adding bigrams (*uni+bigram*) and trigrams (*uni+bi+trigram*) to the baseline increased the precision and specificity by 4%. Recall and NPV remained the same. Azzam et. al.'s rule-based baseline generated higher recall but lower precision when compared to n-gram features. The best f-score (64.45%) was achieved with the *uni+bi+trigram* representation.

4.4 Feature Selection Experiments

To understand the effect of large feature space on classification performance, we studied how the performance of our system evolves for various threshold values (*N*) on the different combinations of χ^2 ranked unigram, bigram, and trigram features. Table 6 includes a subset of the results we collected for different values of *N*. As listed

System configuration	TP	TN	FP	FN	Precision/ PPV	Recall/ Sensitivity	NPV	Specificity	F-Score	Accuracy
Baseline#1–Azzam et. al. (2009)	201	184	191	53	51.27	79.13	77.64	49.07	62.23	61.21
Baseline#2–*unigram*	156	288	87	98	64.20	61.42	74.61	76.80	62.78	70.59
Uni+bigram	156	296	79	98	66.38	61.42	75.13	78.93	63.80	71.86
Uni+bi+trigram	155	303	72	99	68.28	61.02	75.37	80.80	64.45	72.81

Table 5 Performance evaluation on development set with no feature selection. TP: True positive, TN: True negative, FP: False positive, FN: False negative, PPV: Positive predictive value, NPV: Negative predictive value. The row with the heighted F-Score is highlighted.

in this table, for *N*=100, the *unigram* representation performed better than *uni+bigram*, *uni+bi+trigram* feature combinations; however, as *N* increased, the performance of *uni+bi+trigram* performed better, reaching the best f-score (78.53%) at *N*=800. When compared to the two defined baselines, the performance results of *uni+bi+trigram* at *N*=800 were significantly better than those of the baselines.

4.5 Assertion Analysis Experiments

We ran a series of experiments to understand the effect of assertion analysis on the classification performance. We used the best performing clas-

N	Feature configuration	TP	TN	FP	FN	Precision/ PPV	Recall/ Sensitivity	NPV	Specificity	F-Score	Accuracy
	Unigram	191	316	59	63	76.40	75.20	83.38	84.27	75.79	80.60
100	Uni+bigram	180	313	62	74	74.38	70.87	80.88	83.47	72.58	78.38
	Uni+bi+trigram	183	317	58	71	75.93	72.05	81.70	84.53	73.94	79.49
	Unigram	189	312	63	65	75.00	74.41	82.76	83.20	74.70	79.65
200	Uni+bigram	183	321	54	71	77.22	72.05	81.89	85.60	74.54	80.13
	Uni+bi+trigram	190	322	53	64	78.19	74.80	83.42	85.87	76.46	81.40
	Unigram	185	311	64	69	74.30	72.83	81.84	82.93	73.56	78.86
300	Uni+bigram	188	322	53	66	78.01	74.02	82.99	85.87	75.96	81.08
	Uni+bi+trigram	187	331	44	67	80.95	73.62	83.17	88.27	77.11	82.35
	Unigram	179	315	60	75	74.90	70.47	80.77	84.00	72.62	78.54
400	Uni+bigram	184	319	56	70	76.67	72.44	82.01	85.07	74.49	79.97
	Uni+bi+trigram	184	325	50	70	78.63	72.44	82.28	86.67	75.41	80.92
	Unigram	177	310	65	77	73.14	69.69	80.10	82.67	71.37	77.42
500	Uni+bigram	178	321	54	76	76.72	70.08	80.86	85.60	73.25	79.33
	Uni+bi+trigram	187	325	50	67	78.90	73.62	82.91	86.67	76.17	81.40
	Unigram	179	305	70	75	71.89	70.47	80.26	81.33	71.17	76.95
600	Uni+bigram	177	320	55	77	76.29	69.69	80.60	85.33	72.84	79.01
	Uni+bi+trigram	189	325	50	65	79.08	74.41	83.33	86.67	76.67	81.72
	Unigram	176	308	67	78	72.43	69.29	79.79	82.13	70.82	76.95
700	Uni+bigram	180	323	52	74	77.59	70.87	81.36	86.13	74.07	79.97
	Uni+bi+trigram	189	328	47	65	80.08	74.41	83.46	87.47	77.14	82.19
	Unigram	172	311	64	82	72.88	67.72	79.13	82.93	70.20	76.79
800	Uni+bigram	180	327	48	74	78.95	70.87	81.55	87.20	74.69	80.60
	Uni+bi+trigram	192	332	43	62	81.70	75.59	84.26	88.53	78.53	83.31
	Unigram	174	311	64	80	73.11	68.50	79.54	82.93	70.73	77.11
900	Uni+bigram	182	328	47	72	79.48	71.65	82.00	87.47	75.36	81.08
	Uni+bi+trigram	187	333	42	67	81.66	73.62	83.25	88.80	77.43	82.67
	Unigram	177	313	62	77	74.06	69.69	80.26	83.47	71.81	77.90
1000	Uni+bigram	185	326	49	69	79.06	72.83	82.53	86.93	75.82	81.24
	Uni+bi+trigram	190	327	48	64	79.83	74.80	83.63	87.20	77.24	82.19

Table 6 Performance evaluation on development set with feature selection. TP: True positive, TN: True negative, FP: False positive, FN: False negative, PPV: Positive predictive value, NPV: Negative predictive value. The row with the heighted F-Score is highlighted.

Assertion configuration	TP	TN	FP	FN	Precision/ PPV	Recall/ Sensitivity	NPV	Specificity	F-Score	Accuracy
Assertion_none	192	332	43	62	81.70	75.59	84.26	88.53	78.53	83.31
Assertion_all	188	328	47	66	80.00	74.02	83.25	87.47	76.89	82.03
Assertion_top_10	191	328	47	63	80.25	75.20	83.89	87.47	77.64	82.51
Assertion_top_20	190	329	46	64	80.51	74.80	83.72	87.73	77.55	82.51
Assertion_top_30	190	331	44	64	81.20	74.80	83.80	88.27	77.87	82.83
Assertion_top_40	190	328	47	64	80.17	74.80	83.67	87.47	77.39	82.35
Assertion_top_50	190	330	45	65	80.85	74.51	83.54	88.00	77.55	82.54

Table 7 Performance evaluation on development set with the assertion feature (uni+bi+trigram at *N*=800). TP: True positive, TN: True negative, FP: False positive, FN: False negative, PPV: Positive predictive value, NPV: Negative predictive value. The row with the heighted F-Score is highlighted.

System configuration	TP	TN	FP	FN	Precision/ PPV	Recall/ Sensitivity	NPV	Specificity	F-Score	Accuracy
Baseline#1–Azzam et. al. (2009)	10	18	16	11	38.46	47.62	62.07	52.94	42.55	50.91
Baseline#2–*unigram*	12	29	5	9	70.53	57.14	76.32	85.29	63.16	74.55
Uni+bi+trigram at k=800	9	30	4	12	69.23	42.86	71.43	88.24	52.94	70.91

Table 8 Performance evaluation on validation set. TP: True positive, TN: True negative, FP: False positive, FN: False negative, PPV: Positive predictive value, NPV: Negative predictive value. The row with the heighted F-Score is highlighted.

sifier with *uni+bi+trigram* at *N*=800 in our experiments. We applied assertion analysis to all 800 features as well as only a small set of top ranked 10×k (1≤k≤5) features which were observed to be closely related to ALI (e.g., *diffuse, opacities, pulmonary edema*). We hypothesized applying assertion analysis would inform the classifier on the presence and absence of those terms which would potentially decrease the false positive and negative counts.

Table 7 summarizes the results of our experiments. When we applied assertion analysis to all 800 features, the performance slightly dropped when compared to the performance with no assertion analysis. When assertion analysis applied to only top ranked features, the best f-score performance was achieved with assertion analysis with top 30 features; however, it was still slightly lower than the f-score with no assertion analysis. The differences are not statistically significant.

4.6 Experiments with Validation Set

We used the validation set to explore the generalizability of the proposed approach. To accomplish this we run the best performing classifier (*uni+bi+trigram* at *N=800*) and two defined baselines on the validation set. We re-trained the *uni+bi+trigram* at *N=800* classifier and unigram baseline on the complete development set.

Table 8 includes the performance results. The second baseline with unigrams performed the best and Azzam et. al.'s baseline performed the worst in identifying the patients with ALI in the validation set.

5 Discussion

Our best system achieved an f-score of 78.53 (precision=81.70, recall=75.59) on the development set. While the result is encouraging and significantly better than the f-score of a previously published system (f-score=62.23, precision=51.27, recall=79.13), there is still room for improvement.

There are several important limitations to our current development dataset. First, the annotators who are pulmonary care specialists used only the x-ray images to annotate the patients. However, the classifiers were trained based on the features extracted from the radiologists' free-text interpretation of the x-ray images. In one false positive case, the radiologist has written *"Bilateral diffuse opacities, consistent with pulmonary edema. Bibasilar atelectasis."* in the chest x-ray report, however all three pulmonary care specialists annotated the case as negative based on their interpretation of images. Because the report consisted of many very strong features indicative of ALI, our classifier falsely identified the patient as positive with a very high prediction probability 0.96. Second, although three annotators annotated the development set, there was full agreement on 42.12% (107/254) of the positive patients and 45.33% (170/375) of the negative patients. Table 9 includes the false positive and negative statistics of the best performing classifier (*uni+bi+trigrams* at *N=800*). As can be seen from the table, the classifier made more mistakes on patients where the annotator agreement was not perfect. The classifier predicted 13 of the 28 false positives and 23 of the 39 false negatives with probabilities higher than 0.75. When we investigated the reports of those 13 false positives, we observed that the radiologists used many very strong ALI indicative features (e.g., *diffuse lung opacities, low lung volumes*) to describe the images. On the contrary, radiologists did not use as many ALI indicative features in the reports of 23 false negative cases.

Error Type	Agreement	Frequency	Percentage
False Positives	3	15	10.20% (15/147)
	2	28	26.17% (28/107)
False Negatives	3	24	11.70% (24/205)
	2	39	22.94% (39/170)

Table 9 False positive and false negative statistics at different agreement levels.

In our experiments on the development set, we demonstrated the positive impact of statistical feature selection on the overall classification performance. We achieved the best f-score, when we used only 2.67% (800/29,914) of the complete n-gram feature space. We enriched the highly ranked features with assertion analysis. However, unlike feature selection, assertion analysis did not improve the overall performance. To explore the reasons, we analyzed reports from our corpus and found out that the current six assertion classes (*present, absent, conditional, hypothetical, possible*) were not sufficient to capture true meaning in many cases. For example, our assertion classifier assigned the class *present* to the bigram *bibasilar opacities* based on the sentence *"There are bibasilar opacities that are unchanged"*. Although *present* was the correct assignment for *bibasilar opacities*, the more important piece of information was the change of state in *bibasilar opacities* for ALI diagnosis. X-rays describe a single snapshot of time but the x-ray report narrative makes explicit or, more often implicit references to a previous x-ray. In this way, the sequence of x-ray reports is used not only to assess a patient's health at a moment in time but also to monitor the change. We recently defined a schema to annotate change of state for clinical events in chest x-ray reports (Vanderwende et al., 2013). We will use this annotation schema to create an annotated corpus for training models to enrich the assertion features for ALI classification.

The results on the validation set revealed that the classification performance degraded significantly when training and test data do not come from the same dataset. There are multiple reasons to this effect. First, the two datasets had different language characteristics. Although both development and validation sets included chest x-ray reports, only 2,488 of the 3,305 (75.28%) n-gram features extracted from the validation set overlapped with the 29,914 n-gram features extracted from the development set. We suspect that this is the main reason why our best performing classifier with feature selection trained on the development set did not perform as well as the unigram baseline on the validation set. Second, the validation set included only 55 patients and each patient had only one chest x-ray report unlike the development set where each patient had 2.78 reports on the average. In other words, the classifiers trained on the development set with richer content made poor predictions on the validation set with more restricted content. Third, because the number of patients in the validation set was too small, each false positive and negative case had a huge impact on the overall performance.

6 Conclusion

In this paper, we described a text processing approach to identify patients with ALI from the information available in their corresponding free-text chest x-ray reports. To increase the classification performance, we (1) enhanced the baseline unigram representation with bigram and trigram features, (2) enriched the n-gram features with assertion analysis, and (3) applied statistical feature selection. Our proposed methodology of ranking all the features using statistical hypothesis testing and selecting only the most relevant ones for classification resulted in significantly improving the performance of a previous system for ALI identification. The best performing classifier achieved 81.70% precision (positive predictive value), 75.59% recall (sensitivity), 78.53% f-score, 74.61% negative predictive value, 76.80% specificity in identifying patients with ALI when using the uni+bi+trigram representation at N=800. Our experiments showed that assertion values did not improve the overall performance. For future work, we will work on defining new semantic features that will enhance the current assertion definition and capture the change of important events in radiology reports.

Acknowledgements

The work is partly supported by the Institute of Translational Health Sciences (UL1TR000423), and Microsoft Research Connections. We would also like to thank the anonymous reviewers for helpful comments.

References

Aronsky D, Fiszman M, Chapman WW, Haug PJ. Combining decision support methodologies to diagnose pneumonia. AMIA Annu Symp Proc., 2001:12-16.

Artigas A, Bernard GR, Carlet J, Dreyfuss D, Gattinoni L, Hudson L, Lamy M, Marini JJ, Matthay MA, Pinsky MR, Spragg R, Suter PM. The American-European Consensus Conference on ARDS, part 2: Ventilatory, pharmacologic, supportive therapy, study design strategies, and issues related to recovery and remodeling. Acute respiratory distress syndrome. Am J Respir Crit Care Med. 1998;157(4 Pt1):1332-47.

Azzam HC, Khalsa SS, Urbani R, Shah CV, Christie JD, Lanken PN, Fuchs BD. Validation study of an automated electronic acute lung injury screening tool. J Am Med Inform Assoc. 2009; 16(4):503-8.

Bejan CA, Xia F, Vanderwende L, Wurfel M, Yetisgen-Yildiz M. Pneumonia identification using statistical feature selection. J Am Med Inform Assoc. 2012; 19(5):817-23.

Bejan CA, Vanderwende L, Xia F, Yetisgen-Yildiz M. Assertion Modeling and its role in clinical phenotype identification. J Biomed Inform. 2013; 46(1):68-74.

Berger AL, Pietra SAD, Pietra VJD. A maximum entropy approach to natural language processing. Journal of Computational Linguistics. 1996; 22(1):39-71.

Demner-Fushman D, Chapman WW, McDonald CJ. What can natural language processing do for clinical decision support? J Biomed Inform. 2009; 42(5):760-72.

Dushianthan A, Grocott MPW, Postle AD, Cusack R. Acute respiratory distress syndrome and acute lung injury. Postgrad Med J. 2011; 87:612-622.

Elkin PL, Froehling D, Wahner-Roedler D, Trusko B, Welsh G, Ma H, Asatryan AX, Tokars JI, Rosenbloom ST, Brown SH. NLP-based identification of pneumonia cases from free-text radiological reports. AMIA Annu Symp Proc. 2008; 6:172-6.

Ferguson ND, Frutos-Vivar F, Esteban A, Fernández-Segoviano P, Aramburu JA, Nájera L, Stewart TE. Acute respiratory distress syndrome: underrecognition by clinicians and diagnostic accuracy of three clinical definitions. Crit Care Med. 2005; 33(10):2228-34.

Fiszman M, Chapman WW, Aronsky D, Evans RS, Haug PJ. Automatic detection of acute bacterial pneumonia from chest X-ray reports. J Am Med Inform Assoc. 2000;7(6):593-604.

Glavan BJ, Holden TD, Goss CH, Black RA, Neff MJ, Nathens AB, Martin TR, Wurfel MM; ARDSnet Investigators. Genetic variation in the FAS gene and associations with acute lung injury. Am J Respir Crit Care Med. 2011;183(3):356-63.

Herasevich V, Yilmaz M, Khan H, Hubmayr RD, Gajic O. Validation of an electronic surveillance system for acute lung injury. Intensive Care Med. 2009; 35(6):1018-23.

Manning CD, Schutze H. Foundations of statistical natural language processing. MIT Press 1999.

Ranieri VM, Rubenfeld GD, Thompson BT, Ferguson ND, Caldwell E, Fan E, Camporota L, Slutsky AS. Acute Respiratory Distress Syndrome. The Berlin Definition. JAMA. 2012; 307(23): 2526-2533.

Rubenfeld GD, Caldwell E, Peabody E, Weaver J, Martin DP, Neff M, Stern EJ, Hudson LD. Incidence and outcomes of acute lung injury. N Engl J Med. 2005; 353(16):1685-93.

Rubenfeld GD, Cooper C, Carter G, Thompson BT, Hudson LD. Barriers to providing lung-protective ventilation to patients with acute lung injury. Crit Care Med. 2004; 32(6):1289-93.

Solti I, Cooke CR, Xia F, Wurfel MM. Automated Classification of Radiology Reports for Acute Lung Injury: Comparison of Keyword and Machine Learning Based Natural Language Processing Approaches. Proceedings (IEEE Int Conf Bioinformatics Biomed). 2009;314-319.

Tepper M, Capurro D, Xia F, Vanderwende L, Yetisgen-Yildiz M. Statistical Section Segmentation in Free-Text Clinical Records. Proceedings of the International Conference on Language Resources and Evaluation (LREC), Istanbul, May 2012.

Tepper M, Evans HL, Xia F, Yetisgen-Yildiz M. Modeling Annotator Rationales with Application to Pneumonia Classification. Proceedings of Expanding the Boundaries of Health Informatics Using AI Workshop of AAAI'2013, Bellevue, WA; 2013.

Uzuner O, South BR, Shen S, DuVall SL. 2010 i2b2/VA challenge on concepts, assertions, and relations in clinical text. J Am Med Inform Assoc. 2011; 18(5):552–556.

Vanderwende L, Xia F, Yetisgen-Yildiz M. Annotating Change of State for Clinical Events. Proceedings of the 1st Workshop on EVENTS: Definition, Detection, Coreference, and Representation Workshop of NAACL'2013, Atlanta, June 2013.

Wenqian W, Houkuan H, Haibin Z et al. A novel feature selection algorithm for text categorization. Expert Syst Appl 2007;33:1–5.

Discovering Narrative Containers in Clinical Text

Timothy A. Miller[1], **Steven Bethard**[2], **Dmitriy Dligach**[1],
Sameer Pradhan[1], **Chen Lin**[1], and **Guergana K. Savova**[1]
[1] Children's Hospital Informatics Program, Boston Children's Hospital and Harvard Medical School
firstname.lastname@childrens.harvard.edu
[2] Center for Computational Language and Education Research, University of Colorado Boulder
steven.bethard@colorado.edu

Abstract

The clinical narrative contains a great deal of valuable information that is only understandable in a temporal context. Events, time expressions, and temporal relations convey information about the time course of a patient's clinical record that must be understood for many applications of interest. In this paper, we focus on extracting information about how time expressions and events are related by *narrative containers*. We use support vector machines with composite kernels, which allows for integrating standard feature kernels with tree kernels for representing structured features such as constituency trees. Our experiments show that using tree kernels in addition to standard feature kernels improves F1 classification for this task.

1 Introduction

Clinical narratives are a rich source of unstructured information that hold great potential for impacting clinical research and clinical care. These narratives consist of unstructured natural language descriptions of various stages of clinical care, which makes them information dense but challenging to use computationally. Information extracted from these narratives is already being used for clinical research tasks such as automatic phenotype classification for collecting disease cohorts retrospectively (Ananthakrishnan et al., 2013), which can in turn be used for a variety of studies, including pharmacogenomics (Lin et al., 2012; Wilke et al., 2011). Future applications may use information extracted from the clinical narrative at the point of care to assist physicians in decision-making in a real time fashion.

One of the most interesting and challenging aspects of clinical text is the pervasiveness of temporally grounded information. This includes a number of clinical concepts which are *events* with finite time spans (e.g., *surgery* or *x-ray*), *time expressions* (*December*, *postoperatively*), and links that relate events to times or other events. For example, *surgery last May* relates the time *last May* with the event *surgery* via the CONTAINS relation, while *Vicodin after surgery* relates the medication event *Vicodin* with the procedure event *surgery* via the AFTER relation. There are many potential applications of clinical information extraction that are only possible with an understanding of the ordering and duration of the events in a clinical encounter.

In this work we focus on extracting a particular temporal relation, CONTAINS, that holds between a time expression and an event expression. This level of representation is based on the computational discourse model of *narrative containers* (Pustejovsky and Stubbs, 2011), which are time expressions or events which are central to a section of a text, usually manifested by being relative hubs of temporal relation links. We argue that containment relations are useful as an intermediate level of granularity between full temporal relation extraction and "coarse" temporal bins (Raghavan et al., 2012) like *before admission*, *on admission*, and *after admission*. Correctly extracting CONTAINS relations will, for example, allow for more accurate placement of events on a timeline, to the resolution possible by the number of time expressions in the document. We suspect that this finer grained information will also be more useful for downstream applications like coreference, for which coarse information was found to be useful. The approach we develop is a supervised machine learning approach in which pairs of time expressions and events are classified as CONTAINS or not. The specific approach is a support vector machine using both standard feature kernels and tree kernels, a novel approach to this problem in this domain that has shown promise on other relation extraction tasks.

This work makes use of a new corpus we developed as part of the THYME[1] project (Temporal History of Your Medical Events) focusing on temporal events and relations in clinical text. This corpus consists of clinical and pathology notes on colorectal cancer from Mayo Clinic. Gold standard annotations include Penn Treebank-style phrase structure in addition to clinically relevant temporal annotations like clinical events, temporal expressions, and various temporal relations.

2 Background and Related Work

2.1 Annotation Methodology

The THYME annotation guidelines[2] detail the extension of TimeML (Pustejovsky et al., 2003b) to the annotations of events, temporal expressions and temporal relations in the clinical domain. In summary, an EVENT is anything that is relevant to the clinical timeline. Temporal expressions (TIMEX3s) in the clinical domain are similar to those in the general domain with two exceptions. First, TimeML sets and frequencies occur much more often in the clinical domain, especially with regard to medications and treatments (*Claritin 30mg* ***twice daily***). The second deviation is a new type of TIMEX3 – PREPOSTEXP which covers temporally complex terms like *preoperative*, *postoperative*, and *intraoperative*.

EVENTs and TIMEX3s are ordered on a timeline through temporal TLINKs which range from fairly coarse (the relation to document time creation) to fairly granular (the explicit pairwise TLINKs between EVENTs and/or TIMEX3s). Of note for this work, the CONTAINS relation between a TIMEX3 and an EVENT means that the span of the EVENT is completely within the span of the TIMEX3. The interannotator agreement F1-score for CONTAINS for the set of documents used here was 0.60.

2.2 Narrative Containers

One relatively new concept for marking temporal relations is that of narrative containers, as in Pustejovsky and Stubbs (2011). Narrative containers are time spans which are central to the discourse and often subsume multiple events and time expressions. They are often anchored by a time expression, though more abstract events may also act as anchors. Using the narrative container framework significantly reduces the number of explicit TLINK annotations yet retains a relevant degree of granularity enabling inferencing.

Consider the following clinical text example with DocTime of February 8.

> *The patient recovered well after her initial first surgery on December 16th to remove the adenocarcinoma, although on the evening of January 3rd she was admitted with a fever and treated with antibiotics.*

There are three narrative containers in this snippet – (1) the broad period leading up to the document creation time which includes the events of *recovered* and *adenocarcinoma*, (2) *December 16th*, which includes the events of *surgery* and *remove*, and (3) *January 3rd*, which includes the events of *admitted*, *fever*, and *treated*.

Using only the relation to the document creation time would provide too coarse of a timeline resulting in collapsing the three narrative containers (the coarse time bins of Raghavan et al. (2012) would collapse all events into the *before admission* category). On the other hand, marking explicit links between every pair of events and temporal expressions would be tedious and redundant. In this example, there is no need to explicitly mark that, for instance, *fever* was AFTER *surgery*, because we know that the fever happened on January 3rd and that the surgery happened on December 16th, and that January 3rd is AFTER December 16th. With the grouping of EVENTs in this way, we can infer the links between them and reduce annotator effort. Narrative containers strike the right balance between parsimony and expressiveness.

2.3 Related Work

Of course, the possibility of annotating temporal containment relations was allowed by even the earliest versions of the TimeML specification using TLINKs with the relation type INCLUDES. However, TimeML is a specification not a guideline, and as such, the way in which temporal relations have been annotated has varied widely and no

[1] http://clear.colorado.edu/TemporalWiki

[2] Annotation guidelines are posted on the THYME wiki.

corpus has previously been annotated with narrative containers in mind. In the TimeBank corpus (Pustejovsky et al., 2003a), annotators annotated only a sparse, mostly disconnected graph of the temporal relations that seemed salient to them. In TempEval 2007 and 2010 (Verhagen et al., 2007; Verhagen et al., 2010), annotators annotated only relations in specific constructions – e.g. all pairs of events and times in a sentence – and used a restricted set of relation types that excluded the INCLUDES relation. TempEval 2013 (UzZaman et al., 2013) allowed INCLUDES relations, but again only in particular constructions or when the relation seemed salient to the annotators. The 2012 i2b2 Challenge[3], which provided TimeML annotations on clinical data, annotated the INCLUDES relation, but merged it with other relations for the evaluation due to low inter-annotator agreement.

Since no narrative container-annotated corpora exist, there are also no existing models for extracting narrative container relations. However, we can draw on the various methods applied to related temporal relation tasks. Most relevant is the work on linking events to timestamps. This was one of the subtasks in TempEval 2007 and 2010, and systems used a variety of features including words, part-of-speech tags, and the syntactic path between the event and the time (Bethard and Martin, 2007; Llorens et al., 2010). Syntactic path features were also used in the 2012 i2b2 Challenge, where they provided gains especially for intra-sentential temporal links (Xu et al., 2013).

Recent research has also looked to syntactic tree kernels for temporal relation extraction. Mirroshandel et al. (2009) used a path-enclosed tree (i.e., selecting only the sub-tree containing the event and time), and used various weighting scheme variants of this approach on the TimeBank (Pustejovsky et al., 2003a) and Opinion[4] corpora. Hovy et al. (2012) used a flat tree structure for each event-time pair, including only token-based information (words, part of speech tags) between the event and time, and found that adding such tree kernels on top of a baseline set of features improved event-time linking performance on the TempEval 2007 and Machine Reading corpora (Strassel et al., 2010). While Mirroshandel et al. saw improvements using a representation with syntactic structure, Hovy et al. used the flat tree structure because they found that "using a full-parse syntactic tree as input representation did not help performance." Thus, it remains an open question exactly where and when syntactic tree kernels will help temporal relation extraction.

[3]http://i2b2.org/NLP/TemporalRelations

[4]Also known as the AQUAINT TimeML corpus – http://www.timeml.org

3 Methods

Inspired by this prior work, we treat the narrative container extraction task as a within-sentence relation extraction task between time and event mentions. For each sentence, this approach iterates over every gold standard annotated EVENT, pairing it with each TIMEX3 in the sentence, and uses a supervised machine learning algorithm to classify each pair as related by the CONTAINS relation or not. Training examples are generated in the same way, with pairs corresponding to annotated links marked as positive examples and all others marked as negative. We investigate a variety of features for the classifier as well as a variety of tree kernel combinations.

This straightforward approach does not address all relation pairs, setting aside event-event relations and inter-sentential relations, which are both likely to require different approaches.

3.1 SVM with Tree Kernels

The machine learning approach we use is support vector machine (SVM) with standard feature kernels, tree kernels, and composite kernels that combine the two. SVMs are used extensively for classification tasks in natural language processing, due to robust performance and widely available software packages. We take advantage of the ability in SVMs to represent structured features such as trees using *convolution kernels* (Collins and Duffy, 2001), also known as *tree kernels*. This kernel computes similarity between two tree structures by computing the number of common sub-trees, with a weight parameter to discount the influence of larger structural similarities. The specific formalism we use is sometimes called a *subset tree* kernel (Moschitti, 2006), which checks for similarity on subtrees of all sizes, as long as each subtree has its production rule completely expanded.

A useful property of kernels is that a linear combination of two kernels is guaranteed to be a kernel (Cristianini and Shawe-Taylor, 2000). In addition, the product of two kernels is also a kernel. This means that it is simple to combine traditional feature-based kernels used in SVMs (linear, polynomial, radial basis function) with tree kernels representing structural information. This approach of using *composite kernels* has been widely used in the task of relation extraction where syntactic information is presumed to be useful, but is hard to represent as traditional numeric features.

We investigate a few different composite kernels here, including a linear combination:

$$K_C(o_1, o_2) = \tau * K_T(t_1, t_2) + K_F(f_1, f_2) \quad (1)$$

where a composite kernel K_C operates on objects o_j composed of features f_j and tree t_j, by adding a tree kernel K_T weighted by τ to a feature kernel K_F. We also use a composite kernel that takes the product of kernels:

$$K_C(o_1, o_2) = K_T(t_1, t_2) * K_F(f_1, f_2) \quad (2)$$

Sometimes it is beneficial to make use of multiple syntactic "views" of the same instance. Below we will describe many different tree representations, and the tree kernel framework allows them to all be used simultaneously, by simply summing the similarities of the different representations and taking the combined sum as the tree kernel value:

$$K_T(\{t_1^1, t_1^2 \ldots, t_1^N\}, \{t_2^1, t_2^2, \ldots, t_2^N\}) = \sum_{i=1}^{N} K_T(t_1^i, t_2^i) \quad (3)$$

where i indexes the N different tree views. In all kernel combinations we compute the normalized version of both the feature and tree kernels so that they can be combined on an even footing.

The actual implementations we use for training are the SVM-LIGHT-TK package (Moschitti, 2006), which is a tree kernel extension to SVM^{light} (Joachims, 1999). At test time, we use the SVM-LIGHT-TK bindings of the ClearTK toolkit (Ogren et al., 2009) in a module built on top of Apache cTAKES (Savova et al., 2010), to take advantage of the pre-processing stages.

3.2 Flat Features

The flat features developed for the standard feature kernel include the text of each argument as a whole, the tokens of each argument represented as a bag of words, the first and last word of each argument, and the preceding and following words of each argument as bags of words. The token context between arguments is also represented using the text span as a whole, the first and last words, the set of words represented as a bag of words, and the distance between the arguments. In addition, part of speech (POS) tag features are extracted for each mention, with separate bag of POS tag features for each argument. The POS features are generated by the cTAKES POS tagger.

We also include semantic features of each argument. For event mentions, we include a feature marking the *contextual modality*, which can take on the possible values *Actual*, *Hedged*, *Hypothetical*, or *Generic*, which is part of the gold standard annotations. This feature was included as it was presumed that actual events are more likely to have definite time spans, and thus be related to times, than hypothetical or generic mentions of events. For time mentions we include a feature for the *time class*, with possible values of *Date*, *Time*, *Duration*, *Quantifier*, *Set*, or *Prepostexp*. The time class feature was used as it was hypothesized that dates and times are more likely to contain events than sets (e.g., *once a month*).

3.3 Tree Kernel Representations

We leverage existing tree kernel representations for this work, using some directly and others as starting point to a domain-specific representation.

First, we take advantage of the (relatively) flat structured tree kernel representations of Hovy et al. (2012). This representation uses lexical items such as POS tags rather than constituent structure, but places them into an ordered tree structure, which allows tree kernels to use them as a bag of items while also taking advantage of ordering structure when it is useful. Figure 1 shows an example tree for an event-time pair for which a relation exists, where the lexical information used is POS tag information for each term (the representation that Hovy et al. found most useful). We also used a version of this representation where the surface form is used instead of the POS tag.

While Hovy et al. showed positive results using this representation over just standard features, it is still somewhat constrained in its ability to represent long distance relations. This is because the subset tree kernel compares only complete rule productions, and with long distance relations a flat tree structure will have a production that is too big to learn. Alternatively, tree kernel representations can be based on constituent structure, as is common in the relation extraction literature. This will

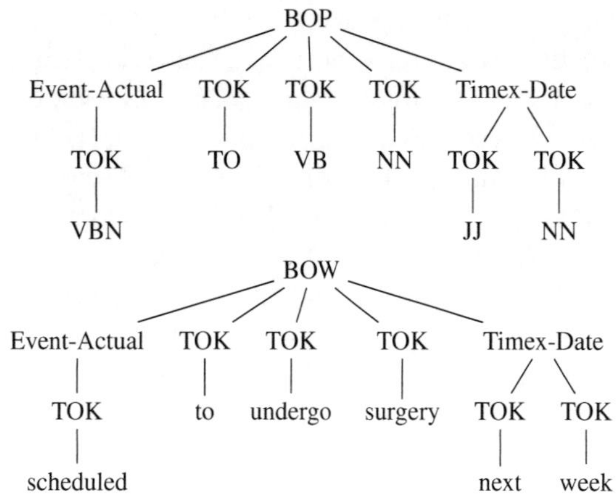

Figure 1: Two trees indicating the flat tree kernel representation. Above is the bag of POS tags version; below is the bag of words version.

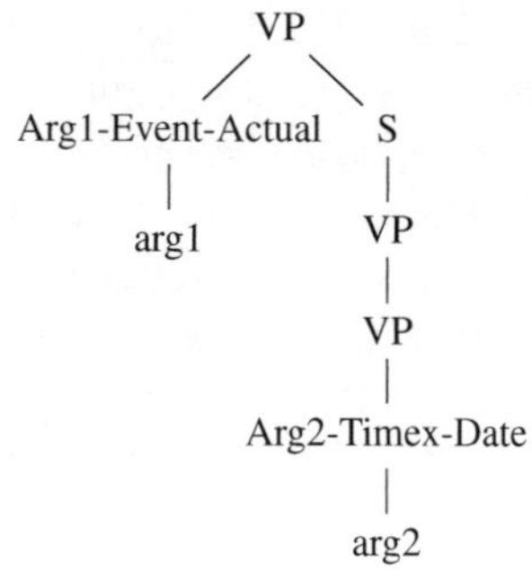

Figure 2: Path Tree (PT) representation

hopefully allow for the representation of longer distance relations by taking advantage of syntactic sub-structure with smaller productions. The representations used here are known as Feature Trees (FT), Path Trees (PT) and Path-Enclosed Trees (PET).

The Feature Tree representation takes the entire syntax tree for the sentence containing both arguments and inserts semantic information about those arguments. That information includes the argument type (EVENT or TIMEX) as an additional tree node above the constituent enclosing the argument. We also append semantic class information to the argument (contextual modality for events, time class for times), as in the flat features.

The Feature Tree representation is not commonly used, as it includes an entire sentence around the arguments of interest, and that may include a great deal of unrelated structure that adds noise to the classifier. Here we include it in an attempt to get to the root of an apparent discrepancy in the tree kernel literature, as explained in Section 2, in which Hovy et al. (2012) report a negative result and Mirroshandel et al. (2009) report a positive result for using constituency structure in tree kernels for temporal relation extraction.

The Path Tree representation uses a sub-tree of the whole constituent tree, but removes all nodes that are not along the path between the two arguments. Path information has been used in standard feature kernels (Pradhan et al., 2008), with each individual path being a possible boolean feature. Another representation making use of the path tree takes contiguous subsections of the path tree, or "path n-grams," in an attempt to combat the sparsity of using the whole path (Zheng et al., 2012). By using the path representation with a tree kernel, the model should get the benefit of all different sizes of path n-grams, up to the size of the whole path. This representation is augmented by adding in argument nodes with event and time features, as in the Feature Tree. Unlike the Feature Tree and the PET below, the Path Tree representation does not include word nodes, because the important aspect of this representation is the labels of the nodes on the path between arguments. Figure 2 shows an example of what this representation looks like.

The Path-Enclosed Tree representation is based on the smallest sub-tree that encloses the two proposed arguments. This is a representation that has shown value in other work using tree kernels for relation extraction (Zhang et al., 2006; Mirroshandel et al., 2009). The information contained in the PET representation is a superset of that contained in the Path Tree representation, since it includes the full path between arguments as well as the structure between arguments and the argument text. This means that it can take into account path information while also considering constituent structure between arguments that may play a role in determining whether the two arguments are related. For example, temporal cue words like *after* or *during* may occur between arguments and will not be captured by Path Trees. Like the PT representation, the PET representation is augmented with the semantic information specified above in the Feature Tree representation. Figure 3 shows an example of this representation.

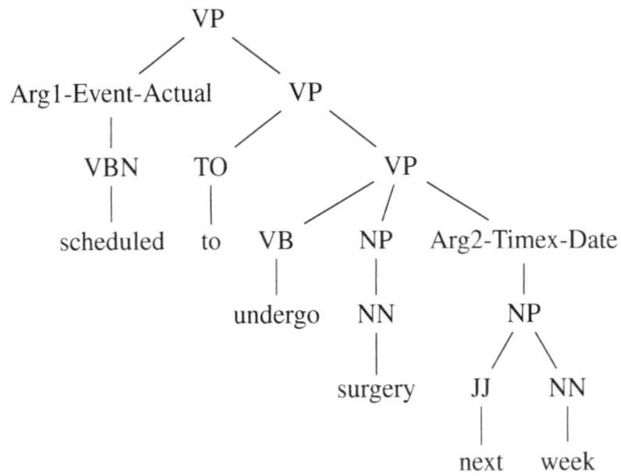

Figure 3: Path-Enclosed Tree representation

4 Evaluation

The corpus we used for evaluations was described in Section 2. There are 78 total notes in the corpus, with three notes for each of 26 patients. The data is split into training (50%), development (25%), and test (25%) sections based on patient number, so that each patient's notes are all in the same section. The combined training and development set used for final training consists of 4378 sentences with 49,050 tokens, and 7372 events, 849 time expressions, and 2287 CONTAINS relations. There were 774 positive instances of CONTAINS in the training data, with 1513 negative instances. For constituent structure and features we use the gold standard treebank and event and time features from our corpus. Preliminary work suggests that automatic parses from cTAKES do not harm performance very much, but the focus of this work is on the relation extraction so we use gold standard parses. All preliminary experiments were done using the development set for testing.

We designed a set of experiments to examine several hypotheses regarding extraction of the CONTAINS relation and the efficacy of different tree kernel representations. The first two configurations test simple rule-based baseline systems, CLOSEST-P and CLOSEST-R, for distance-related decision rule systems meant to optimize precision and recall, respectively. CLOSEST-P hypothesizes a CONTAINS link between every TIMEX3 and the closest annotated EVENT, which will make few links overall. CLOSEST-R hypothesizes a CONTAINS link between every EVENT and the closest TIMEX3, which will make many more links.

The next configuration, *Flat Features*, uses the token and part of speech features along with argument semantics features, as described in Section 3. While this feature set may not seem exhaustive, in preliminary work many traditional relation extraction features were tried and found to not have much effect. This particular configuration was tested because it is most comparable to the bag of word and bag of POS kernels from Hovy et al. (2012), and should help show whether the tree kernel is providing anything over an equivalent set of basic features.

We then examine several composite kernels, all using the same feature kernel, but using different tree kernel-based representations. First, we use a composite kernel which uses the bag of word and bag of POS tree views, as in Hovy et al. (2012). Next, we add in two additional tree views to the tree kernel, Path-Enclosed Tree and Path Tree, which are intended to examine the effect of using traditional syntax, and the long distance features that they enable. The final experimental configuration replaces the PET and PT representations from the last configuration with the Feature Tree representation. This tests the hypothesis that the difference between positive results for tree kernels in this task (as in, say, Mirroshandel et al. (2009)) and negative results reported by Hovy et al. (2012) is the difference between using a full-parse tree and using standard sub-tree representations.

For the rule-based systems, there are no parameters to tune. Our machine-learning systems are based on support vector machines (SVM), which require tuning of several parameters, including kernel type (linear, polynomial, and radial basis function), the parameters for each kernel, and c, the cost of misclassification. Tree kernels introduce an additional parameter λ for weighting large structures, and the use of a composite kernel introduces parameters for which kernel combination operator to use, and how to weight the different kernels for the sum operator.

For each machine learning configuration, we performed a large grid search over the combined parameter space, where we trained on the training set and tested on the development set. For the final experiments, the parameters were chosen that optimized the F1 score on the development set. Qualitatively, the parameter tuning strongly favored configurations which combined the kernels using the sum operator, and recall and precision were strongly correlated with the SVM parameter c. Using these parameters, we then trained on the combined training and development sets and tested on the official test set.

4.1 Evaluation Metrics

The state of evaluating temporal relations has been evolving over the past decade. This is partially due to the inferential properties of temporal relations, because it is possible to define the same set of relations using different set of axioms. To take a very simple example, given a gold set of relations A<B and B<C, and given the system output A<B, A<C and B<C, if one were to compute a plain precision/recall metric, then the axiom A<C would be counted against the system, when one can easily infer from the gold set of relations that it is indeed correct. With more relations the inference process becomes more complex.

Recently there has been some work trying to address the shortcomings of the plain F1 score (Muller and Tannier, 2004; Setzer et al., 2006; UzZaman and Allen, 2011; Tannier and Muller, 2008; Tannier and Muller, 2011). However, the community has not yet come to a consensus on the best evaluation approach. Two recent evaluations, TempEval-3 (UzZaman et al., 2013) and the 2012 i2b2 Challenge (Sun et al., 2013), used an implementation of the proposal by (UzZaman and Allen, 2011). However, as described in Cherry et al. (2013), this algorithm, which uses a greedy graph minimization approach, is sensitive to the order in which the temporal relations are presented to the scorer. In addition, the scorer is not able to give credit for non-redundant, non-minimum links (Cherry et al., 2013) as with the the case of the relation A<C mentioned earlier.

Considering that the measures for evaluating temporal relations are still evolving, we decided to use plain F-score, with recall and precision scores also reported. This score is computed across all intra-sentential EVENT-TIMEX3 pairs in the gold standard, where precision $= \frac{\#\ correct\ predictions}{\#\ predictions}$, recall $= \frac{\#\ correct\ predictions}{\#\ gold\ standard\ relations}$, and F1 score $= \frac{2*precision*recall}{precision+recall}$.

4.2 Experimental Results

Results are shown in Table 1. Rule-based baselines perform reasonably well, but are heavily biased in terms of precision or recall. The machine learning baseline cannot even obtain the same performance as the CLOSEST-R rule-based system, though it is more balanced in terms of precision and recall. Using a composite kernel which adds in the flat token-based tree kernels improves performance over the standard feature kernel by 4.1 points. Adding in the Path Tree and Path-Enclosed Tree constituency-based trees along with the flat trees improves F1 score to our best result of 73.7. Finally, replacing PT and PET representations with the Feature Tree representation does not offer any performance improvement over the Flat Features + Bag Trees configuration.

System	Precision	Recall	F1
CLOSEST-P	0.754	0.537	0.627
CLOSEST-R	0.502	**0.947**	0.656
Flat Features (FF)	0.705	0.593	0.645
FF+Bag Trees (BT)	0.649	0.728	0.686
FF+BT+PET+PT	**0.770**	0.707	**0.737**
FF+BT+FT	0.691	0.691	0.691

Table 1: Table of results of main experiments.

4.3 Error Analysis

We performed error analysis on the outputs of the best-performing system (FF+BT+PET+PT in Table 1). First, we note that the parameter search was optimized for F1. This resulted in the highest-scoring configuration using a composite kernel with the sum operator, polynomial kernel for the secondary kernel, $\lambda = 0.5$, tree kernel weight (T) of 0.1, and $c = 10.0$. This high value of c and low value of T results in higher precision and lower recall, but there were configurations with lower c and higher T which made the opposite tradeoff, with only marginally worse F1-score. For the purposes of error analysis, however, this configuration leads to a focus on false negatives.

First, the false positives contained many relations that were legitimately ambiguous or possible annotator errors. An example ambiguous case is *She is currently being treated on the Surgical Service for...*, in which the system generates the relation CONTAINS(*currently*, *treated*), but the gold standard labels as OVERLAP. This example is ambiguous because it is not clear from just the linguistic context whether the treatment is wholly contained in the small time window denoted by *currently*, or whether it started a while ago or will continue into the future. There are many similar cases where the event is a disease/disorder type, and the specific nature of the disease is important to understanding whether this is a CONTAINS or OVERLAP relation, specifically understanding whether the disease is chronic or more acute.

Another source of false positives were where the event and time were clearly related, but not with CONTAINS. In the example *reports that she has been having intermittent bleeding since May of 1998*, the term *since* clearly indicates that this is a BEGINS-ON relation between *bleeding* and *May of 1998*. This is a case where having other temporal relation classifiers may be useful, as they can compete and the relation can be assigned to whichever classifier is more confident.

False negatives frequently occurred in contexts where the event and time were far apart. Syntactic tree kernels were introduced to help improve recall on longer-distance relations, and were successful up to a limit. However, certain examples are so far apart that the algorithm may have had difficulty sorting noise from important structure. For example, the system did not find the CONTAINS(*October 27, 2010, oophorectomy*) relation in the sentence:

> *October 27, 2010, Dr. XXX performed exploratory laparotomy with an transverse colectomy and Dr. YYY performed a total abdominal hysterectomy with a bilateral salpingo-oophorectomy.*

Here, while the date may be part of the same sentence as the event, the syntactic relation between the pair is not what makes the relation; the date is acting as a kind of discourse marker that indicates that the following events are contained. This suggests that discourse-level features may be useful even for the intra-sentential classification task.

Other false negatives occurred where there was syntactic complexity, even on shorter examples. The subset tree kernel used here matches complete rule productions, and across complex structure with large productions, the chances of finding similarity decreases substantially. Thus, events within coordination or separated from the time by clause breaks are more difficult to relate to the time due to the multiple different ways of relating these different syntactic elements.

Finally, there are some examples where the anchor of a narrative container is an event with multiple sub-events. In these cases, the system performs well at relating a time expression to the anchor event, but may miss the sub-events that are farther away. This is a case where having an event-event TLINK classifier, then applying deterministic closure rules, would allow a combined system to link the sub-events to the time expression.

5 Discussion and Conclusion

In this paper we have developed a system for automatically identifying CONTAINS relations in clinical text. The experiments show first that a machine learning approach that intelligently integrates constituency information can greatly improve performance over rule-based baselines. We also show that the tree kernel approach, which can model sequence better than a bag of tokens-style approach, is beneficial even when it uses the same features. Finally, the experiments show that choosing the correct representation is important for tree kernel approaches, and specifically that using a full parse tree may give inferior performance compared to sub-trees focused on the structure of interest.

In general, there is much work to be done in the area of representing temporal information in clinical records. Many of the inputs to the algorithm described in this paper need to be extracted automatically, including time expressions and events. Work on relations will focus on adding features to represent discourse information and richer representation of event semantics. Discourse information may help with the longer-distance errors, where the time expression acts almost as a topic for an extended description of events. Better understanding of event semantics, such as whether a disease is chronic or acute, or typical duration for a treatment, may help constrain relations. In addition, we will explore the effectiveness of using dependency tree structure, which has been useful in the domain of extracting relations from the biomedical literature (Tikk et al., 2013).

Acknowledgements

The work described was supported by Temporal History of Your Medical Events (THYME) NLM R01LM010090 and Integrating Informatics and Biology to the Bedside (i2b2) NCBO U54LM008748. Thanks to the anonymous reviewers for thorough and insightful comments.

References

Naushad UzZaman, Hector Llorens, et al. 2013. Semeval-2013 task 1: Tempeval-3: Evaluating time expressions, events, and temporal relations. In *Second Joint Conference on Lexical and Computational Semantics (*SEM)*,

Volume 2: Proceedings of the Seventh International Workshop on Semantic Evaluation (SemEval 2013), pages 1–9, Atlanta, Georgia, USA, June. Association for Computational Linguistics.

Ashwin N Ananthakrishnan, Tianxi Cai, et al. 2013. Improving case definition of Crohn's disease and ulcerative colitis in electronic medical records using natural language processing: a novel informatics approach. *Inflammatory bowel diseases*.

Steven Bethard and James H. Martin. 2007. CU-TMP: Temporal relation classification using syntactic and semantic features. In *Proceedings of the 4th International Workshop on Semantic Evaluations (SemEval-2007)*, pages 129–132.

Colin Cherry, Xiaodan Zhu, et al. 2013. A la recherche du temps perdu: extracting temporal relations from medical text in the 2012 i2b2 NLP challenge. *Journal of the American Medical Informatics Association*, March.

Michael Collins and Nigel Duffy. 2001. Convolution kernels for natural language. In *Neural Information Processing Systems*.

Nello Cristianini and John Shawe-Taylor. 2000. *An Introduction to Support Vector Machines and Other Kernel-based Learning Methods*. Cambridge University Press.

Dirk Hovy, James Fan, et al. 2012. When did that happen?: linking events and relations to timestamps. In *Proceedings of the 13th Conference of the European Chapter of the Association for Computational Linguistics*, pages 185–193. Association for Computational Linguistics.

Thorsten Joachims. 1999. Making large scale svm learning practical. In B. Schlkopf, C. Burges, and A. Smola, editors, *Advances in Kernel Methods - Support Vector Learning*. Universität Dortmund.

Chen Lin, Helena Canhao, et al. 2012. Feature engineering and selection for rheumatoid arthritis disease activity classification using electronic medical records. In *Proceedings of ICML Workshop on Machine Learning for Clinical Data*.

Hector Llorens, Estela Saquete, and Borja Navarro. 2010. TIPSem (english and spanish): Evaluating crfs and semantic roles in tempeval-2. In *Proceedings of the 5th International Workshop on Semantic Evaluation*, pages 284–291. Association for Computational Linguistics.

Seyed Abolghasem Mirroshandel, M Khayyamian, and GR Ghassem-Sani. 2009. Using tree kernels for classifying temporal relations between events. *Proc. of the PACLIC23*, pages 355–364.

Alessandro Moschitti. 2006. Efficient convolution kernels for dependency and constituent syntactic trees. In *Machine Learning: ECML 2006*, pages 318–329. Springer.

Philippe Muller and Xavier Tannier. 2004. Annotating and measuring temporal relations in texts. In *Proceedings of the 20th international conference on Computational Linguistics*, COLING '04, Stroudsburg, PA, USA. Association for Computational Linguistics.

Philip V. Ogren, Philipp G. Wetzler, and Steven J. Bethard. 2009. ClearTK: a framework for statistical natural language processing. In *Unstructured Information Management Architecture Workshop at the Conference of the German Society for Computational Linguistics and Language Technology*, 9.

Sameer S Pradhan, Wayne Ward, and James H Martin. 2008. Towards robust semantic role labeling. *Computational Linguistics*, 34(2):289–310.

James Pustejovsky and Amber Stubbs. 2011. Increasing informativeness in temporal annotation. In *Proceedings of the 5th Linguistic Annotation Workshop*, pages 152–160.

James Pustejovsky, Patrick Hanks, et al. 2003a. The timebank corpus. In *Corpus linguistics*, volume 2003, page 40.

James Pustejovsky, José Casta no, et al. 2003b. Timeml: Robust specification of event and temporal expressions in text. In *Fifth International Workshop on Computational Semantics (IWCS-5)*.

Preethi Raghavan, Eric Fosler-Lussier, and Albert M Lai. 2012. Temporal classification of medical events. In *Proceedings of the 2012 Workshop on Biomedical Natural Language Processing*, pages 29–37. Association for Computational Linguistics.

Guergana K. Savova, James J. Masanz, et al. 2010. Mayo clinical text analysis and knowledge extraction system (cTAKES): architecture, component evaluation and applications. *J Am Med Inform Assoc*, 17(5):507–513.

Andrea Setzer, Robert Gaizauskas, and Mark Hepple. 2006. The role of inference in the temporal annotation and analysis of text. *Language Resources and Evaluation*, 39(2-3):243–265, February.

Stephanie Strassel, Dan Adams, et al. 2010. The DARPA machine reading program - encouraging linguistic and reasoning research with a series of reading tasks. In *Proceedings of the Seventh International Conference on Language Resources and Evaluation (LREC'10)*, Valletta, Malta.

Weiyi Sun, Anna Rumshisky, and Ozlem Uzuner. 2013. Evaluating temporal relations in clinical text: 2012 i2b2 challenge. *Journal of the American Medical Informatics Association*, April.

Xavier Tannier and Philippe Muller. 2008. Evaluation metrics for automatic temporal annotation of texts. *Proceedings of the Proceedings of the Sixth International Language Resources and Evaluation (LREC'08)*.

Xavier Tannier and Philippe Muller. 2011. Evaluating temporal graphs built from texts via transitive reduction. *J. Artif. Int. Res.*, 40(1):375413, January.

Domonkos Tikk, Illés Solt, et al. 2013. A detailed error analysis of 13 kernel methods for protein-protein interaction extraction. *BMC bioinformatics*, 14(1):12.

Naushad UzZaman and James Allen. 2011. Temporal evaluation. In *Proceedings of the 49th Annual Meeting of the Association for Computational Linguistics: Human Language Technologies*, page 351–356.

Marc Verhagen, Robert Gaizauskas, et al. 2007. Semeval-2007 task 15: Tempeval temporal relation identification. In *Proceedings of the Fourth International Workshop on Semantic Evaluations (SemEval-2007)*, pages 75–80.

Marc Verhagen, Roser Sauri, et al. 2010. Semeval-2010 task 13: Tempeval-2. In *Proceedings of the 5th International Workshop on Semantic Evaluation*, pages 57–62, Uppsala, Sweden, July. Association for Computational Linguistics.

RA Wilke, H Xu, et al. 2011. The emerging role of electronic medical records in pharmacogenomics. *Clinical Pharmacology & Therapeutics*, 89(3):379–386.

Yan Xu, Yining Wang, et al. 2013. An end-to-end system to identify temporal relation in discharge summaries: 2012 i2b2 challenge. *Journal of the American Medical Informatics Association : JAMIA*.

Min Zhang, Jie Zhang, and Jian Su. 2006. Exploring syntactic features for relation extraction using a convolution tree kernel. In *Proceedings of the Human Language Technology Conference of the North American Chapter of the ACL*, pages 288–295.

Jiaping Zheng, Wendy W Chapman, et al. 2012. A system for coreference resolution for the clinical narrative. *Journal of the American Medical Informatics Association*, 19:660–667.

Identifying pathological findings in German radiology reports using a syntacto-semantic parsing approach

Claudia Bretschneider[1,2], Sonja Zillner[1] and Matthias Hammon[3]
[1] Siemens AG, Corporate Technology, 81739 Munich, Germany
[2] University Munich, Center for Information and Language Processing, 80538 Munich, Germany
[3] University Hospital Erlangen, Department of Radiology, 91054 Erlangen, Germany
{claudia.bretschneider.ext,sonja.zillner}@siemens.com,
matthias.hammon@uk-erlangen.de

Abstract

In order to integrate heterogeneous clinical information sources, semantically correlating information entities have to be linked. Our discussions with radiologists revealed that anatomical entities with pathological findings are of particular interest when linking radiology text and images. Previous research to identify pathological findings focused on simplistic approaches that recognize diseases or negated findings, but failed to establish a holistic approach. In this paper, we introduce our syntacto-semantic parsing approach to classify sentences in radiology reports as either pathological or non-pathological based on the findings they describe. Although we operate with an incomplete, RadLex-based linguistic resource, the obtained results show the effectiveness of our approach by identifying a recall value of 74.3% for the classification task.

1 Introduction

In radiology, descriptions of the patient's health status are stored in heterogeneous formats. They range from radiology images - which are the primary source for radiologists - over dictated reports about the image findings up to written texts.

Although the various data items describe the same status, they are distributed in non-linked systems. This is hindering the radiologist's workflow. Especially when reading reports, radiologists want to link back from the described finding (in the text) to the related body location (in the images). Today, they establish the link manually. This is obviously time-consuming when state-of-the-art imaging modalities deliver a mass of stacked images.

In order to link radiology images and reports, each information source needs to be annotated with semantic meta-information about the anatomical entities they describe. The necessary semantic image annotations for the integration have been made available as a result of the Theseus MEDICO project (Seifert, 2010). Introduced algorithms automatically detect anatomical entities in radiology images and annotate those with the corresponding RadLex IDs (Seifert et al., 2009). The semantic annotations from the reports have to be in line with those image annotations. Therefore, the final result of the text analysis system need to be anatomical annotations based on RadLex. We introduce a mechanism that extracts those semantic annotations from the radiology reports to enable the integration.

We identified three challenges, which a text analysis system has to consider when extracting the relevant anatomical entities from text:

1. The linguistic characteristics of the reports differ significantly from standard free-text,
2. the underlying German linguistic resource (the RadLex taxonomy) is incomplete and
3. only a subset of the named anatomical entities in the reports are relevant for annotating.

First, the special *linguistic characteristics* of the handled German reports have to be taken into account. While the linguistic characteristics English radiology reports have been intensively studied (Friedman et al., 1994; Friedman et al., 2002; Sager et al., 1994), German ones are still a young research area. German reports are comparable to English ones when it comes to structural particularities. One can observe two characteristics in both languages: syntactic shortness and reduced semantic complexity. But the reports differ in richness of the language used. German language is rich in inflection form; the same is true for German medical language. Additionally, clinical texts extend the variety in inflection forms by introducing a huge amount of Greek- and Latin-rooted vocabulary. Further linguistic particularities will be introduced in a later section.

Second, the anatomical annotations will be established based on the controlled vocabulary of the *RadLex* taxonomy. Anatomical annotations of the images (based on RadLex) are already available and hence impose the mandatory condition to use RadLex annotations for the reports. We operate on German radiology reports that is why we use the German RadLex taxonomy. Compared to the English version, the German RadLex is lacking in terminology. This is an obstacle, we have to overcome.

Third, we have to find a way to filter *relevant anatomical annotations*. According to the radiologists we worked with, it is inappropriate to extract *all* anatomical entities from the text to link them with the image annotations. A large portion of the anatomies is described with normal or absent findings, which do not describe pathologies. Those findings are included in the reports in order to exclude differential diagnoses. However, radiologists are interested in images of anatomical entities described with pathological findings. Thus, a crucial part of our work is to extract the anatomical entities with pathological findings in order to link only those with the image positions.

The core contribution of this paper is the description of a syntacto-semantic parsing approach to identify the sentences that describe pathological findings by using the German version of the RadLex taxonomy. The results of this approach are used to integrate relevant semantic information from heterogeneous data sources and support radiologists significantly in their work routine.

To introduce our solution, the remainder of this paper is organized as follows: Section 2 refers to related work in the field and shows where sub-problems are still unsolved. In Section 3, we analyze the linguistic characteristics of the reports. Section 4 introduces the text analysis system for integrating radiology text and images. The system handles both the linguistic particularities of the reports and the shortcomings of RadLex as linguistic resource and filters relevant anatomical entities from the reports. Section 5 evaluates and discusses the classification and extraction results. Finally, Section 6 concludes with possible future work.

2 Related work

Medical grammar-based text analysis systems Information extraction from medical texts is a well-researched task in medical natural language processing (Meystre et al, 2008). Especially radiology reports play an important role.

Theoretical work in the linguistic characteristics of the medical sublanguage has been conducted on the adaption of theories of Harris by (Friedman et al., 2002). Early systems of (Sager et al., 1994; Friedman et al., 1994) are adaptations of the theories and implement own (context-free) medical language grammar for radiology reports. They show that parsing of medical texts based on a combined semantic-syntactic grammar can be successfully conducted – but they conducted their research using English reports. Even today, advances in grammar-based parsing of medical texts are reached (Fan et al., 2011).

More recently, sophisticated semantic medical text analysis systems have integrated a component to parse texts. (Savova et al., 2010) They take the output of the parsing process to extract semantic relationships between the medical concepts described.

All those systems work with elaborated lexicons that fully cover the vocabulary used in English report.

Detecting diseases and Negated finding Most systems cover the problem of detecting pathological findings in the reports just partially: In order to detect pathologies, they automate the assignment of codes for diseases listed in ontologies such as UMLS (Aronson, 2001; Lindberg, 1990; Long, 2005) or ICD (Computational Medicine Center, 2007; Pestian et al., 2007).

Non-pathological findings are identified using negation detection algorithms. Available approaches range from simple algorithms based on dictionary lookup and regular expressions (Chapman et al., 2001; Mutalik et al., 2001) through machine learning (Goryachev et al., 2006) up to advanced approaches that apply a context-free "negation grammar" (Huang, 2007).

Gap analysis While the grammar-based analysis of radiology reports has proven to be successful with complete lexical resources, we have to face the shortcomings of an incomplete lexicon. Furthermore, in other systems the grammar is used to analyze the syntax of the reports. Our approach to use it for classification is novel and has not been applied so far.

Working with German clinical texts is another challenge in the field. English texts have been made available by a number of shared tasks and gained more and more interest in the last decade. Medical corpora in languages other than English are not available to that extent.

That is perhaps also the reason for the tremendous lack of German medical ontologies. While great effort is put into the advance of English ontologies, German language versions are rare.

Terminology acquisition and semantic classification Semantic classifications beyond the hierarchical information encoded in taxonomies and ontologies are still rare for ontology concepts. In particular, semantic classifications such as information about the pathological nature of the concepts are missing so far.

Several approaches address this lack of semantic information: Corpus-based approaches base their methods on statistical analyses about the coverage and usage frequency of UMLS ontology concepts (Liu et al., 2012; Wu et al., 2012). (Johnson, 1999) derives semantic classes from ontology mapping and disambiguates multiple senses in contexts of discharge summaries. (Campbell et al., 1999) applies pattern-based rules and combines them with UMLS concepts to acquire new and semantically classified terminology. However, this approach is limited to noun phrases.

Finally, (Zweigenbaum et al., 2003) introduce approaches to automatically extending the existing English UMLS ontology with non-English concepts based on statistical algorithms.

3 Corpus analysis

3.1 Reference corpus

Since a publicly available corpus of German radiology reports is missing, we build our own annotated corpus based on 2713 de-identified reports from our clinical partner, the University Hospital Erlangen. The reports result from radiology examinations of lymphoma patients and range from April 2002 to July 2007. Each report contains two free-text sections: The first one describes findings observed in the images. In the second sections, the radiologist provides an overall evaluation about the findings, derives probable diagnoses and excludes differential diagnoses.

3.2 Development set of reports

From the corpus, we selected 174 reports for the development set. They are uniformly distributed across time and length.

The development set serves multiple purposes:

1. It is used for the linguistic analysis.
2. We use it for grammar derivation.
3. And pathology classifications and additional vocabulary are learned from the sentences.

A radiologist classified each of the contained sentences either as pathological or non-pathological. This is done based on the characteristics of the findings described in the sentence. Sentences describing normal or negated findings are classified as 'non-pathological' and those containing descriptions of abnormalities are classified as 'pathological'. In cases where sentences include both types of findings, they are classified as 'pathological'. Hence, each sentence in the development set was annotated with the classification information.

3.3 Statistics of the development set

The 174 reports in the development set contain 4295 sentences of which less than half are classified as 'pathological'. This ratio is in line with the radiologists' experience. As from their intuition, the majority of the findings described in radiology reports is noted as absent or has normal status. In the reports, they complement pathological findings in order to note the absence of finding and to exclude suspected diseases. However, those sentences classified as 'non-pathological' are irrelevant for our setting of linking the containing anatomies to the images.

Table 1 shows additional results of the statistical corpus analysis.

	Sentence classification	
Corpus characteristic	*pathological*	*non-pathological*
Sentences	1943	2352
Tokens used	16437	11572
Average sentence length	8.46	4.92
Distinct word types	2398	1581

Table 1: Results of statistical corpus analysis based on the development set

Another significant characteristic of the sentences is their average length. Pathological sentences are about as twice as long as non-pathological ones and thus are more complex in their syntax. The pathology classifier has to cover this complexity.

Furthermore, from comparing the distinct word types used, we conclude that the description of pathological findings requires a richer language than those of normal states and absent findings in non-pathological sentences. The linguistic resource has to cover this required rich language.

3.4 Semantic and syntactic characteristics

One of the most apparent syntactic characteristics of the reports is the elliptical style of the sentences. The texts are rich in omission of verbs; verbs are dispensable as they only underline the absence or presence of symptoms. An example that illustrates the facts is shown below.

General language
In der Lunge sind keine Ergüsse zu finden.
In the lung, there are no effusions found.
Radiologist's style
Lunge: Kein Erguss.
Lung: No effusions.

The observation of the syntactic structure of the sentences is in line with (Friedman et al., 2002) and will simplify the classification of the sentences.

The second observation we made is that the medical language uses a high amount of domain-specific vocabulary. This vocabulary is rarely used in every-day language and is highly connected with (implicit) medical domain knowledge. Thus, the linguistic handling of the reports requires a domain-specific lexicon. Furthermore, the vocabulary can be categorized into only a few semantic classes representing the content, such as measurements, dates, anatomies, modifier of the anatomies, diseases, etc.

Third, one feature of the medical language is very domain-specific: It uses a high amount of Greek- and Latin-rooted words. This is important, because those terms follow their own specific inflection forms. Furthermore, for many terms there exist both German and Latin-/Greek-rooted descriptions which are used interchangeably (e.g. descriptions of anatomical entities or diseases). However, most lexicons only contain a single term - not the complete list of synonyms.

Like the German language, the medical language is also rich in compound terms such as *Nasenseptumdeviation* (deviation of the nasal septum) or *Glukosestoffwechselsteigerung* (increase in glucose metabolism). Especially radiologists use a high number of compounds to describe pathological findings. They will be of particular importance for the identification of pathological findings. In many cases, only after determining the pathology classification of each subtoken, the classification of the compound can be determined.

Systems that mine information from radiology reports have to consider the named syntactic and semantic characteristics and handle them as language-specifics. In particular, the short length of the sentences simplifies the development of a grammar with a limited number of rules.

4 Methods

4.1 Grammar-based classification approach

Based on the observations from the corpus analysis, we derive and apply a semantic context-free grammar (CFG) to classify sentences.

Using a grammar to classify the sentences may not seem intuitive for every-day language sentences. Nevertheless, the language used in radiology reports allows this approach. There are several facts that support the usage of a grammar.

1. The structure of the sentences created by radiologists differs significantly from the structure of general German language. To model this language an own (sublanguage) grammar is necessary.

2. Since the sentences are short in length, a relatively small number of grammar rules can represent their syntax. In particular, the omission of verbs allows us to create and use a simplified grammar.

3. As already researched by (Friedman et al., 2002), the sentences contain a limited number of semantic classes which are combined into few rules.

These observations support the approach to create a grammar with few rules to classify the sentences.

4.2 Overview of the building blocks of the text analysis system

After having analyzed the linguistic characteristics, we designed a text analysis system to extract the relevant information from the reports. The classification is based on a grammar whose components are setup first: The **grammar rules are created** and **lexicon is setup**. To overcome the incompleteness of the lexicon and to enhance the grammar with probabilities, we introduce an additional **learning step**. These first three steps can be regarded as preparation steps for the subsequent integration steps: Finally, the system is able to **classify** report sentences and **extracts** anatomical annotations from the sentences classified as 'pathological'. In the end, the semantic annotations from text and images are **linked** across the data sources. The described steps of the target system are shown in Figure 1.

This paper focuses on the details of the created grammar: how the parsing algorithm is adapted to learn new linguistic knowledge and how the probabilistic parsing algorithm is used to derive a classification for an input sentence.

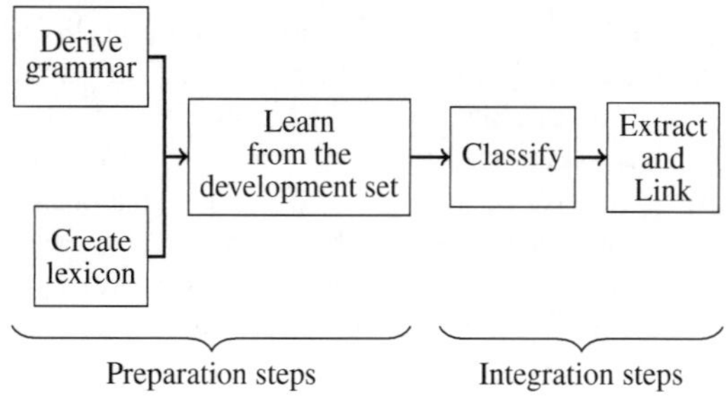

Figure 1: Processing steps in text analysis system

The following sections describe the details of the individual processing steps.

4.3 Derive grammar

The core component of the text processing system is the grammar. Our grammar has two functions:

1. It is used to describe the structure of a given input sentence, and

2. using the results of the parsing process, an input sentence can be classified as either 'pathological' or 'non-pathological'.

We use a *semantic* grammar for the description of the syntactic structure of the sentences. That means, instead of mapping syntactic categories from part-of-speech tags as non-terminal symbols, we use semantic representations of the content. E.g., the term *Niere* [spleen] gets assigned the non-terminal symbol ANATOMIE.

Following the proposal of (Friedman et al., 1994), we create semantic classes that represent the content of the radiology reports. However, we do not need their fine-grained semantic class definition. Our task of pathology classification requires only a reduced number of classes. We drop classes that do not change the pathology classification result (such as degree, quantity, technique, etc.) and introduce the generalized semantic classes MOD (modifier) and TERM. The list of semantic classes derived is shown in Table 2.

The grammar has to fulfill one condition to be able to classify sentences. Only non-terminal symbols used for classification are directly derived from the start symbol (S). We use the non-terminal symbols PATH for classifying sentences as 'pathological' and NOPATH for classifying as 'non-pathological'. Hence, the following unary rules designate the classification in our grammar:

$$S \rightarrow PATH$$
$$S \rightarrow NOPATH$$

Any subsequent rules have to be hierarchically embedded into those rules.

During the subsequent (manual) grammar derivation process, we use the listed semantic classes as non-terminal symbols and derive the grammar rules from

Structural non-terminals	
ROOT	
S	
KOMMA	
ENUM	
FIND_CONNECT	
Classification non-terminals	
PATH	*Constituents*
NOPATH	*(sentence-level,*
MOD_PATH	*modifier and term)*
MOD_NOPATH	*with pathology*
TERM_PATH	*classification*
TERM_NOPATH	*information*
FINDING_NOPATH	
FINDING_PATH	
Semantic non-terminals	
LOCATION	
DATE	*Non-terminals*
MEASUREMENT	*representing*
ANATOMIE	*constituents with*
NEGATION	*specific semantic*
DISEASE	*meaning*
Linguistic non-terminals	
ARTICLE	*Article non-terminal*
ARTICLE_GENITIV	
PREP_DATE	*Preposition*
PREP_LOCATION	*non-terminals*
PREP_MEASUREMENT	*indicating different*
	semantic units
Mapping semantic class - regular expression	
DATE_VALUE	
MEASUREMENT_VALUE	
IMAGE_VALUE	

Table 2: List of semantic non-terminals

the development corpus. Because of the limited number of semantic classes and the elliptical sentence style, a small set of 238 grammar rules suffices to describe the sentence syntax. The resulting grammar rules consider the syntactic complexity of the sentences describing pathological findings: 52% of the rules model the constituent structure of pathological sentences.

4.4 Create lexicon

The linguistic resource of our system is a lexicon, created based on the German version of the RadLex taxonomy.

RadLex (RSNA, 2012) is a taxonomy published by the Radiological Society of North America (RNSA) in order to deliver a uniform controlled vocabulary for indexing and retrieval of radiology information sources. The current English version 3.8 contains 39976 classes. A German version has been worked-out (Marwede et al., 2009) in 2007. The contained terms are organized in 13 major categories: anatomical entity as one among others such as treatment, image observation and imaging observation characteristics. But as the development of the German language version has been stopped, the latest version 2.0 contains only a subset of classes (n=10003). This lack in terminology is an obstacle to overcome.

Linguistic resource From the German RadLex we created a lexicon (n=9479), which we use as linguistic resource. Each entry is represented by a list of properties.

Besides the structural properties *label* and *RID*, we apply several steps of linguistic and semantic processing to enrich the lexical entries. The *normalized stem* of each entry results from an own tokenization, normalization and stemming algorithm.

The normalization aligns German and Latin style spellings (e.g. *Karzinom/Carzinom*, *Okzipitallappen/-Occipitallappen*). The stemmer adapts the German Porter stemmer and incorporates additional rules for suffixes and inflection that are derived from Latin and Greek. E.g., this extension enabled the mapping of *Mediastinum* and *mediastinal* to the same stem *mediastin-*, which would not have been possible with the German Porter stemmer.

Furthermore, during lexicon setup each entry is enriched with *semantic classification* information. The semantic class is used during parsing. We use reasoning methods and the hierarchical *is-a* structure of the RadLex taxonomy in order to deduct a semantic class for each entry from the major categories. For example, this mechanism enables us to assign to deduct the semantic class ANATOMIE for sub-entities of the major category 'Anatomical entity' (such as *Prostata* [prostate]).

We apply a similar reasoning mechanism for the *pathology classification*. As the lexicon entries are initially unclassified according to their pathological information, we analyzed them and found the following mechanism: It is feasible to classify each of the major categories unambiguously either as 'pathological' or 'non-pathological'. For example, entries with semantic class ANATOMIE are classified as 'non-pathological'. This pathological classification information is added to 10 out of 13 major RadLex categories and inferred to all hyponyms. For three of the categories, the classification is ambiguous. The determination of the pathology classification results in the distribution shown in Table 3.

Classification	#	
non-pathological	6001	63.3%
pathological	1714	18.1%
not to be determined	1764	18.6%
	9479	100%

Table 3: Results of the initial pathology classification of RadLex-based lexicon entries

The algorithm is able to classify 81.4 % of the lexicon

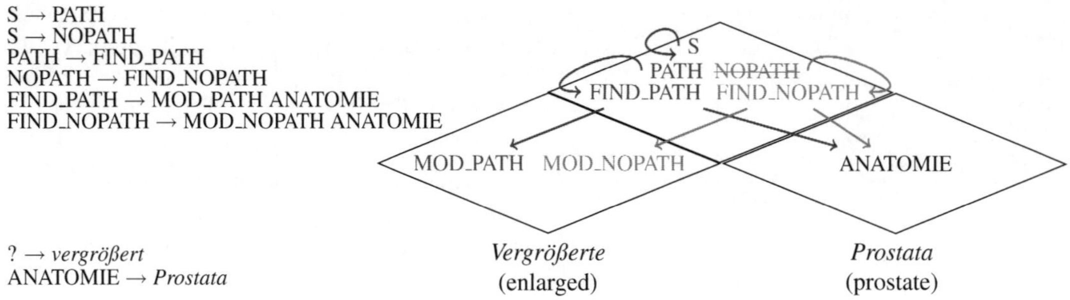

Figure 2: Learning lexical knowledge from sentence *Vergrößerte Prostata* (enlarged prostate)

entries. We have to find a way to classify the remaining unclassified entries. Only when all the lexical entries are classified, the sentence classification algorithm produces reliable results.

The finally derived lexical resource contains 9479 entries with 23588 tokens of which 6326 are distinct. Comparing this number with the distinct word types used in the development set (n=3172), one assumes that the lexicon could cover the vocabulary used in the reports. However, this is not the case. Important terms that occur quite frequently in the development set and have high relevance for the pathology classification are either not included in the lexicon (e.g. *Läsion/lesion*) or are included but are not classified (e.g. *sklerosiert* | RID 5906 [sclerosing]).

That is why we argue that an additional corpus-based learning step to extend the vocabulary and its classification is mandatory.

4.5 Learn from the development set

We introduce an additional learning step to extend the lexicon with missing items and to classify existing item missing a pathology classification. At the same time, the probabilities of the grammar rules are trained during this step. The learning is conducted using an adapted probabilistic CKY algorithm.

Extending the lexical resource How parsing is adapted to learn from the sentences is illustrated in Figure 2. The sentence *Vergrößerte Prostata* [Enlarged prostate] is input to the learning. From the sentence's annotation, we know that this sentence describes a pathological finding (PATH). The subset of the grammar necessary to parse this sentence is shown on the left-hand side of the figure. The non-terminal mapping of the words is shown below the grammar rules. Currently, only the mapping of the word *Prostata* to the non-terminal symbol ANATOMIE can be derived from the lexicon. Mapping *vergrößert* is not possible. The lexical entry has a semantic classification (*Modifier*) assigned, but no pathology classification. However, in this case both information items are necessary to determine the non-terminal mapping. In order to *learn* the missing pathology classification of this word, we apply an adapted CKY parsing algorithm.

The standard CKY algorithm (Kasami, 1965) operates bottom-up and uses two complete components to determine the parse tree of a given input sentence:

1. A complete lexicon to determine the non-terminal mapping of the words, and

2. a complete list of all grammar rules.

Our setting is missing the complete lexicon. That is why we adapt the standard algorithm and introduce a top-down analysis in order to extend the linguistic resource while parsing.

There are two possible non-terminal mappings for the word *vergrößert*: MOD_PATH (indicating a modifier for pathologies) or MOD_NOPATH (indicating a modifier not describing pathologies). Both of the options are used to determine the parse tree of the sentence. The ambiguity is resolved at the top-most parsing level: The sentence is annotated as 'pathological', hence, only rewritings that include the corresponding non-terminal symbol PATH are allowed. Finally, the parse tree of the sentence can be derived (as shown in Figure 3).

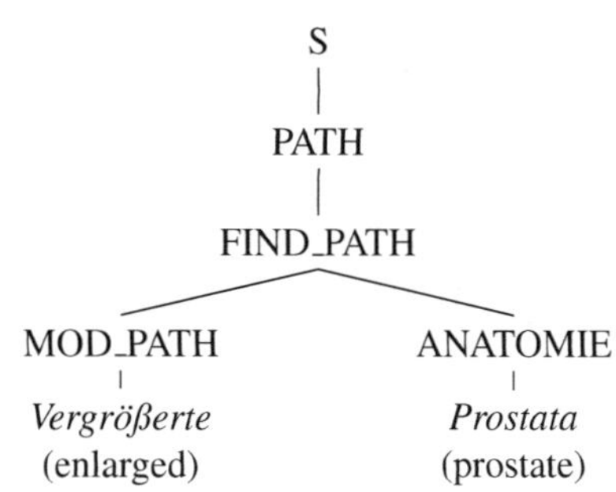

Figure 3: Parse tree derived from sentence *Vergrößerte Prostata* (Enlarged prostate)

In addition, the (formerly unknown) non-terminal mapping of the word *vergrößert* to MOD_PATH is deducted from the parse tree and the corresponding lexical entry is updated. Using this algorithm, we are also able to learn vocabulary that was not available in the lexicon before.

Training the grammar's probabilities The parse tree is also used as input for extending the grammar to a probabilistic context-free grammar. Each of the grammar rules used to form the parse tree is used to re-calculate the probabilities of the grammar rules.

After the learning step, the lexicon is extended to 10344 entries (before 9479). But even more important, the overall amount of lexicon entries classified as 'pathological' increased by 18.8 % to now 2036 entries (before 1714). We consider this a key success of the learning, as our classification depends on this encoded knowledge.

4.6 Classify

After conducting the previous steps,

1. the extended lexicon,
2. the trained P-CFG, and
3. the standard probabilistic CKY parsing algorithm

are applied to parse unclassified sentences.

The sentence classification is conducted based on the lexicon and the grammar rules. The lexicon helps to assign non-terminal symbols to the words in the sentence. Depending on non-terminal symbols assigned and the grammar rules applied during the subsequent parsing process, the parse tree will reveal the classification of the sentence.

As parsing algorithm we apply the standard probabilistic CKY (P-CKY) algorithm. It resolves both syntactic and classification ambiguities. In case, the sentence contains unknown words, the probabilistic parsing feature helps to disambiguate the non-terminal assignment. The derived parse tree describes both the syntactic structure of the sentence and the derived pathology classification.

4.7 Extract and Link

Finally, in case a sentence is classified as 'pathological', the contained anatomical entities are extracted. The sentences are annotated with the extracted anatomical information. An external system combines the anatomical annotations from images and reports. Thus, links are created successfully and the correlating image positions for pathological findings can be accessed from the text.

5 Evaluation

We evaluate the classification system using 40 randomly-chosen reports containing 1296 sentences.

5.1 Precision and recall measurements

We evaluate the classification results and the success of the alignment of radiology reports and images using precision and recall values. Only for sentences classified as 'pathological', the contained anatomical entities are extracted and anatomical annotations are created. That is why we prefer high recall values. If sentences are misclassified as 'pathological' – although they describe non-pathological findings (FP) – this is a minor issue. This misclassification results in alignment of anatomical entities in text and images without pathological findings. We accept lower precision values that yield those additional, but not intended alignments.

5.2 Baseline evaluation

We compare the evaluation results of the classification system with the results of a semantically-informed baseline algorithm. This algorithm detects negations and classifies the containing sentences as 'non-pathological'. Sentences containing diseases (determined based on Latin suffixes such as *-itis*, *-ose*, etc.) or a pathological RadLex concepts (as determined during the lexicon creation step) are classified as 'pathological'. Any remaining sentences are assumed to describe non-pathological findings.

The results of the baseline classification are shown in Table 4. The headings denote 'non-pathological' sentences (NOPATH) respectively 'pathological' sentences (PATH).

		expected classification	
		PATH	*NOPATH*
observed	*PATH*	17	0
classification	*NOPATH*	446	833

Table 4: Classification results using baseline algorithm

This baseline approach has the advantage of 100% precision value. However, it produces a low recall value of 3.67 %, which shows that this approach is not applicable for the alignment of text and images. The results show that the identification of pathologies is not feasible by only using (1) suffixes to determine diseases and (2) available pathology descriptions from the RadLex taxonomy.

5.3 Evaluation of the parsing-based classification results

Table 5 shows the system results of classifying the 1296 report sentences using the syntacto-semantic parsing approach.

		expected classification	
		PATH	*NOPATH*
observed	*PATH*	344	288
classification	*NOPATH*	119	545

Table 5: Sentence classification results using syntacto-semantic parsing approach

Taking into account the impact of the (still) incomplete lexicon, the recall value of 74.3 % indicates that the chosen approach to classify pathological sentences is successful. However, the precision value of 54.4 %

indicates that the classification of almost half of the 'pathological' sentences is incorrect.

Compared to the baseline, the acquisition of additional, pathology classified vocabulary and its incorporation into a parsing-based approach significantly improves the recall value. That is why we regard the enrichment of the lexicon at the crucial step for (further) improvement of the classification results. However, a large amount of sentences was classified incorrectly as 'pathological'. The error analysis will reveals some causes.

5.4 Error analysis

We identified four error types that produce incorrectly classified results.

1. Some of the pathology classification of the semantic knowledge acquired during learning is incorrect.

   Terms that do not describe pathological properties such as *Voraufnahme* [previous examination] or *Lymphknoten* [lymph node] were classified as 'pathological'; also, pathological findings such as *Läsion* [lesion] or *Infiltrat* [infiltrate] could not be classified correctly. Because of their high usage frequency (26, 116, 20, 7 times), these four terms are accountable for 169 of the misclassified sentences (both FP and FN) from the evaluation.

   The disambiguation of (word-level) pathology classification using sentence-level annotations is obviously very vague and imprecise. In order to improve the terminology acquisition results, we will include distribution information and probabilistic features into the learning process as future work.

2. The terminology acquisition leads to an extended lexicon, but still, terminology remains uncovered. In particular, the description of pathological findings requires a richer language, its lack inhibits their correct classification. Even though our corpus is limited to reports of lymphoma patients (i.e., contains limited medical vocabulary), still, the test set contains vocabulary that is not used in the training set. For a further elaborated lexicon, the training set has to be extended in size and also in content.

3. Furthermore, the majority of long sentences is not successfully parsed because of missing grammar rules. Those long sentences are more likely describing pathological findings, which leads to false negatives. We found that sentences longer than 8 tokens are rather incorrectly classified than correctly; nevertheless, this concerns only 8 % (99/1296) of all sentences. Thus, we regard this as a minor issues.

4. Finally, our assumption of covering the semantics with a limited number of non-terminals was disproven. The oversimplification of semantic classes is insufficient to parse the complex sentence structures in the reports. In particular, the structure of long sentences requires a wider range of non-terminals (and more grammar rules) in order to disambiguate the pathology classification. E.g., the defined semantic classes do nor distinguish modifiers of locations or size for anatomical entities or temporal modifier for pathologies. Their introduction will increase the resolution of dependencies in complex sentences and the overall classification.

The learning step is *the* crucial step for improvement of the classification results. It enriches the vocabulary. If the pathology classification of the learned vocabulary is optimized, the system will deliver even better results. The optimization of the vocabulary learning step will be future work.

6 Conclusion

We designed and implemented a system that aligns findings from radiology reports to findings in images based on semantic annotations. Providing the system, we assume to reduce the time necessary to find correlating descriptions of one finding in heterogeneous data sources.

We build our system on tailored NLP algorithms that extract relevant anatomical annotations with pathological findings. To identify sentences that describe pathological findings, we introduce a new, semantic grammar-based classification approach. To bridge the gap of the incomplete German terminology, a vocabulary acquisition step is introduced. Incorporating this newly learned vocabulary, the grammar-based classification delivers a recall value of 74.3%.

We identified a major issue relevant for further work on German clinical texts: The evaluation results reveal a large gap in coverage between the vocabulary used in non-English radiology texts and the controlled vocabulary delivered by RadLex. Furthermore, we believe that lexicons will be crucial resources for language processing in the medical domain. We will focus our future work on enriching existing lexicons and establishing new resources for linguistic analysis.

Acknowledgements

This research has been supported in part by the THESEUS Program in the MEDICO Project, which is funded by the German Federal Ministry of Economics and Technology under grant number 01MQ07016. The responsibility for this publication lies with the authors.

References

A. R. Aronson. 2001. Effective mapping of biomedical text to the UMLS Metathesaurus: the MetaMap program. *Proc AMIA Symp*, 17–21.

D. A. Campbell, S. B. Johnson. 1999. A technique for semantic classification of unknown words using UMLS resources.. *Proc AMIA Symp*, 716–20.

W. W. Chapman, W. Bridewell, P. Hanbury, G. F. Cooper, and B. G. Buchanan. 2001. A simple algorithm for identifying negated findings and diseases in discharge summaries. *J Biomed Inform*, 34:301–310.

W. W. Chapman, W. Bridewell, P. Hanbury, G. F. Cooper, and B. G. Buchanan. 2001. Evaluation of negation phrases in narrative clinical reports. *Proc AMIA Symp.*, 105-109.

Computational Medicine Center. 2007. International Challenge: Classifying Clinical Free Text Using Natural Language Processing.. `http://www.computationalmedicine.org/challenge/index.php`.

J. W. Fan and C. Friedman. 2011. Deriving a probabilistic syntacto-semantic grammar for biomedicine based on domain-specific terminologies.. *J Biomed Inform*, 44(5):805–14.

C. Friedman, P. O. Alderson, J. H. M. Austin, J. J. Cimino, and S. B. Johnson. 1994. A General Natural-Language Text Processor for Clinical Radiology. *J Am Med Inform Assoc*, 1:161–174.

C. Friedman, P. Kra, and A. Rzhetksy. 2002. Two biomedical sublanguages: a description based on the theories of Zellig Harris. *J Biomed Inform*, 35:222–235.

S. Goryachev, M. Sordo, Q. T. Zeng, and L. Ngo. 2006. Implementation and evaluation of four different methods of negation detection.. Technical report, DSG.

Y. Huang and H. J. Lowe. 2007. A Novel Hybrid Approach to Automated Negation Detection in Clinical Radiology Reports. *J Am Med Inform Assoc*, 14:304–311.

S. B. Johnson. 1999. A semantic lexicon for medical language processing.. *J Am Med Inform Assoc*, 6(3):205-18.

T. Kasami. 1965. An efficient recognition and syntax-analysis algorithm for context-free languages. *Scientific Report AFCRL-65-758*, Air Force Cambridge Research Lab.

C. Lindberg. 1990. The Unified Medical Language System (UMLS) of the National Library of Medicine.. *J Am Med Rec Assoc*, 61(5):40–42.

H. Liu, S. T. Wu, D. Li, S. Jonnalagadda, S. Sohn, K. Wagholikar, P. J. Haug, S. M. Huff, and C. G. Chute. 2012. Towards a semantic lexicon for clinical natural language processing.. *AMIA Annu Symp Proc*, 568-576.

W. Long. 2005. Extracting diagnoses from discharge summaries. *AMIA Annu Symp Proc*, 470–4.

D. Marwede, P. Daumke, K. Marko, D. Lobsien, S. Schulz, and T. Kahn. 2009. RadLex - German version: a radiological lexicon for indexing image and report information. *Fortschr Röntgenstr*, 181(1): 38–44.

S. M. Meystre, G. K. Savova, K. C. Kipper-Schuler, and J. F. Hurdle. 2008. Extracting Information from Textual Documents in the Electronic Health Record: A Review of Recent Research. *Yearb Med Inform*, 24(11):128–144.

P. G. Mutalik, A. Deshpande, P. M. Nadkarni. 2001. Use of general-purpose negation detection to augment concept indexing of medical documents: a quantitative study using the UMLS.. *J Am Med Inform Assoc*, 8(6):598–609.

J. P. Pestian, C. Brew, P. Matykiewicz, D. J. Hovermale, N. Johnson, K. B. Cohen, and W. Duch. 2007. A Shared Task Involving Multi-label Classification of Clinical Free Text.. *BioNLP 2007: Biological, translational, and clinical language processing.*.

Radiological Society of North America. 2012. RadLex. `http://rsna.org/RadLex.aspx`.

N. Sager, M. Lyman, C. Bucknall, N. Nhan, and L. J. Tick. 1994. Natural Language Processing and the Representation of Clinical Data. *J Am Med Inform Assoc*, 1:142–160.

G. K. Savova, J. J. Masanz, P. V. Ogren, J. Zheng, S. Sohn, K. C. Kipper-Schuler, and C. G. Chute. 2010. Mayo clinical Text Analysis and Knowledge Extraction System (cTAKES): architecture, component evaluation and applications.. *J Am Med Inform Assoc*, 17(5):507–13.

S. Seifert. 2010. THESEUS-Anwendungsszenario MEDICO. `http://www.joint-research.org/das-theseus-forschungsprogramm/medico/`.

S. Seifert, A. Barbu, K. Zhou, D. Liu, J. Feulner, M. Huber, M. Suehling, A. Cavallaro, and D. Comaniciu. 2009. Hierarchical Parsing and Semantic Navigation of Full Body CT Data. *SPIE Medical Imaging*.

S. T. Wu, H. Liu, D. Li, C. Tao, M. A. Musen, C. G. Chute, N. H. Shah. 2012. Unified Medical Language System term occurrences in clinical notes: a large-scale corpus analysis.. *J Am Med Inform Assoc*, 19(1):149–56.

P. Zweigenbaum, R. Baud, A. Burgun, F. Namer, E. Jarrousse N. Grabar, P. Ruch, F. Le Duff, B. Thirion, and S. Darmoni. 2003. UMLF: a Unified Medical Lexicon for French. *AMIA Annu Symp Proc*, 1062.

Corpus-Driven Terminology Development: Populating Swedish SNOMED CT with Synonyms Extracted from Electronic Health Records

Aron Henriksson[1], **Maria Skeppstedt**[1], **Maria Kvist**[1,2], **Martin Duneld**[1], **Mike Conway**[3]

[1]Department of Computer and Systems Sciences (DSV), Stockholm University, Sweden
[2]Department of Learning, Informatics, Management and Ethics (LIME), Karolinska Institute, Sweden
[3]Division of Biomedical Informatics, University of California San Diego, USA

Abstract

The various ways in which one can refer to the same clinical concept needs to be accounted for in a semantic resource such as SNOMED CT. Developing terminological resources manually is, however, prohibitively expensive and likely to result in low coverage, especially given the high variability of language use in clinical text. To support this process, distributional methods can be employed in conjunction with a large corpus of electronic health records to extract synonym candidates for clinical terms. In this paper, we exemplify the potential of our proposed method using the Swedish version of SNOMED CT, which currently lacks synonyms. A medical expert inspects two thousand term pairs generated by two semantic spaces – one of which models multiword terms in addition to single words – for one hundred preferred terms of the semantic types *disorder* and *finding*.

1 Introduction

In recent years, the adoption of standardized terminologies for the representation of clinical concepts – and their textual instantiations – has enabled meaning-based retrieval of information from electronic health records (EHRs). By identifying and linking key facts in health records, the ever-growing stores of clinical documentation now available to us can more readily be processed and, ultimately, leveraged to improve the quality of care. SNOMED CT[1] has emerged as the *de facto* international terminology for representing clinical concepts in EHRs and is today used in more than fifty countries, despite only being available in a handful of languages[2]. Translations into several other languages are, however, under way[3]. This translation effort is essential for more widespread integration of SNOMED CT in EHR systems globally.

Translating a comprehensive[4] terminology such as SNOMED CT to an additional language is, however, a massive and expensive undertaking. A substantial part of this process involves enriching the terminology with synonyms in the target language. SNOMED CT has, for instance, recently been translated into Swedish; however, the Swedish version does not as yet contain synonyms. Methods and tools that can accelerate the language porting process in general and the synonym identification task in particular are clearly needed, not only to lower costs but also to increase the coverage of SNOMED CT in clinical text. Methods that can account for real-world language use in the clinical setting, then, as well as to changes over time, are particularly valuable.

This paper evaluates a semi-automatic method for the extraction of synonyms of SNOMED CT preferred terms using models of distributional semantics to induce semantic spaces from a large corpus of clinical text. In contrast to most approaches that exploit the notion of distributional similarity for synonym extraction, this method addresses the key problem of identifying synonymy between terms of varying length: a simple solution is proposed that effectively incorporates the notion of paraphrasing in a distributional framework. The semantic spaces – and, by extension, the method – are evaluated for their ability to extract synonyms of SNOMED CT terms of the semantic types *disorder* and *finding* in Swedish.

[1]`http://www.ihtsdo.org/snomed-ct/`

[2]SNOMED CT is currently available in US English, UK English, Spanish, Danish and Swedish.

[3]`http://www.ihtsdo.org/snomed-ct/snomed-ct0/different-languages/`

[4]SNOMED CT contains more than 300,000 active concepts and over a million relations.

2 Background

Synonymy is an aspect of semantics that concerns the fact that concepts can be instantiated using multiple linguistic expressions, or, viewed conversely, that multiple linguistic expressions can refer to the same concept. As synonymous expressions do not necessarily consist of single words, we sometimes speak of paraphrasing rather than synonymy (Androutsopoulos and Malakasiotis, 2010). This variability of language use needs to be accounted for in order to build high-quality natural language processing (NLP) and text mining systems. This is typically achieved by using thesauri or encoding textual instantiations of concepts in a semantic resource, e.g. an ontology. Creating such resources manually is, however, prohibitively expensive and likely to lead to low coverage, especially in the clinical genre where language use variability is exceptionally high (Meystre et al., 2008).

2.1 Synonym Extraction

As a result, the task of extracting synonyms – and other semantic relations – has long been a central challenge in the NLP research community, not least in the biomedical (Cohen and Hersh, 2005) and clinical (Meystre et al., 2008) domains. A wide range of techniques has been proposed for relation extraction in general and synonym extraction in particular – lexico-syntactic patterns (Hearst, 1992), distributional semantics (Dumais and Landauer, 1997) and graph-based models (Blondel et al., 2004) – from a variety of sources, including dictionaries (Blondel et al., 2004), linked data such as Wikipedia (Nakayama et al., 2007), as well as both monolingual (Hindle, 1990) and multilingual (van der Plas and Tiedemann, 2006) corpora. In recent years, ensemble methods have been applied to obtain better performance on the synonym extraction task, combining models from different families (Peirsman and Geeraerts, 2009), with different parameter settings (Henriksson et al., 2012) and induced from different data sources (Wu and Zhou, 2003).

In the context of biomedicine, the goal has often been to extract synonyms of gene and protein names from the biomedical literature (Yu and Agichtein, 2003; Cohen et al., 2005; McCrae and Collier, 2008). In the clinical domain, Conway and Chapman (2012) used a rule-based approach to generate potential synonyms from the BioPortal ontology web service, verifying candidate synonyms against a large clinical corpus. Zeng et al. (2012) used three query expansion methods for information retrieval of clinical documents and found that a model of distributional semantics – LDA-based topic modeling – generated the best synonyms. Henriksson et al. (2012) combined models of distributional semantics – random indexing and random permutation – to extract synonym candidates for Swedish MeSH[5] terms and possible abbreviation-definition pairs. In the context of SNOMED CT, distributional methods have been applied to capture synonymous relations between terms of varying length: 16-24% of English SNOMED CT synonyms present in a large clinical corpus were successfully identified in a list of twenty suggestions (Henriksson et al., 2013).

2.2 Distributional Semantics

Models of distributional semantics (see Cohen and Widdows (2009) for an overview of methods and their application in the biomedical domain) were initially motivated by the inability of the vector space model to account for synonymy, which had a negative impact on recall in information retrieval systems (Deerwester et al., 1990). The theoretical foundation underpinning such models of semantics is the *distributional hypothesis* (Harris, 1954), according to which words with similar meanings tend to appear in similar contexts. By exploiting the availability of large corpora, the meaning of terms can be modeled based on their distribution in different contexts. An estimate of the semantic relatedness between terms can then be quantified, thereby, in some sense, rendering semantics computable.

An obvious application of distributional semantics is the extraction of semantic relations between terms, such as synonymy, hyp(o/er)nymy and cohyponymy (Panchenko, 2013). As synonyms are interchangeable in some contexts – and thus have similar distributional profiles – synonymy is certainly a semantic relation that should be captured. However, since hyp(o/er)nyms and co-hyponyms – in fact, even antonyms – are also likely to have similar distributional profiles, such semantic relations will be extracted too.

Many models of distributional semantics differ in how context vectors, representing term

[5] **M**edical **S**ubject **H**eadings (`http://www.nlm.nih.gov/mesh`).

meaning, are constructed. They are typically derived from a term-context matrix that contains the (weighted, normalized) frequency with which terms occur in different contexts. Partly due to the intractability of working with such high-dimensional data, it is projected into a lower-dimensional (semantic) space, while approximately preserving the relative distances between data points. Methods that rely on computationally expensive dimensionality reduction techniques suffer from scalability issues.

Random Indexing

Random indexing (RI) (Kanerva et al., 2000) is a scalable and computationally efficient alternative in which explicit dimensionality reduction is avoided: a lower dimensionality d is instead chosen *a priori* as a model parameter and the d-dimensional context vectors are then constructed incrementally. Each unique term in the corpus is assigned a static index vector, consisting of zeros and a small number of randomly placed 1s and -1s[6]. Each term is also assigned an initially empty context vector, which is incrementally updated by adding the index vectors of the surrounding words within a sliding window, weighted by their distance to the target term. The semantic relatedness between two terms is then estimated by calculating, for instance, the cosine similarity between their context vectors.

Random Permutation

Random permutation (RP) (Sahlgren et al., 2008) is a modification of RI that attempts to take into account term order information by simply *permuting* (i.e. shifting) the index vectors according to their direction and distance from the target term before they are added to the context vector. RP has been shown to outperform RI on the synonym part of the TOEFL[7] test.

Model Parameters

The model parameters need to be configured for the task that the semantic space is to be used for. For instance, with a document-level context definition, *syntagmatic* relations are modeled, i.e. terms that belong to the same topic (<*car, motor, race*>), whereas, with a sliding window context definition, *paradigmatic* relations are modeled (<*car, automobile, vehicle*>) (Sahlgren, 2006). Synonymy is an instance of a paradigmatic relation.

The dimensionality has also been shown to be potentially very important, especially when the size of the vocabulary and the number of contexts[8] are large (Henriksson and Hassel, 2013).

3 Materials and Methods

The task of semi-automatically identifying synonyms of SNOMED CT preferred terms is here approached by, first, statistically identifying multiword terms in the data and treating them as compounds; then, performing a distributional analysis of a preprocessed clinical corpus to induce a semantic term space; and, finally, extracting the semantically most similar terms for each preferred term of interest.

The experimental setup can be broken down into the following steps: (1) data preparation, (2) term recognition, (3) model parameter tuning and (4) evaluation. Semantic spaces are induced with different parameter configurations on two dataset variants: one with unigram terms only and one that also includes multiword terms. The model parameters are tuned using MeSH, which contains synonyms for Swedish. The best parameter settings for each of the two dataset variants are then employed in the final evaluation, where a medical expert inspects one hundred term lists extracted for SNOMED CT preferred terms belonging to the semantic types *disorder* and *finding*.

3.1 Data Preparation

The data used to induce the semantic spaces is extracted from the Stockholm EPR Corpus (Dalianis et al., 2009), which contains Swedish health records from the Karolinska University Hospital in Stockholm[9]. The subset (~33 million tokens) used in these experiments comprises all forms of text-based records – i.e., clinical notes – from a large variety of clinical practices. The documents in the corpus are initially preprocessed by simply lowercasing tokens and removing punctuation and digits. Lemmatization is not performed, as we want to be able to capture morphological

[6] By generating sparse vectors of a sufficiently high dimensionality in this way, the context representations will be *nearly* orthogonal.

[7] Test Of English as a Foreign Language

[8] The vocabulary size and the number of contexts are equivalent when employing a window context definition.

[9] This research has been approved by the Regional Ethical Review Board in Stockholm (Etikprövningsnämnden i Stockholm), permission number 2012/834-31/5.

variants of terms; stop-word filtering is not performed, as traditional stop words – for instance, high-frequency function words – could potentially be constituents of multiword terms.

3.2 Term Recognition

Multiword terms are extracted statistically from the corpus using the C-value statistic (Frantzi and Ananiadou, 1996; Frantzi et al., 2000). This technique has been used successfully for term recognition in the biomedical domain, largely due to its ability to handle nested terms (Zhang et al., 2008). Using the C-value statistic for term recognition first requires a list of candidate terms, for which the C-value can then be calculated. Here, this is simply produced by extracting n-grams – unigrams, bigrams and trigrams – from the corpus with TEXT-NSP (Banerjee and Pedersen, 2003). The statistic is based on term frequency and term length (number of words); if a candidate term is part of a longer candidate term (as will be the case for practically all unigram and bigram terms), the number and frequency of those longer terms are also taken into account (Figure 1).

In order to improve the quality of the extracted terms, a number of filtering rules is applied to the generated term list: terms that begin and/or end with certain words, e.g. prepositions and articles, are removed. The term list – ranked according to C-value – is further modified by giving priority to terms of particular interest, e.g. SNOMED CT *disorder* and *finding* preferred terms: these are moved to the top of the list, regardless of their C-value. As a result, the statistical foundation on which the distributional method bases its semantic representation will effectively be strengthened.

The term list is then used to perform exact string matching on the entire corpus: multiword terms with a higher C-value than their constituents are concatenated. We thereby treat multiword terms as separate (term) types with distinct distributions in the data, different from those of their constituents.

3.3 Model Parameter Tuning

Term spaces with different parameter configurations are induced from the two dataset variants: one containing only unigram terms (*Unigram Word Spaces*) and one containing also multiword terms (*Multiword Term Spaces*). The following model parameters are tuned:

- Distributional Model: Random indexing (RI) vs. Random permutation (RP)
- Context Window Size: 2+2, 4+4, 8+8 surrounding terms (*left+right* of the target term)
- Dimensionality: 1000, 2000, 3000

As the Swedish version of SNOMED CT currently does not contain synonyms, it cannot be used to perform the parameter tuning automatically. This is instead done with the Swedish version of MeSH, which is one of the very few standard terminologies that contains synonyms for medical terms in Swedish. However, as the optimal parameter configurations for capturing synonymy are not necessarily identical for all semantic types, the parameter tuning is performed by evaluating the semantic spaces for their ability to identify synonyms of MeSH terms that belong to the categories *Disease or Syndrome* and *Sign or Symptom*. These particular categories are simply chosen as they, to a reasonable extent, seem to correspond to the SNOMED CT semantic types studied in this paper, namely *Disorder* and *Finding*. Only synonym pairs that appear at least fifty times in each of the dataset variants are included (155 for *Unigram Word Spaces* and 123 for *Multiword Term Spaces*), as the statistical foundation for terms that only occur rarely in the data may not be sufficiently solid. In these *Multiword Term Spaces*, the MeSH terms – but not the synonyms – are given precedence in the term list. A term is provided as input to a semantic space and the twenty semantically most similar terms are output, provided that they also appear at least fifty times in the data. Recall Top 20 is calculated for each input term: *what proportion of the MeSH synonyms are identified in a list of twenty suggestions?* Since each synonym pair must appear at least fifty times in the corresponding dataset variant, it should be duly noted that the optimization sets will not be identical, which in turn means that the results of the *Unigram Word Spaces* and the *Multiword Term Spaces* are not directly comparable. The optimal parameter configuration, then, may be different when also multiword terms are modeled.

3.4 Evaluation

The optimal parameter configuration for each dataset variant is employed in the final evaluation. In this *Multiword Term Space*, the SNOMED CT

$$C\text{-}value(a) = \begin{cases} \log_2 |a| \cdot f(a) & \text{if a is not nested} \\ \log_2 |a| \cdot (f(a) - \frac{1}{P(Ta)} \sum_{b \epsilon Ta} f(b)) & \text{otherwise} \end{cases}$$

a	= candidate term	Ta	= set of extracted candidate terms that contain a
b	= longer candidate terms	$P(Ta)$	= number of candidate terms in Ta
$f(a)$	= term frequency of a	$f(b)$	= term frequency of longer candidate term b
$\|a\|$	= length of candidate term (number of words)		

Figure 1: *C-Value Formula.* The formula for calculating C-value of candidate terms.

preferred terms of interest, rather than the MeSH terms, are prioritized in the term list. The semantic spaces – and, in effect, the method – are primarily evaluated for their ability to identify synonyms of SNOMED CT preferred terms, in this case of concepts that belong to the semantic types *disorder* and *finding*. The need to identify synonyms for these semantic types is clear, as it has been shown that the coverage of SNOMED CT for mentions of disorders (38%) and, in particular, findings (23%) in Swedish clinical text is low (Skeppstedt et al., 2012). Since the Swedish version of SNOMED CT currently lacks synonyms, the evaluation reasonably needs to be manual, as there is no reference standard. One option, then, could be to choose a random sample of preferred terms to use in the evaluation. A potential drawback of such a(n) (unguided) selection is that many concepts in the English version of SNOMED CT do not have any synonymous terms, which might lead to evaluators spending valuable time looking for something which does not exist. An alternative approach, which is assumed here, is to inspect concepts that have many synonyms in the English version of SNOMED CT. The fact that some concepts have many textual instantiations in one language does not necessarily imply that they also have many textual instantiations in another language. This, however, seems to be the case when comparing the English and Swedish versions of MeSH: terms[10] that have the most synonyms in the English version tend to have at least one synonym in the Swedish version to a larger extent than a random selection of terms (60% and 62% of the terms in the Swedish version have at least one synonym when looking at the top 100 and top 50 terms with the most synonyms in the English version, compared to 41% overall in the Swedish version).

For the two dataset variants, we thus select 25 SNOMED CT preferred terms for each semantic type – *disorder* and *finding* – that (1) have the most synonyms in the English version and (2) occur at least fifty times in the data. In total, fifty terms are input to the *Unigram Word Space* and another fifty terms (potentially with some overlap) are input to the *Multiword Term Space*. A medical expert inspects the twenty semantically most similar terms for each input term. Synonymy is here the primary semantic relation of interest, but the semantic spaces are also evaluated for their ability, or tendency, to extract other semantic term relations: hypernyms or hyponyms, co-hyponyms, antonyms, as well as *disorder-finding* relations.

4 Results

The term recognition and concatenation of multiword terms naturally affect some properties of the dataset variants, such as the vocabulary size (number of types) and the type-token ratio. The *Unigram Word Space* contains 381,553 types and an average of 86.54 tokens/type, while the *Multiword Term Space* contains 2,223,953 types and an average of 9.72 tokens/type. This, in turn, may have an effect on which parameter configuration is 'optimal' for the synonym extraction task. In fact, this seems to be the case when tuning the parameters for the two dataset variants. For the *Unigram Word Spaces*, random indexing with a sliding context window of 8+8 terms and a dimensionality of 2000 seems to work best, whereas for the *Multiword Term Spaces*, random permutation with a sliding window context of 4+4 terms and a dimensionality of 3000 works better (Table 1).

When these parameter configurations are applied to the SNOMED CT terms, a total of 40 synonyms are extracted by the *Unigram Word Space* and 33 synonyms by the *Multiword Term Space* (Table 2). On average, 0.80 and 0.66 synonyms are extracted per preferred term, respectively. The number of identified synonyms per input term varies significantly: for some, none; for others, up to ten. Other semantic relations are also extracted

[10]These calculations are based on MeSH terms that belong to the categories *Disease or Syndrome* and *Sign or Symptom*.

	Unigram Word Spaces						Multiword Term Spaces					
	RI			RP			RI			RP		
Sliding Window →	**2+2**	**4+4**	**8+8**	**2+2**	**4+4**	**8+8**	**2+2**	**4+4**	**8+8**	**2+2**	**4+4**	**8+8**
1000 dimensions	0.43	0.47	0.48	0.41	0.45	0.42	0.21	0.25	0.26	0.25	0.26	0.24
2000 dimensions	0.43	0.48	**0.49**	0.48	0.48	0.43	0.21	0.24	0.25	0.25	0.25	0.24
3000 dimensions	0.44	0.47	0.48	0.46	0.45	0.43	0.22	0.24	0.24	0.23	**0.27**	0.25

Table 1: *Model Parameter Tuning*. Results, reported as recall top 20, for MeSH synonyms that appear at least 50 times in each of the dataset variants (unigram vs. multiword). Random indexing (RI) and Random permutation (RP) term spaces were built with different context window sizes (2+2, 4+4, 8+8 surrounding terms) and dimensionality (1000, 2000, 3000).

by the semantic spaces: mainly co-hyponyms, but also hypernyms and hyponyms, antonyms and *disorder-finding* relations. The *Unigram Word Space* extracts, on average, 0.52 hypernyms or hyponyms, 1.8 co-hyponyms, 0.1 antonyms and 0.34 *disorder-finding* relations. The *Multiword Term Space* extracts, on average, 0.16 hypernyms or hyponyms, 1.1 co-hyponyms, 0.14 antonyms and 0.66 *disorder-finding* relations. In general, more of the above semantic relations are extracted by the *Unigram Word Space* than by the *Multiword Term Space* (178 vs. 136). It is, however, interesting to note that almost twice as many *disorder-finding* relations are extracted by the latter compared to the former. Of course, none of the relations extracted by the *Unigram Word Space* involve a multiword term; on the other hand, more than half (around 57%) of the relations extracted by the *Multiword Term Space* involve at least one multiword term.

Both semantic spaces identify more synonyms of preferred terms that belong to the semantic type *finding* than *disorder* (in total 56 vs. 39). The same holds true for hyp(er/o)nyms and co-hypnoyms; however, the converse is true for antonyms and *disorder-finding* relations.

5 Discussion

The results demonstrate that it is indeed possible to extract synonyms of medical terms by performing a distributional analysis of a large corpus of clinical text – unigram-unigram relations, as well as unigram-multiword and multiword-unigram relations. It is also clear, however, that other semantically related terms share distributional profiles to a similar degree as synonymous terms. The predominance of the other semantic relations, except for antonymy, in the term lists can reasonably be explained by the simple fact that there exist more hypernyms, hyponyms, co-hyponyms and *disorder-finding* relations than synonyms (or antonyms).

It is also evident that more semantic relations, and indeed more synonyms, are extracted by the *Unigram Word Space* than the *Multiword Term Space*. Again, it is important to underline that the results cannot be compared without due qualification since the evaluation sets are not identical: the *Unigram Word Space* does not contain any multiword terms, for instance. The ability to model multiword terms in a distributional framework and to handle semantic composition – i.e., how meaning is, and sometimes is not, composed by the meaning of its constituents – has long been an endeavor in the NLP research community (Sag et al., 2002; Baroni and Zamparelli, 2010; Grefenstette and Sadrzadeh, 2011; Mitchell, 2011). Treating multiword terms as compound tokens is a simple and rather straightforward approach, which also makes intuitive sense: rather than treat individual words as clearly delineated bearers of meaning, identify *semantic units* – regardless of term length – and model their distributional profiles. Unfortunately, there are problems with this approach. First, the attendant increase in vocabulary size entails a lower tokens-type ratio, which in turn means that the statistical foundation for terms will weaken. In this case, the average token-type ratio decreased from 86.54 to 9.72. This approach therefore requires access to a sufficiently large corpus. Second, the inflation in vocabulary size entails a corresponding increase in the number of vectors in the semantic space. This not only requires more memory; to ensure that the crucial *near-orthogonality* property[11] of RI-based models is maintained, the dimensionality has to be suffi-

[11]Random indexing assumes that the index vectors – representing distinct contexts – are *nearly* orthogonal.

	Unigram Word Space		Multiword Term Space	
	DISORDER	*FINDING*	*DISORDER*	*FINDING*
Synonyms				
sum	18	22	16	17
average	0.72	0.88	0.64	0.68
≥ 1 / preferred term	12	12	8	6
involves mwe	-	-	10	13
Hyp(er/o)nyms				
sum	12	14	4	4
average	0.48	0.56	0.16	0.16
≥ 1 / preferred term	6	8	4	3
involves mwe	-	-	3	3
Co-hyponyms				
sum	34	56	22	33
average	1.36	2.24	0.88	1.32
≥ 1 / preferred term	14	17	10	13
involves mwe	-	-	19	15
Antonyms				
sum	3	2	4	3
average	0.12	0.08	0.16	0.12
≥ 1 / preferred term	3	2	3	3
involves mwe	-	-	0	1
Disorder-Finding				
sum	11	6	28	5
average	0.44	0.24	1.12	0.2
≥ 1 / preferred term	6	5	12	5
involves mwe	-	-	11	2

Table 2: *Evaluation Results.* The types of semantic relations extracted among the twenty most semantically similar terms of 25 *DISORDER* and 25 *FINDING* SNOMED CT preferred terms from each semantic space. *Sum* is the total number of identified relevant terms. *Average* is the average number of relevant terms per preferred term. *≥ 1 / preferred term* is the number of preferred terms for which at least one relevant term is identified. *Involves mwe* is the number of relevant relations where either the preferred term or the relevant term is a multiword expression.

ciently large in relation to the number of contexts (represented by index vectors). In the *Multiword Term Space* the vocabulary size is over two million (compared to less than 400,000 in the *Unigram Word Space*). A dimensionality of 3000 is likely insufficient to ensure that each term type has an initial distinct and uncorrelated representation. In the evaluation, there were several examples where two groups of terms – semantically homogenous within each group, but semantically heterogenous across groups – co-existed in the same term list: these 'topics' had seemingly collapsed into the same subspace. Despite these problems, it should be recognized that the *Multiword Term Space* is, in fact, able to retrieve 23 synonymous relations that involve at least one multiword term. The *Unigram Word Space* cannot retrieve any such relations.

The ability to extract high-quality terms would seem to be an important prerequisite for this approach to modeling multiword terms in a distributional framework. However, despite employing a rather simple means of extracting terms – without using any syntactic information – the terms that actually appeared in the lists of semantically related terms were mostly reasonable. This perhaps indicates that the term recognition task does not need to be perfect: terms of interest, of course, need to be identified, but some noise in the form of bad terms might be acceptable. A weakness of the term recognition part is, however, that too many terms were identified, which in turn led to the aforementioned inflation in vocabulary size.

Limiting the number of multiword terms in the initial term list – for instance by extracting syntactic phrases as candidate terms – could provide a possible solution to this problem.

Overall, more synonyms were identified for the semantic type *finding* than for *disorder*. One possible explanation for this could be that there are more ways of describing a finding than a disorder – not all semantic types can be assumed to have the same number of synonyms. The same holds true for all other semantic relations except for *disorder-finding*, where disorders generated a much larger number of distributionally similar findings than vice versa. This could perhaps also be explained by the possible higher number of synonyms for *finding* than *disorder*.

When this method was evaluated using the English version of SNOMED CT, 16-24% of known synonyms were identified (Henriksson et al., 2013). In this case, however, we extracted synonym candidates for terms that may or may not have synonyms. This is thus a scenario that more closely resembles how this method would actually be used in a real-life setting to populate a terminology with synonyms. Although the comparison with MeSH showed that terms with many synonyms in English also tend to have at least one synonym in Swedish, approximately 40% of them did not have any synonyms. It is thus not certain that the terms used in this evaluation all have at least one synonym, which was also noted by the evaluator in this study.

6 Conclusions

In this study, we have demonstrated a method that could potentially be used to expedite the language porting process of terminologies such as SNOMED CT. With access to a large corpus of clinical text in the target language and an initial set of terms, this language-independent method is able to extract and present candidate synonyms to the lexicographer, thereby providing valuable support for semi-automatic terminology development. A means to model multiword terms in a distributional framework is an important feature of the method and is crucial for the synonym extraction task.

Acknowledgments

This work was partly supported by the Swedish Foundation for Strategic Research through the project High-Performance Data Mining for Drug Effect Detection (ref. no. IIS11-0053) at Stockholm University, Sweden, and partly funded by the Stockholm University Academic Initiative through the Interlock project. Finally, we would like to thank the reviewers for their constructive feedback.

References

Ion Androutsopoulos and Prodromos Malakasiotis. 2010. A Survey of Paraphrasing and Textual Entailment Methods. *Journal of Artificial Intelligence Research*, 38:135–187.

Satanjeev Banerjee and Ted Pedersen. 2003. The Design, Implementation, and Use of the Ngram Statistic Package. In *Proceedings of CICLing*, pages 370–381.

Marco Baroni and Roberto Zamparelli. 2010. Nouns are Vectors, Adjectives are Matrices: Representing Adjective-Noun Constructions in Semantic Space. In *Proceedings of EMNLP*, pages 1183–1193.

Vincent D. Blondel, Anahí Gajardo, Maureen Heymans, Pierre Senellart, and Paul Van Dooren. 2004. A Measure of Similarity between Graph Vertices: Applications to Synonym Extraction and Web Searching. *SIAM Review*, 46(4):647–666.

Aaron M. Cohen and William R. Hersh. 2005. A Survey of Current Work in Biomedical Text Mining. *Briefings in Bioinformatics*, 6(1):57–71.

Trevor Cohen and Dominic Widdows. 2009. Empirical Distributional Semantics: Methods and Biomedical Applications. *J Biomed Inform*, 42(2):390–405.

AM Cohen, WR Hersh, C Dubay, and K Spackman. 2005. Using co-occurrence network structure to extract synonymous gene and protein names from medline abstracts. *BMC Bioinformatics*, 6(1):103.

Mike Conway and Wendy W. Chapman. 2012. Discovering Lexical Instantiations of Clinical Concepts using Web Services, WordNet and Corpus Resources. In *AMIA Fall Symposium*, page 1604.

Hercules Dalianis, Martin Hassel, and Sumithra Velupillai. 2009. The Stockholm EPR Corpus: Characteristics and Some Initial Findings. In *Proceedings of ISHIMR*, pages 243–249.

Scott Deerwester, Susan T. Dumais, George W Furnas, Thomas K Landauer, and Richard Harshman. 1990. Indexing by Latent Semantic Analysis. *Journal of the American Society for Information Science*, 41(6):391–407.

Susan T. Dumais and Thomas K. Landauer. 1997. A Solution to Plato's Problem: The Latent Semantic

Analysis Theory of Acquisition, Induction and Representation of Knowledge. *Psychological Review*, 104(2):211–240.

Katerina Frantzi and Sophia Ananiadou. 1996. Extracting Nested Collocations. In *Proceedings of COLING*, pages 41–46.

Katerina Frantzi, Sophia Ananiadou, and Hideki Mima. 2000. Automatic Recognition of Multi-Word Terms: The C-value/NC-value Method. *International Journal on Digital Libraries*, 3(2):115–130.

Edward Grefenstette and Mehrnoosh Sadrzadeh. 2011. Experimental Support for a Categorical Compositional Distributional Model of Meaning. In *Proceedings of EMNLP*, pages 1394–1404.

Zellig S. Harris. 1954. Distributional Structure. *Word*, 10:146–162.

Marti Hearst. 1992. Automatic Acquisition of Hyponyms from Large Text Corpora. In *Proceedings of COLING*, pages 539–545.

Aron Henriksson and Martin Hassel. 2013. Optimizing the Dimensionality of Clinical Term Spaces for Improved Diagnosis Coding Support. In *Proceedings of Louhi*.

Aron Henriksson, Hans Moen, Maria Skeppstedt, Ann-Marie Eklund, and Vidas Daudaravicius. 2012. Synonym Extraction of Medical Terms from Clinical Text Using Combinations of Word Space Models. In *Proceedings of SMBM*, pages 10–17.

Aron Henriksson, Mike Conway, Martin Duneld, and Wendy W. Chapman. 2013. Identifying Synonymy between SNOMED Clinical Terms of Varying Length Using Distributional Analysis of Electronic Health Records. In *AMIA Annual Symposium (submitted)*.

Donald Hindle. 1990. Noun Classification from Predicate-Argument Structures. In *Proceedings of ACL*, pages 268–275.

Pentti Kanerva, Jan Kristofersson, and Anders Holst. 2000. Random Indexing of Text Samples for Latent Semantic Analysis. In *Proceedings CogSci*, page 1036.

John McCrae and Nigel Collier. 2008. Synonym Set Extraction from the Biomedical Literature by Lexical Pattern Discovery. *BMC Bioinformatics*, 9(1):159.

Stéphane M. Meystre, Guergana K. Savova, Karin C. Kipper-Schuler, John F. Hurdle, et al. 2008. Extracting Information from Textual Documents in the Electronic Health Record: A Review of Recent Research. *Yearb Med Inform*, 35:128–44.

Jeffrey Mitchell. 2011. *Composition in Distributional Models of Semantics*. Ph.D. thesis, University of Edinburgh.

Kotaro Nakayama, Takahiro Hara, and Shojiro Nishio. 2007. Wikipedia Mining for an Association Web Thesaurus Construction. In *Proceedings of WISE*, pages 322–334.

Alexander Panchenko. 2013. *Similarity Measures for Semantic Relation Extraction*. Ph.D. thesis, PhD thesis, Université catholique de Louvain & Bauman Moscow State Technical University.

Yves Peirsman and Dirk Geeraerts. 2009. Predicting Strong Associations on the Basis of Corpus Data. In *Proceedings of EACL*, pages 648–656.

Ivan A. Sag, Timothy Baldwin, Francis Bond, Ann Copestake, and Dan Flickinger. 2002. Multiword Expressions: A Pain in the Neck for NLP. In *Proceedings of CICLing*, pages 1–15.

Magnus Sahlgren, Anders Holst, and Pentti Kanerva. 2008. Permutations as a Means to Encode Order in Word Space. In *Proceedings of CogSci*, pages 1300–1305.

Magnus Sahlgren. 2006. *The Word-Space Model: Using Distributional Analysis to Represent Syntagmatic and Paradigmatic Relations between Words in High-Dimensional Vector Spaces*. Ph.D. thesis, PhD thesis, Stockholm University.

Maria Skeppstedt, Maria Kvist, and Hercules Dalianis. 2012. Rule-based Entity Recognition and Coverage of SNOMED CT in Swedish Clinical Text. In *Proceedings of LREC*, pages 1250–1257.

Lonneke van der Plas and Jörg Tiedemann. 2006. Finding Synonyms Using Automatic Word Alignment and Measures of Distributional Similarity. In *Proceedings of COLING/ACL*, pages 866–873.

Hua Wu and Ming Zhou. 2003. Optimizing Synonym Extraction Using Monolingual and Bilingual Resources. In *Proceedings of the Second International Workshop on Paraphrasing*, pages 72–79.

Hong Yu and Eugene Agichtein. 2003. Extracting Synonymous Gene and Protein Terms from Biological Literature. *Bioinformatics*, 19(suppl 1):i340–i349.

Qing T Zeng, Doug Redd, Thomas Rindflesch, and Jonathan Nebeker. 2012. Synonym, Topic Model and Predicate-Based Query Expansion for Retrieving Clinical Documents. In *Proceedings AMIA Annual Symposium*, pages 1050–9.

Ziqi Zhang, José Iria, Christopher Brewster, and Fabio Ciravegna. 2008. A Comparative Evaluation of Term Recognition Algorithms. In *Proceedings of LREC*.

Unsupervised Linguistically-Driven Reliable Dependency Parses Detection and Self-Training for Adaptation to the Biomedical Domain

Felice Dell'Orletta, Giulia Venturi, Simonetta Montemagni
Istituto di Linguistica Computazionale "Antonio Zampolli" (ILC–CNR)
Via G. Moruzzi, 1 – Pisa (Italy)
{felice.dellorletta,giulia.venturi,simonetta.montemagni}@ilc.cnr.it

Abstract

In this paper, a new self–training method for domain adaptation is illustrated, where the selection of reliable parses is carried out by an unsupervised linguistically–driven algorithm, ULISSE. The method has been tested on biomedical texts with results showing a significant improvement with respect to considered baselines, which demonstrates its ability to capture both reliability of parses and domain–specificity of linguistic constructions.

1 Introduction

As firstly demonstrated by (Gildea, 2001), parsing systems have a drop of accuracy when tested against domain corpora outside of the data from which they were trained. This is a real problem in the biomedical domain where, due to the rapidly expanding body of biomedical literature, the need for increasingly sophisticated and efficient biomedical text mining systems is becoming more and more pressing. In particular, the existence of natural language parsers reliably dealing with biomedical texts represents the prerequiste for identifying and extracting knowledge embedded in them. Over the last years, this problem has been tackled within the biomedical NLP community from different perspectives. The development of a domain–specific annotated corpus, i.e. the Genia Treebank (Tateisi, Yakushiji, Ohta, & Tsujii, 2005), played a key role by providing a sound basis for empirical performance evaluation as well as training of parsers. On the other hand, several attempts have been made to adapt general parsers to the biomedical domain. First experiments in this direction are reported in (Clegg & Shepherd, 2005) who first compared the performance of three different parsers against the Genia treebank and a sample of the Penn Treebank (PTB) (Mitchell P. Marcus & Santorini, 1993) in order to carry out an inter–domain analysis of the typology of errors made by each parser and demonstrated that by integrating the output of the three parsers they achieved statistically significant performance gains. Three different methods of parser adaptation for the biomedical domain have been proposed by (Lease & Charniak, 2005) who, starting from the results of unknown word rate experiments carried out on the Genia treebank, adapted a PTB–trained parser by improving the Part–Of–Speech tagging accuracy and by relying on an external domain–specific lexicon. More recently, (McClosky, Charniak, & Johnson, 2010) and (Plank & van Noord, 2011) devised adaptation methods based on domain similarity measures. In particular, both of them adopted lexical similarity measures to automatically select from an annotated collection of texts those training data which is more relevant, i.e. lexically closer, to adapt the parser to the target domain.

A variety of semi–supervised approaches, where unlabeled data is used in addition to labeled training data, have been recently proposed in the literature in order to adapt parsing systems to new domains. Among these approaches, the last few years have seen a growing interest in self–training for domain adaptation, i.e. a method for using automatically annotated data from a target domain when training supervised models. Self–training methods proposed so far mainly differ at the level of the selection of parse trees to be added to the in–domain gold trees as further training data. Depending on whether or not external supervised classifiers are used to select the parses to be added to the gold–training set, two types of methods are envisaged in the literature. The first is the case, among others, of: (Kawahara & Uchimoto, 2008), using a machine learning classifier to predict the reliability of parses on the basis of different feature types; or (Sagae & Tsujii, 2007), selecting identical analyses for the same sentence within the output of different parsing models trained on the same dataset; or (McClosky, Charniak, & Johnson, 2006), using a discriminative reranker against the output of a n–best generative parser for selecting the best parse for each sentence to be used as further training data. Yet, due to the fact that several supervised classifiers are resorted to for improving the base supervised parser, this class of methods cannot be seen as a genuine istance of self–training. The second type of methods is exemplified, among others, by (Reichart & Rappoport, 2007) who use the whole set of automatically analyzed sentences, and by (McClosky & Charniak, 2008) and (Sagae, 2010) who add different amounts of automatically parsed data without any selection strategy. Note that (McClosky & Charniak, 2008) tested their self–training approach on the Genia Treebank: they self–trained a PTB–trained costituency parser using a random selection of Medline abstracts.

In this paper, we address the second scenario with a main novelty: we use an unsupervised approach to select reliable parses from automatically parsed target domain texts to be combined with the gold–training set. Two unsupervised algorithms have been proposed so far in the literature for selecting reliable parses, namely: PUPA (*POS–based Unsupervised Parse Assessment Algorithm*) (Reichart & Rappoport, 2009) and ULISSE (*Unsupervised LInguiStically–driven Selection of dEpendency parses*) (Dell'Orletta, Venturi, & Montemagni, 2011). Both algorithms assign a quality score to each parse tree based on statistics collected from a large automatically parsed corpus, with a main difference: whereas PUPA operates on costituency trees and uses statistics about sequences of part–of–speech tags, ULISSE uses statistics about linguistic features checked against dependency–based representations. The self–training strategy presented in this paper is based on an augmented version of ULISSE. The reasons for this choice are twofold: if on the one hand ULISSE appears to outperform PUPA (namely, a dependency–based version of PUPA implemented in (Dell'Orletta et al., 2011)), on the other hand the linguistically–driven nature of ULISSE makes our self–training strategy for domain adaptation able to capture reliable parses which are also representative of the syntactic peculiarities of the target domain.

After introducing the in– and out–domain corpora used in this study (Section 2), we discuss the results of the multi–level linguistic analysis of these corpora carried out (Section 3) with a view to identifying the main features differentiating the biomedical language from ordinary language. In Section 4, the algorithm used to select reliable parses from automatically parsed domain–specific texts is described. In Section 5 the proposed self–training method is illustrated, followed by a discussion of achieved results (Section 6).

2 Corpora

Used domain corpora include *i)* the two out–domain datasets used for the "Domain Adaptation Track" of the CoNLL 2007 Shared Task (Nivre et al., 2007) and *ii)* the dependency–based version of the Genia Treebank (Tateisi et al., 2005). The CoNLL 2007 datasets are represented by chemical (CHEM) and biomedical abstracts (BIO), made of 5,001 tokens (195 sentences) and of 5,017 tokens (200 sentences) respectively. The dependency–based version of Genia includes $\sim$493k tokens and $\sim$18k sentences which was generated by converting the PTB version of Genia created by Illes Solt[1] using the (Johansson & Nugues, 2007) tool with the *-conll2007* option to produce annotations in line with the CoNLL 2007 data set[2]. As unlabelled data, we used the datasets distributed in the framework of the CoNLL 2007 Domain Adaptation Track. For CHEM the set of unlabelled data consists of 10,482,247 tokens (396,128 sentences) and for BIO of 9,776,890 tokens (375,421 sentences). For the experiments using Genia as test set, we used the BIO unlabelled data. This was possible due to the fact that both the Genia Treebank and the BIO dataset consist of biomedical abstracts extracted (though using different query terms) from PubMed.com.

As in–domain training data we have used the CoNLL 2007 dependency–based version of Sections 2–11 of the Wall Street Journal (WSJ) partition of the Penn Treebank (PTB), for a total of 447,000 tokens and about 18,600 sentences. For testing, we used the subset of Section 23 of WSJ consisting of 5,003 tokens (214 sentences).

All corpora have been morpho–syntactically tagged and lemmatized by a customized version

[1] http://categorizer.tmit.bme.hu/~illes/genia_ptb/

[2] In order to be fully compliant with the PTB PoS tagset, we changed the PoS label of all punctuation marks.

of the pos–tagger described in (Dell'Orletta, n.d.) and dependency parsed by the DeSR parser using Multi–Layer Perceptron (MLP) as learning algorithm (Attardi, Dell'Orletta, Simi, & Turian, n.d.), a state–of–the–art linear–time Shift–Reduce dependency parser following a "stepwise" approach (Buchholz & Marsi, 2006).

3 Linguistic analysis of biomedical abstrats vs newspaper articles

For the specific concerns of this study, we carried out a comparative linguistic analysis of four different corpora, taken as representative of ordinary language and biomedical language. In each case, we took into account a *gold* (i.e. manually annotated) corpus, and an *unlabelled* corpus, which was automatically annotated. By comparing the results obtained with respect to gold and automatically annotated texts, we intend to demonstrate the reliability of features extracted from automatically annotated texts. As data representative of ordinary language we took *i)* the whole WSJ section of the Penn Treebank[3] including 39,285,425 tokens (1,625,606 sentences) and *ii)* the sections 2–11 of the WSJ. For what concerns the biomedical domain, we relied on the Genia Treebank in order to guarantee comparability of the results of our linguistic analysis with previous studies carried out on this reference corpus. As automatically annotated data we used the corpus of biomedical abstract (BIO) distributed as out–domain dataset used for the "Domain Adaptation Track" of the CoNLL 2007 Shared Task.

In order to get evidence of the differences holding between the WSJ newspaper articles and the selected biomedical abstracts, the four corpora have been compared with respect to a wide typology of features (i.e. raw text, lexical, morpho–syntactic and syntactic). Let us start from raw text features, in particular from average sentence length (calculated as the average number of words per sentence): as Figure 1 shows, both the corpus of automatically parsed newspaper articles (*WSJ_unlab*) and the manually annotated one (*WSJ_gold*) contain shorter sentences with respect to both the automatically parsed biomedical abstrats (*BIO_unlab*) and the manually annotated ones (*Genia_gold*), a result which is in line

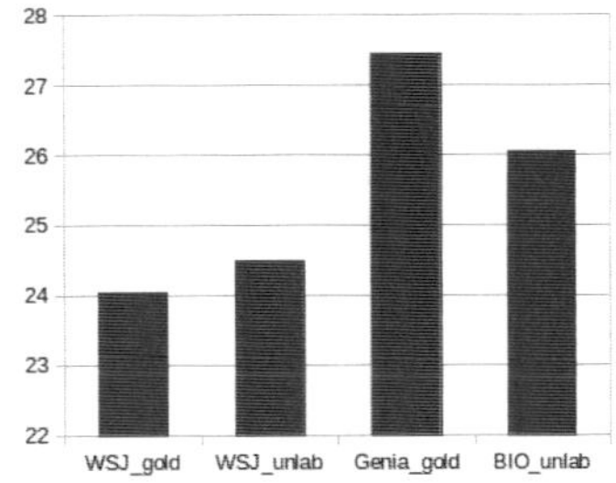

Figure 1: Average sentence length in biomedical and newspaper corpora.

with (Clegg & Shepherd, 2005) findings. When we focus on the lexical level, *BIO_unlab* and *Genia_gold* appear to have quite a similar percentage of lexical items which is not contained in *WSJ_gold* (23.13% and 26.14% respectively) while the out–of–vocabulary rate of *WSJ_unlab* is much lower, i.e. 8.69%. Similar results were recorded by (Lease & Charniak, 2005) who report the unknown word rate for various genres of tecnical literature.

Let us focus now on the morpho–syntactic level. If we consider the distribution of nouns, verbs and adjectives, three features typically representing stylistic markers associated with different linguistic varieties (Biber & Conrad, 2009), it can be noticed (see Figures 2(a) and 2(c)) that the biomedical abstracts contain a higher percentage of nouns and adjectives while showing a significantly lower percentage of verbs (Figure 2(b)). The syntactic counterpart of the different distribution of morpho–syntactic categories can be observed in Table 1, reporting the percentage distribution of the first ten Parts–of–Speech dependency triplets occurring in the biomedical and newspaper corpora: each triplet is described as the sequence of the PoS of a dependent and a head linked by a depedency arc, by also considering the PoS of the head father. It turned out that biomedical abstracts are characterized by *nominal* dependency triplets, e.g. two nouns and a preposition (NN–NN–IN) or noun, preposition, noun (NN–IN–NN) or adjective, noun and preposition (JJ–NN–IN), which occur more frequently than *verbal* triplets, such as determiner, noun and verb (DT–NN–VBZ) or a verbal root (.–VBD–ROOT)[4]. Interestingly, in *Genia_gold* no verbal triplet occurs within the top ten triplets, which cover the 21% of the total amount

[3]This corpus represents to the unlabelled data set distributed for the CoNLL 2007 Shared Task on Dependency Parsing, domain adaptation track.

[4]We named 'ROOT' the artificial root node.

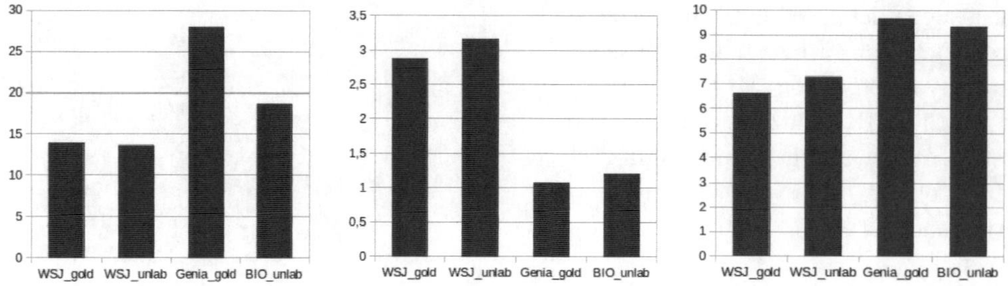

(a) Distribution of Nouns (b) Distribution of Verbs (c) Distribution of Adjectives

Figure 2: Distribution of some Parts–of–Speech in biomedical and newspaper corpora.

of triplets occurring in the corpus. By contrast, the same top ten triplets represent only ∼11% in *WSJ_gold*, testifying the wider variety of syntactic constructions occurring in newspaper articles with respect to texts of the biomedical domain. This is also proved by the total amount of different PoS dependency triplets occurring in the two gold datasets, i.e. 7,827 in *WSJ_gold* and 5,064 in *Genia_gold* even though the Genia Treebank is ∼50,000–tokens bigger.

Further differences can be observed at a deeper syntactic level of analysis. This is the case of the average depth of embedded complement 'chains' governed by a nominal head. Figure 3(a) shows that biomedical abstracts are characterized by an average depth which is higher than the one observed in newspaper articles. A similar trend can be observed for what concerns the distribution of 'chains' by depth. In Figure 3(b) shows that *WSJ_unlab* and *WSJ_gold* 'chains', on the one hand, and *BIO_unlab* and *Genia_gold* 'chains', on the other hand, overlap. The corpora have also been compared with respect to *i)* the average length of dependency links, measured in terms of the words occurring between the syntactic head and the dependent (excluding punctuation marks), and *ii)* the average depth of the whole parse tree, calculated in terms of the longest path from the root of the dependency tree to a leaf. In both cases it can be noted that *i)* the biomedical abstracts contain much longer dependency links than newswire texts (Figure 3(c)) and *ii)* the average depth of *BIO_unlab* and *Genia_gold* parse trees is higher than in the case of the *WSJ_unlab* and *WSJ_gold* (Figure 3(d)). A further distinguishing feature of the biomedical abstracts concerns the average depth of 'chains' of embedded subordinate clauses, calculated here by taking into account both clausal arguments and complements linked to a verbal sentence root. As Figure 3(e) shows, both *BIO_unlab* and *Genia_gold* have shorter 'chains' with respect to the ones contained in the newspaper articles. Interestingly, a careful analysis of the distributions by depth of 'chains' of embedded subordinate clauses shows that the biomedical abstracts appear to have *i)* a higher occurrence of 'chains' including just one subordinate clause and *ii)* a lower percentage of deep 'chains' with respect to newswire texts. Finally, we compared the two types of corpora with respect to the distribution of verbal roots. The biomedical abstracts resulted to be characterised by a lower percentage of verbal roots with respect to newspaper articles (see Figure 3(f)). This is in line with the distribution of verbs as well as of the *nominal* dependency triplets observed in the biomedical abstracts at the morpho–syntactic level of analysis.

Interestingly, the results obtained with respect to automatically parsed and manually annotated data show similar trends for both considered in– and out–domain corpora, thus demonstrating the reliability of features monitored against automatically annotated data. In what follows, we will show how detected linguistic peculiarities can be exploited in a domain adaptation scenario.

4 Linguistically–driven Unsupervised Ranking of Parses for Self–training

In the self–training approach illustrated in this paper, the selection of parses from the automatically annotated target domain dataset is guided by an augmented version of ULISSE, an unsupervised linguistically–driven algorithm to select reliable parses from the output of dependency annotated texts (Dell'Orletta et al., 2011) which has shown a good performance for two different languages

WSJ_gold		WSJ_unlab		Genia_gold		BIO_unlab	
Triplet	% Freq	Triplet	% Freq	Triplet	% Freq	Triplet	% Freq
DT-NN-IN	2.03	DT-NN-IN	1.72	NN-NN-IN	3.66	DT-NN-IN	2.87
.-VBD-ROOT	1.61	.-VBD-ROOT	1.30	NN-IN-NN	2.93	NN-IN-NN	2.39
NN-IN-NN	1.11	JJ-NN-IN	0.99	DT-NN-IN	2.48	JJ-NN-IN	2.08
JJ-NN-IN	1.10	NN-IN-NN	0.97	JJ-NN-IN	1.96	NN-NN-IN	1.73
.-VBZ-ROOT	1.09	NNP-NNP-IN	0.87	NN-NNS-IN	1.88	IN-NN-IN	1.72
NNP-NNP-IN	0.95	DT-NN-VBD	0.85	JJ-NNS-IN	1.77	JJ-NNS-IN	1.36
DT-NN-VBZ	0.89	NN-VBD-ROOT	0.80	IN-NN-IN	1.65	.-VBD-ROOT	1.33
DT-NN-VBD	0.87	JJ-NNS-IN	0.79	NN-CC-IN	1.64	NNS-IN-NN	1.13
JJ-NNS-IN	0.87	NNP-NNP-VBD	0.78	NNS-IN-NN	1.56	NNP-NN-IN	1.03
IN-NN-IN	0.87	.-VBZ-ROOT	0.75	NN-NN-CC	1.47	NN-IN-VBN	0.93

Table 1: Frequency distribution of the first ten Parts–of–Speech dependency triplets in biomedical and newspaper corpora.

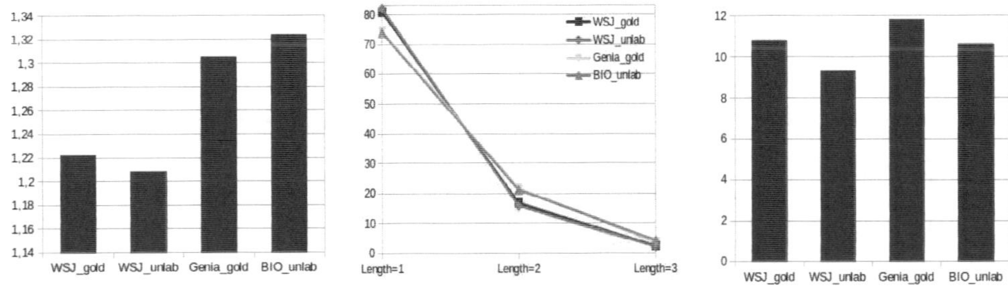

(a) Depth of embedded complement 'chains'

(b) Distribution of embedded complement 'chains' by depth

(c) Length of dependency links

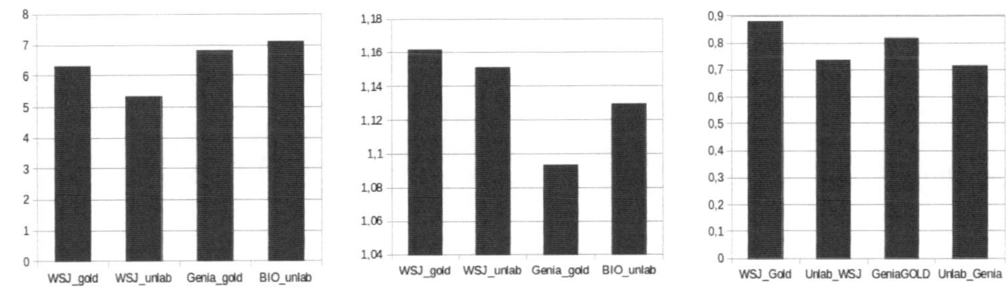

(d) Parse tree depth

(e) Depth of embedded subordinate clauses 'chains'

(f) Distribution of verbal roots

Figure 3: Syntactic features in biomedical and newspaper corpora.

(English and Italian) against the output of two supervised parsers (MST, (McDonald, Lerman, & Pereira, 2006) and DeSR, (Attardi, 2006)) selected for their behavioral differences (McDonald & Nivre, 2007). ULISSE assigns to each dependency tree a score quantifying its reliability based on a wide range of linguistic features. After collecting statistics about selected features from a corpus of automatically parsed sentences, for each newly parsed sentence ULISSE computes a reliability score using the previously extracted feature statistics. In its reliability assessment, ULISSE exploits both global and local features, where global features (listed in Table 2 and discussed in Section 3) are computed with respect to each sentence and averaged over all sentences in the corpus, and the local features with respect to individual dependency links and averaged over all of them. Local features include the plausibility of a dependency link calculated by considering selected features of the dependent and its governing head as well as of the head father: whereas in ULISSE the selected features were circumscribed to part–of–speech information (so–called "ArcPOSFeat" feature), in this version of the algorithm a new local feature has been introduced, named "ArcLemmaFeat", which exploits lemma information. "ArcPOSFeat" is able to capture the different distribution of PoS dependency triplets (see Table 1), along with the type of dependency link, while the newly introduced "ArcLemmaFeat" is meant to capture the lexical peculiarities of the target domain (see Section 3). As demonstrated in (Dell'Orletta et al., 2011), both global and local linguistic features contribute to the selection of reliable parses. Due to the typology of linguistic features underlying ULISSE, selected reliable parses typically include domain–specific constructions. This peculiarity of the ULISSE algorithm turned out to be particularly useful to maximize the self–training effect in improving the parsing performance in a domain adaptation scenario.

The reliability score assigned by this augmented version of ULISSE to newly parsed sentences results from a combination of the weights associated with individual features, both global and local ones. In this study, the reliability score was computed as a simple product of the individual feature weights: in this way, one low weight feature is sufficient to qualify a parse as low quality and thus to exclude it from the self–training dataset[5].

Feature
Parse tree depth
Embedded complement 'chains' headed by a noun
- Average depth
- Distribution by depth
Verbal roots
Arity of verbal predicates
- Distribution by arity
Subordinate vs main clauses
- Relative ordering of subordinate clauses with respect to the main clause
- Average depth of 'chains' of embedded subordinate clauses
- Distribution of embedded subordinate clauses 'chains' by depth
Length of dependency links

Table 2: Global features underlying ULISSE.

5 Experimental set–up

In the reported experiments, we used the DeSR parser. Its performance using the proposed domain adaptation strategy was tested against *i)* the two out–domain datasets distributed for the "Domain Adaptation Track" of the CoNLL 2007 Shared Task and *ii)* the dependency–based version of the Genia Treebank, described in Section 2. For testing purposes, we selected from the dependency–based version of the Genia Treebank sentences with a maximum length of 39 tokens (for a total of 375,912 tokens and 15,623 sentences).

Results achieved with respect to the CHEM and BIO test sets were evaluated in terms of "Labelled Attachment Score" (LAS), whereas for Genia the only possible evaluation was in terms of "Unlabelled Attachment Score" (UAS). This follows from the fact that, as reported by Illes, this version of Genia is annotated with a Penn Treebank–style phrase–structure, where a number of functional tags are missing: this influences the type of evaluation which can be carried out against the Genia test set.

[5]See (Dell'Orletta et al., 2011) for a detailed description of the quality score computation.

Test corpus	LAS	UAS
PTB	86.09%	87.29%
CHEM	78.50%	81.10%
BIO	78.65%	79.97%
GENIA	n/a	80.25%

Table 3: The *BASE* model tested on PTB, CHEM, BIO and GENIA.

Achieved results were compared with two baselines, represented by: i) the *Baseline model* (*BASE*), i.e. the parsing model trained on the PTB training set only; ii) the *Random Selection* (*RS*) of parses from automatically parsed out–domain corpora, calculated as the mean of a *10*–fold cross–validation process. As proved by (Sagae, 2010) and by (McClosky & Charniak, 2008) for the biomedical domain, the latter represents a strong unsupervised baseline showing a significant accuracy improvement which was obtained by adding incremental amounts of automatically parsed out–domain data to the training dataset without any selection strategy.

The experiments we carried out to test the effectiveness of our self–training strategy were organised as follows. ULISSE and the baseline algorithms were used to produce different rankings of parses of the unlabelled target domain corpora. From the top of these rankings different pools of parses were selected to be used for training. In particular, two different sets of experiments were carried out, namely: i) using only automatically parsed data as training corpus and ii) combining automatically parsed data with the PTB training set. For each set of experiments, different amounts of unlabelled data were used to create the self–training models.

6 Results

Table 3 reports the results of the *BASE* model tested on PTB, CHEM, BIO and GENIA. When applied without adaptation to the out–domain CHEM, BIO and GENIA test sets, the *BASE* parsing model has a drop of about 7.5% of LAS in both CHEM and BIO cases. For what concerns UAS, the drop is about 6% for CHEM and about 7% for BIO and GENIA.

The results of the performed experiments are shown in Figures 4 and 5, where each plot reports the accuracy scores (LAS and UAS respectively) of the self–trained parser using the ULISSE

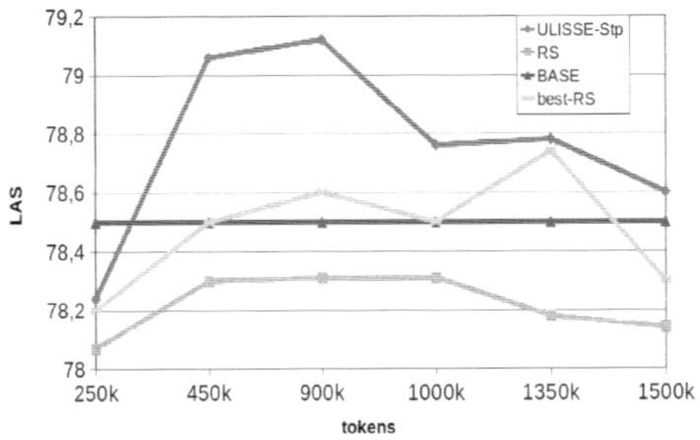

(a) LAS for CHEM without PTB training set.

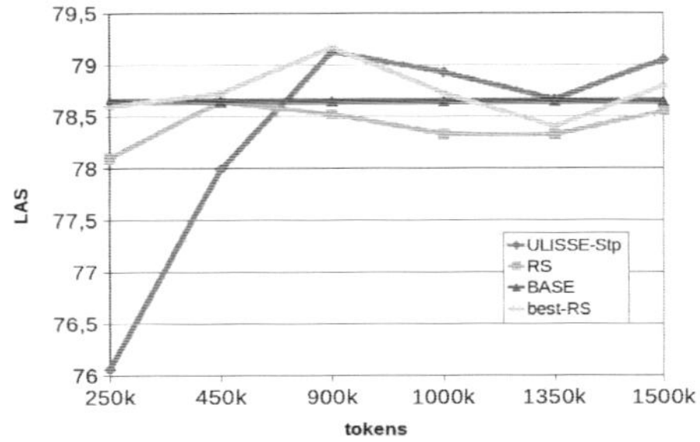

(b) LAS for BIO without the PTB training set.

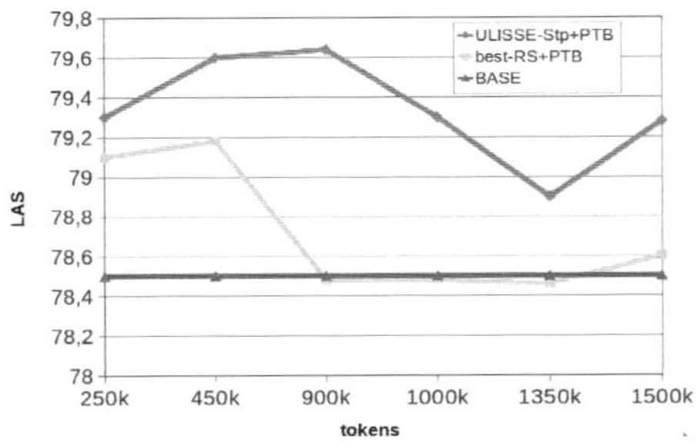

(c) LAS for CHEM with the PTB training set.

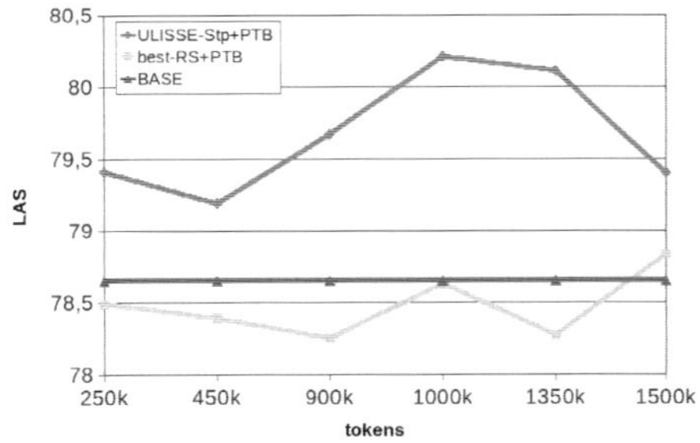

(d) LAS for BIO with the PTB training set.

Figure 4: LAS of the different self–training models in the two sets of performed experiments.

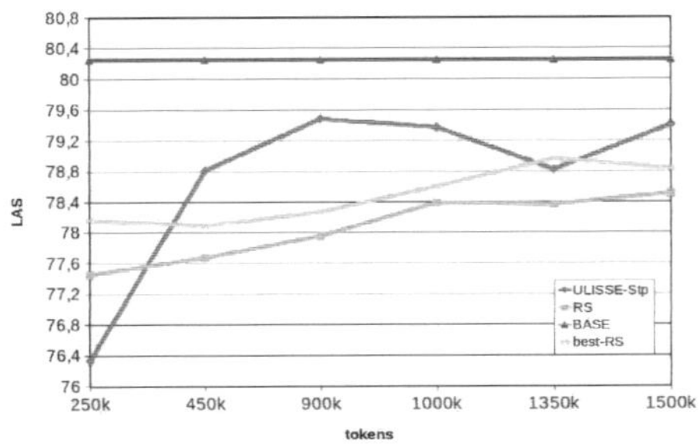

(a) UAS for GENIA without the PTB training set.

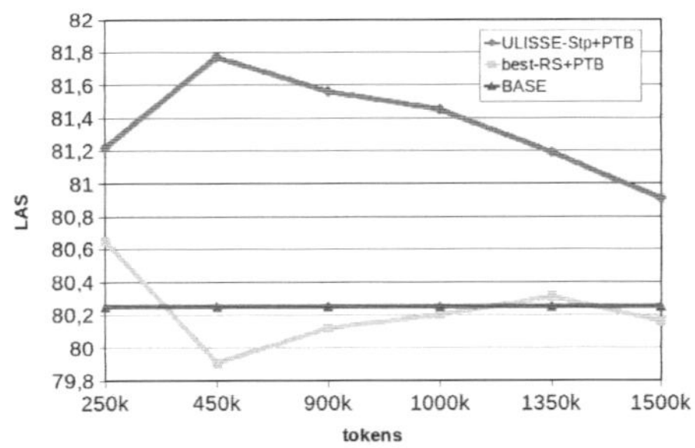

(b) UAS for GENIA with the PTB training set.

Figure 5: UAS of the different self–training models for GENIA.

algorithm (henceforth, ULISSE–Stp) and of the baseline models (*RS* and *BASE*). The parser accuracy was computed with respect to different amounts of automatically parsed data which were used to create the self–trained parsing model. For this purpose, we considered six different pools of 250k, 450k, 900k, 1000k, 1350k and 1500k tokens. Plots are organized by experiment type: i.e. the results in subfigures 4(a), 4(b) and 5(a) are achieved by using only automatically parsed data as training corpus, whereas those reported in the other subfigures refer to models trained on automatically parsed data combined with PTB. Note that in all figures the line named *best–RS* represents the best *RS* score for each pool of *k* tokens in the *10*–fold cross–validation process.

For what concerns BIO and CHEM, in the first set of experiments ULISSE–Stp turned out to be the best self–training algorithm: this is always the case for CHEM (see subfigure 4(a)), whereas for BIO (see subfigure 4(b)) it outperforms all baselines only when pools of tokens $>= 900k$ are added. When 900k tokens are used, ULISSE–Stp allows a LAS improvement of 0.81% on CHEM and of 0.61% on BIO with respect to *RS*, and of 0.62% on CHEM and of 0.48% on BIO with respect to *BASE*. It is interesting to note that ULISSE–Stp using only automatically parsed data for training achieves better results than *BASE* (using the PTB gold training set): to our knowledge, a similar result has never been reported in the literature. The behaviour is similar also when the experiments are evaluated in terms of UAS[6].

The results achieved in the first set of experiments carried out on the GENIA test set (see 5(a)) differ significantly from what we observed for CHEM and BIO: in this case, the *BASE* model appears to outperform all the other algorithms, with the ULISSE–Stp algorithm being however more effective than the *RS* baselines.

Figures 4(c), 4(d) and 5(b) report the results of the second set of experiments, i.e. those carried out by also including PTB in the training set. Note that in these plots the *RS+PTB* lines represent the score of the parser models trained on the pools of tokens used to obtain the *best–RS* line combined with the PTB gold training set. It can be observed that the ULISSE–Stp+PTB self–training model outperforms all baselines for CHEM, BIO and GENIA for all the different sizes of pools of selected tokens. For each pool of parsed data, Table 4 records the improvement and the error reduction observed with respect to the *BASE* model.

Pool of tokens	CHEM	Err. red.	BIO	Err. red.	GENIA	Err. red.
250k	0.8	3.72	0.76	3.55	0.97	4.91
450k	1.1	5.12	0.54	2.53	1.52	7.7
900k	1.14	5.3	1.02	4.77	1.31	6.63
1000k	0.8	3.72	1.56	7.29	1.2	6.08
1350k	0.4	1.49	1.46	6.82	0.94	4.76
1500k	0.78	3.62	0.75	3.37	0.66	3.34

Table 4: % improvement of ULISSE–Stp+PTB vs *BASE* reported in terms of LAS for CHEM and BIO and of UAS for GENIA.

Differently from (Sagae, 2010) (with a constituency–based parser), in this set of experiments the self–training approach based on random selection of sentences (i.e. the *best–RS+PTB* baseline) doesn't achieve any improvement with respect to the *BASE* model with only minor exceptions (observed e.g. with 250k and 450k pools of added tokens for CHEM and with 250k for GENIA). Moreover, even when the *best–RS* LAS is higher than the ULISSE–Stp score (e.g. in the first pools of *k* of Figure 4(b)), ULISSE–Stp+PTB turns out to be more effective than the *best–RS+PTB* baseline (Figure 4(d)). These results may follow from the fact that ULISSE–Stp is able to capture not only reliable parses but also, and more significantly here, parses which reflect the syntactic peculiarities of the target domain.

Table 5 shows the results of the different *ULISSE–Stp+PTB* models tested on the PTB test set: no LAS improvement is observed with respect to the results obtained with the *BASE* model, i.e. 86.09% (see Table 3). This result is in line with (McClosky et al., 2010) and (Plank & van Noord, 2011) who proved that parsers trained on the union of gold corpora belonging to different domains achieve a lower accuracy with respect to the same parsers trained on data belonging to a single target domain. Last but not least, it should be noted that the performance of ULISSE–Stp across the experiments carried out with pools of automatically parsed tokens of different sizes is in line with the behaviour of the ULISSE ranking algorithm (Dell'Orletta et al., 2011), where increasingly wider top lists of parsed tokens show decreasing LAS scores. This helps explaining why the performance of ULISSE–Stp starts decreasing after a certain threshold when wider top–lists of tokens are added to the parser training data.

Pool of tokens	CHEM	BIO
250k	83.53	85.55
450k	85.53	86.01
900k	85.95	84.79
1000k	86.03	85.45
1350k	85.49	85.71
1500k	85.67	86.39

Table 5: ULISSE–Stp+PTB on PTB test set with automatically parsed data.

Conclusion

In this paper we explored a new self–training method for domain adaptation where the selection of reliable parses within automatically annotated texts is carried out by an unsupervised linguistically–driven algorithm, ULISSE. Results achieved for the CoNLL 2007 datasets as well as for the larger test set represented by GENIA show a significant improvement with respect to considered baselines. This demonstrates a two–fold property of ULISSE, namely its reliablity and effectiveness both in capturing peculiarities of biomedical texts, and in selecting high quality parses. Thanks to these properties the proposed self–training method is able to improve the parser performances when tested in an out–domain scenario. The same approach could in principle be applied to deal with biomedical sub–domain variation: as reported by (Lippincott, Séaghdha, & Korhonen, 2011), biomedical texts belonging to different sub–domains do vary along many linguistic dimensions, with a potential negative impact on biomedical NLP tools.

[6]In this paper, for CHEM and BIO experiments we report only the LAS scores since this is the standard evaluation metric for dependency parsing.

References

Attardi, G. (2006). Experiments with a multi-language non-projective dependency parser. In *Proceedings of CoNLL-X '06* (pp. 166–170). New York City, New York.

Attardi, G., Dell'Orletta, F., Simi, M., & Turian, J. (n.d.). Accurate dependency parsing with a stacked multilayer perceptron. In *Proceedings of EVALITA 2009.*

Biber, D., & Conrad, S. (2009). *Genre, register, style.* Cambridge: Cambridge University Press.

Buchholz, S., & Marsi, E. (2006). CoNLL-X shared task on multilingual dependency parsing. In *Proceedings of CoNLL 2006.*

Clegg, A. B., & Shepherd, A. J. (2005). Evaluating and integrating treebank parsers on a biomedical corpus. In *In proceedings of the ACL 2005 workshop on software.*

Dell'Orletta, F. (n.d.). Ensemble system for part-of-speech tagging. In *Proceedings of EVALITA 2009.*

Dell'Orletta, F., Venturi, G., & Montemagni, S. (2011). Ulisse: an unsupervised algorithm for detecting reliable dependency parses. In *Proceedings of CoNLL 2011* (pp. 115–124). Portland, Oregon.

Gildea, D. (2001). Corpus variation and parser performance. In *Proceedings of EMNLP 2001* (p. 167-202). Pittsburgh, PA.

Johansson, R., & Nugues, P. (2007). Extended constituent-to-dependency conversion for english. In *Proceedings of NODALIDA 2007.* Tartu, Estonia.

Kawahara, D., & Uchimoto, K. (2008). Learning reliability of parses for domain adaptation of dependency parsing. In *Proceedings of IJCNLP 2008* (pp. 709–714).

Lease, M., & Charniak, E. (2005). Parsing biomedical literature. In *Proceedings of the second international joint conference on natural language processing (IJCNLP-05), Jeju Island, Korea* (pp. 58–69).

Lippincott, T., Séaghdha, D. Ó., & Korhonen, A. (2011). Exploring subdomain variation in biomedical language. *BMC Bioinformatics, 12*, 212–233.

McClosky, D., & Charniak, E. (2008). Self-training for biomedical parsing. In *Proceedings of ACL–HLT 2008* (pp. 101–104).

McClosky, D., Charniak, E., & Johnson, M. (2006). Reranking and self-training for parser adaptation. In *Proceedings of ACL 2006* (pp. 337–344). Sydney, Australia.

McClosky, D., Charniak, E., & Johnson, M. (2010). Automatic domain adaptation for parsing. In *Proceedings of NAACL–HLT 2010* (pp. 28–36). Los Angeles, California.

McDonald, R., Lerman, K., & Pereira, F. (2006). Multilingual dependency analysis with a two-stage discriminative parser. In *Proceedings of CoNLL 2006.*

McDonald, R., & Nivre, J. (2007). Characterizing the errors of data-driven dependency parsing models. In *Proceedings of EMNLP-CoNLL 2007* (p. 122-131).

Mitchell P. Marcus, M. A. M., & Santorini, B. (1993). Building a large annotated corpus of english: the penn treebank. *Comput. Linguist., 19*(2), 313–330.

Nivre, J., Hall, J., Kübler, S., McDonald, R., Nilsson, J., Riedel, S., & Yuret, D. (2007). The conll 2007 shared task on dependency parsing. In *Proceedings of EMNLP-CoNLL 2007* (pp. 915–932).

Plank, B., & van Noord, G. (2011). Effective measures of domain similarity for parsing. In *Proceedings of ACL 2011* (pp. 1566–1576). Portland, Oregon.

Reichart, R., & Rappoport, A. (2007). Self–training for enhancement and domain adaptation of statistical parsers trained on small datasets. In *Proceedings of ACL 2007* (pp. 616–623).

Reichart, R., & Rappoport, A. (2009). Automatic selection of high quality parses created by a fully unsupervised parser. In *Proceedings of CoNLL 2009* (pp. 156–164).

Sagae, K. (2010). Self-training without reranking for parser domain adaptation and its impact on semantic role labeling. In *Proceedings of the 2010 workshop on domain adaptation for natural language processing (DANLP 2010)* (pp. 37–44). Uppsala, Sweden.

Sagae, K., & Tsujii, J. (2007). Dependency parsing and domain adaptation with lr models and parser ensemble. In *Proceedings of EMNLP–CoNLL 2007* (pp. 1044–1050).

Tateisi, Y., Yakushiji, A., Ohta, T., & Tsujii, J. (2005). Syntax annotation for the GENIA corpus. In *Proceedings of IJCNLP'05* (pp. 222–227). Jeju Island, Korea.

Interpreting Consumer Health Questions: The Role of Anaphora and Ellipsis

Halil Kilicoglu, Marcelo Fiszman, Dina Demner-Fushman
Lister Hill National Center for Biomedical Communications
National Library of Medicine
Bethesda, MD, USA
{kilicogluh, fiszmanm, ddemner}@mail.nih.gov

Abstract

While interest in biomedical question answering has been growing, research in consumer health question answering remains relatively sparse. In this paper, we focus on the task of consumer health question understanding. We present a rule-based methodology that relies on lexical and syntactic information as well as anaphora/ellipsis resolution to construct structured representations of questions (frames). Our results indicate the viability of our approach and demonstrate the important role played by anaphora and ellipsis in interpreting consumer health questions.

1 Introduction

Question understanding is a major challenge in automatic question answering. An array of approaches has been developed for this task in the course of TREC Question Answering evaluations (see Prager (2006) for an overview). These collectively developed approaches to question understanding were successfully applied and expanded upon in IBM's Watson system (Lally *et al.*, 2012). Currently, Watson is being retargeted towards biomedical question answering, joining the ongoing research in domain-specific question answering (for a review, see Simpson and Demner-Fushman, 2012).

Much research in automatic question answering has focused on answering well-formed factoid questions. However, real-life questions that need to be handled by such systems are often posed by lay people and are not necessarily well-formed or explicit. This is particularly evident in questions involving health issues. Zhang (2010), focusing on health-related questions submitted to Yahoo Answers, found that these questions primarily described diseases and symptoms (accompanied by some demographic information), were fairly long, dense (incorporating more than one question), and contained many abbreviations and misspellings. For example, consider the following question posed by a consumer:

(1) *my question is this: I was born w/a esophagus atresia w/dextrocardia. While the heart hasn't caused problems,the other has. I get food caught all the time. My question is...is there anything that can fix it cause I can't eat anything lately without getting it caught. I need help or will starve!*

It is clear that the person asking this question is mainly interested in learning about treatment options for his/her disease, in particular with respect to his/her esophagus. Most of the textual content is not particularly relevant in understanding the question (*I need help or will starve*! or *I get food caught all the time*). In addition, note the presence of anaphora (*it* referring to *esophagus atresia*) and ellipsis (*the other has* $_{[caused\ problems]}$), which should be resolved in order to automatically interpret the question. Finally, note the informal *fix* instead of the more formal *treat*, and *cause* instead of *because*.

The National Library of Medicine® (NLM®) receives questions from consumers on a variety of health-related topics. These questions are currently manually answered by customer support services. The overall goal of our work is to assist the customer support services by automatically interpreting these questions, using information retrieval techniques to find relevant documents and passages, and presenting the information in concise form for their assessment.

In this paper, we specifically focus on question understanding, rather than information retrieval aspects of our ongoing work. Our goal in question understanding is to capture the core aspects of the question in a structured representation (*question frame*), which can then be used to form a query for the search engine. In the current work, we primarily investigate and evaluate the role of anaphora and ellipsis resolution in understanding the questions. Our results confirm the viability of rule-based question understanding based on exploiting lexico-syntactic patterns and clearly demonstrate that anaphora and ellipsis resolution are beneficial for this task.

2 Background

Despite the growing interest to biomedical question answering (Cairns *et al.*, 2012; Ni *et al.*, 2012; Bauer and Berleant, 2012), consumer health question answering remains a fairly understudied area of research. The initial research has focused on the analysis of consumer language (McCray *et al.*, 1999) and the types of questions they asked. Spink *et al.* (2004) found that health-related queries submitted to three web search engines in 2001 were often advice seeking and personalized, and fell into five major categories: general health, weight issues, reproductive health and puberty, pregnancy/obstetrics, and human relationships. Observing that health queries constituted no more than 9.5% of all queries and declined over time, they concluded that the users turn more to the specialized resources for the answers to health-related questions. Similar to the findings of Zhang (2010), Beloborodov e*t al.* (2013) found that diseases and symptoms were the most popular topics in a resource similar to Yahoo Answers, Otvety@Mail.Ru. They analyzed Otvety@Mail.Ru questions by mapping questions to body parts and organs, applying Latent Dirichlet Allocation method with Gibbs sampling to discover topics, and using a knowledge-based method to classify questions as evidence-directed or hypothesis-directed.

First efforts in automated consumer health question processing were to classify the questions using machine learning techniques. In one study, frequently asked questions about diabetes were classified according to two somewhat orthogonal taxonomies: according to the "medical type of the question" (Causes, Diagnostic, Prevention, Symptoms, Treatment, etc.) and according to the "expected answer type" (Boolean, Causal, Definition, Factoid, Person, Place, etc.) (Cruchet *et al.*, 2008). Support Vector Machine (SVM) classification achieved an F-score in low 80s in classifying English questions to the expected answer type. The results for French and medical type classification in both languages were much lower. Liu *et al.* (2011) found that SVM trained to distinguish questions asked by consumers from those posed by healthcare professionals achieve F-scores in the high 80s - low 90s. One of distinguishing characteristics of the consumer questions in Liu *et al.*'s study was the significantly higher use of personal pronouns (compared to professional questions). This feature was found to be useful for machine learning; however, the abundance of pronouns in the long dense questions is also a potential source of failure in understanding the question.

Vicedo and Ferrández (2000) have shown that pronominal anaphora resolution improves several aspects of the QA systems' performance. This observation was supported by Harabagiu *et al.* (2005) who have manually resolved coreference and ellipsis for 14 of the 25 scenarios in the TREC 2005 evaluation. Hickl *et al.* (2006) have incorporated into their question answering system a heuristic based question coreference module that resolved referring expressions in the question series to antecedents mentioned in previous questions or in the target description. To our knowledge, coreference and ellipsis resolution has not been previously attempted in consumer health question understanding.

Another essential aspect in processing consumer questions is defining a formal representation capable of capturing all important points needed for further processing in automatic query generation (in the systems that use document passage retrieval to find a set of potential answers) and answer extraction and unification. Ontologies provide effective representation mechanisms for concepts, whereas relations are better captured in frame-like or event-related structures (Hunter and Cohen, 2006). Frame-based representation of extracted knowledge has a long-standing tradition in the biomedical domain, for example, in MedLEE (Friedman *et al.*, 1994). Demner-Fushman *et al.* (2011) showed that frame-based representation of clinical questions improve identification of patients eligible for cohort inclusion. Demner-Fushman and Abhyankar (2012) extracted frames in four steps: 1) identification of domain concepts, 2) extraction of patient demographics (e.g., age, gender) and social history, 3) establishing dependencies between the concepts using the Stanford dependency parser (de Marneffe *et al.*, 2006), and 4) adding concepts not involved in the relations to the frame as a list of keywords. Event-based representations have also seen increasing use in recent years in biomedical text mining, with the availability of biological event corpora, including GENIA event (Kim *et al.*, 2008) and GREC (Thompson *et al.*, 2009), and shared task challenges (Kim *et al.*, 2012). Most state-of-the-art systems address the event extraction task by adopting machine learning techniques, such as dual composition-based models (Riedel and McCallum, 2011), stacking-based model integration (McClosky *et al.*, 2012), and domain adaptation (Miwa *et al.*, 2012). Good performance has also been reported with some rule-based systems (Kilicoglu and Bergler, 2012). Syntactic dependency parsing has been a key component in all state-of-the-art event extraction systems, as well. The role of coreference resolution in event extraction has recently been acknowledged (Kim *et al.*, 2012), even though efforts in integrating coreference resolution into event extraction pipelines have generally resulted in only modest improvements (Yoshikawa *et al.*, 2011; Miwa *et al.*, 2012; Kilicoglu and Bergler, 2012).

Coreference resolution has also been tackled in open domain natural language processing. State-of-the-art systems often employ a combination of lexical, syntactic, shallow semantic and discourse information (e.g., speaker identification) with deterministic rules (Lee *et al.*, 2011). Interestingly, coreference resolution is one research area, in which deterministic frameworks generally outperform machine learning models (Haghighi and Klein, 2009; Lee *et al.*, 2011).

In contrast to coreference resolution, ellipsis resolution remains an understudied NLP problem. One type of ellipsis that received some attention is *null instantiation* (Fillmore and Baker, 2001), whereby the goal is to recover the referents for an uninstantiated semantic role of a target predicate from the wider discourse context. A semantic evaluation challenge that focused on null instantiation was proposed, although participation was limited (Ruppenhofer *et al.*, 2010). Gerber and Chai (2012) focused on implicit argumentation (i.e., *null instantiation*) for nominal predicates. They annotated a corpus of implicit arguments for a small number of nominal predicates and trained a discriminative model based on syntactic, semantic and discourse features collected from various linguistic resources. Focusing on a different type of ellipsis, Bos and Spenader (2011) annotated a corpus of verb phrase ellipsis; however, so far there have been little work in verb phrase ellipsis resolution. We are also not aware of any work in ellipsis resolution in biomedical NLP.

3 Methods

We use a pipeline model for question analysis, which results in frame annotations that capture the content of the question. Our rule-based method begins with identifying terms (named entities/triggers) in question text. Next, we recognize anaphoric mentions and, if any, perform anaphora resolution. The next step is to link frame triggers with their *theme* and *question cue* by exploiting syntactic dependency relations. Finally, if frames with implicit arguments exist (that is, frames in which *theme* or *question cue* was not instantiated), we attempt to recover these arguments by ellipsis resolution. In this section, we first describe our data selection. Then, we explain the steps in our pipeline, with particular emphasis on anaphora and ellipsis. The pipeline diagram is illustrated in Figure 1.

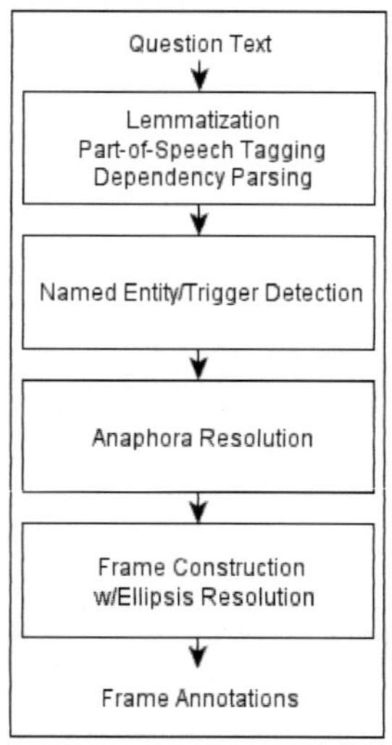

Figure 1. The system pipeline diagram

3.1 Data Selection and Annotation

In this study, we focused on questions about genetic diseases, due to their increasing prevalence. Since the majority of the consumers' questions submitted to NLM are about treatment and prognosis, we selected mainly these types of questions for our training set. Note that while these questions mostly focused on treatment and prognosis, some of them also include other types of questions, asking for general information or about diagnosis, etiology, and susceptibility (thus, confirming the finding of Zhang (2010)). The majority of selected questions were asked by real consumers in 2012. Due to our interest in genetics questions, we augmented this set with some frequently asked questions from the Genetic and Rare Disease Information Center (GARD)[1]. Our selection yielded 32 treatment and 22 prognosis questions. An example treatment question was provided earlier (1). The following is a training question on prognosis:

(2) *They have diagnosed my niece with Salla disease. I understand that this is a very rare disease and that its main origin is Finland. Can you please let me know what to expect? My niece is 7 years old. It has taken them 6 years to finally come up with this diagnosis.*

We used training questions to gain linguistic insights into the problem, to develop and refine our methodology, and as the basis of a trigger/question cue dictionary.

After the system was developed, we selected 29 previously unseen treatment-focused questions posed to GARD for testing. We annotated them with target frames (41 instances) using *brat* annotation tool (Stenetorp *et al.*, 2012) and evaluated our system results against these frames. 29 of the target frames were treatment frames. Additionally, there were 1 etiology, 6 general information, 2 diagnosis, and 3 prognosis frames.

3.2 Syntactic Dependency Parsing

Our question analysis module uses typed dependency relations as the basis of syntactic information. We extract syntactic dependencies using Stanford Parser (de Marneffe *et al.*, 2006) and use its collapsed dependency format. We rely on Stanford Parser for tokenization, lemmatization, and part-of-speech tagging, as well.

3.3 Named Entity/Trigger Detection

We use simple dictionary lookup to map entity mentions in text to UMLS Metathesaurus concepts (Lindberg, 1993). So far, we have focused on recognizing three mention categories: problems, interventions, and patients. Based on UMLS 2007AC release, we constructed a dictionary of string/concept pairs. We limited the dictionary to concepts with predefined semantic types. For example, all problems in the dictionary have a semantic type that belongs to the Disorders semantic group (McCray *et al.*, 2001), such as Neoplastic Process and Congenital Abnormality. Currently our dictionary contains approximately 260K string/concept pairs.

Dictionary lookup is also used to detect triggers and question cues. We constructed a trigger and question cue dictionary based on training data and limited expansion. The dictionary currently contains 117 triggers and 14 question cues.

3.4 Recognizing Anaphoric Mentions

We focus on identifying two types of anaphoric phenomena: *pronominal anaphora* (including anaphora of personal and demonstrative pronouns) and *sortal anaphora*. The following examples from the training questions illustrate these types. Anaphoric mentions are underlined and their antecedents are in bold.

- Personal pronominal anaphora: *My daughter has just been diagnosed with* ***Meier-Gorlin syndrome.*** *I would like to learn more about* <u>*it*</u>*...*
- Demonstrative pronominal anaphora: *We just found out that our grandson has* ***48,XXYY syndrome****. ... I was wondering if you could give us some information on what to expect and the prognosis for* <u>*this*</u> *and ..*
- Sortal anaphora: *I have a 24-month-old niece who has the following symptoms of* ***Cohen syndrome****: ... I would like seek your help in learning more about* <u>*this condition*</u>*.*

To recognize mentions of personal pronominal and sortal anaphora, we mainly adapted the rule-based techniques outlined in Kilicoglu and Bergler (2012), itself based on the deterministic coreference resolution approach described in Haghighi and Klein (2009). While Kilicoglu and Bergler (2012) focused on anaphora involving gene/protein terms, our adaptation focuses on those involving problems and patients. In addition, we expanded their work by developing rules to recognize demonstrative pronominal anaphora.

3.4.1 Personal Pronouns

Kilicoglu and Bergler (2012) focused on only resolving *it* and *they*, since, in scientific article genre, resolving other third person pronouns (*he, she*) was less relevant. We currently recognize these two pronouns, as well. For personal pronouns, we merely tag the word as a pronominal anaphor if it is tagged as a pronoun and is in third person (i.e., *she, he, it, they*).

3.4.2 Demonstrative Pronouns

We rely on typed syntactic dependencies as well as part-of-speech tags to recognize demonstrative pronominal anaphora. A word is tagged as demonstrative pronominal anaphor if it is one of *this, that, those,* or *these* and if it is not the de-

[1] https://rarediseases.info.nih.gov/GARD/

pendent in a *det* (determiner) dependency (in other words, it is not a pronominal modifier). Furthermore, we ensure that the pronoun *that* does not act as a complementizer, requiring that it not be the dependent in a *complm* (complementizer) dependency.

3.4.3 Sortal Anaphora

In the current work, we limited sortal anaphora to problem terms. As in Kilicoglu and Bergler (2012), we require that the anaphoric noun phrases not include any named entity terms. Thus, we allow *the syndrome* as an anaphoric mention, while blocking *the Stickler syndrome.* To recognize sortal anaphora, we look for the presence of *det* dependency, where the dependent is one of *this, that, these, those,* or *the.*

Once the named entities, question cues, triggers, and anaphoric mentions are identified in a sentence, we collapse the syntactic dependencies from the sentence to simplify further processing. This is illustrated in Table 1 for the sentence in (3).

(3) My partner is a carrier for Simpson-Golabi-Behmel syndrome and her son was diagnosed with this rare condition.

Dependencies before	Dependencies after
amod (syndrome, simpson-golabi-behmel)	*prep_for(carrier, simpson-golabi-behmel syndrome)*
prep_for(carrier,syndrome)	
det(condition,this)	*prep_with (diagnosed, this rare condition)*
amod(condition, rare)	
prep_with(diagnosed, condition)	

Table 1: Syntactic dependency transformations

3.5 Anaphora Resolution

Anaphora resolution is the task of finding the antecedent for an anaphoric mention in prior discourse. Our anaphora resolution method is again based on the work of Kilicoglu and Bergler (2012). However, we made simplifying assumptions based on our examination of the training questions. First observation is that each question is mainly about one salient topic (problem) and anaphoric mentions are highly likely to refer to this topic. Secondly, the salient topic often appears as the first named entity in the question. Based on these observations, we did not attempt to use the relatively complex, semantic graph-based resolution strategies (e.g., graph distance) outlined in that work. Furthermore, we have not attempted to address *set-instance anaphora* or *event anaphora* in this work, since we did not see examples of these in the training data.

Anaphora resolution begins with identifying the candidate antecedents (problems, patients) in prior discourse, which are then evaluated for syntactic and semantic compatibility. For pronominal anaphora, compatibility involves person and number agreement between the anaphoric mention and the antecedent. For sortal anaphora, number agreement as well as satisfying one of the following constraints is required:

- *Head word constraint:* The head of the anaphoric NP and the antecedent NP match. This constraint allows *Wolf-Hirschhorn Syndrome* as an antecedent for *this syndrome,* matching on the word *syndrome.*
- *Hypernymy constraint:* The head of the anaphoric NP is a problem hypernym and the antecedent is a problem term. Similar to gene/protein hypernym list in Kilicoglu and Bergler (2012), we used a small list of problem hypernym words, including *disease, disorder, illness, syndrome, condition,* and *problem.* This constraint allows *Simpson-Golabi-Behmel syndrome* as an antecedent for *this rare condition* in example (3).

We expanded number agreement test to include singular mass nouns, so that plural anaphora (e.g., *they*) can refer to mass nouns such as *family, group, population.* In addition, we defined lists of gendered nouns (e.g., *son, father, nephew,* etc. for male and *wife, daughter, niece,* etc. for female) and required gender agreement for pronominal anaphora.

After the candidate antecedents are identified, we assign them *salience scores* based on the order in which they appear in the question and their frequency in the question. The terms that appear earlier in the question and occur more frequently receive higher scores. The most salient antecedent is then taken to be the coreferent.

3.6 Frame Construction

We adapted the frame extraction process based on lexico-syntactic information outlined in Demner-Fushman *et al.* (2012) and somewhat modified the frames to accommodate consumer health questions. For each question posed, we aim to construct a frame which consists of the following elements: *type*, *theme*, and *question cue*: *theme* refers to the topic of the question (problem name, etc.), while *type* refers to the aspect of the theme that the question is about (treatment, prognosis, etc.) and question cue to the question words (*what, how, are there*, etc.). Theme element is semantically typed and is restricted to the UMLS semantic group Disorders. From the question in (1), the following frame should be extracted:

Treatment	*fix*
Theme	*Esophageal atresia (Disease or Syndrome)*
QCue	*Is there*

Table 2: Frame example

We rely on syntactic dependencies to link frame indicators to their themes and question cues. We currently search for the following types of syntactic dependencies between the indicator mention and the argument mentions: *dobj* (direct object), *nsubjpass* (passive nominal subject), *nn* (noun compound modifier), *rcmod* (relative clause modifier), *xcomp* (open clausal complement), *acomp* (adjectival complement), *prep_of, prep_to, prep_for, prep_on, prep_from, prep_with, prep_regarding, prep_about* (prepositional modifier cued by *of, to, for, on, from, with, regarding, about,* respectively). Two special rules address the following cases:

- If the dependency exists between a trigger of type T and another of type General Information, the General Information trigger becomes a question cue for the frame type T. This handles cases such as '*Is there information regarding prognosis..*' where there is a *prep_regarding* dependency between the General Information trigger '*information*' and the Prognosis trigger '*prognosis*'. This results in '*information*' becoming the question cue for the Prognosis frame.
- If a dependency exists between a trigger T and a patient term P and another between the patient term P and a potential theme argument A, the potential theme argument A is assigned as the theme of the frame indicated by T. This handles cases such as '*What is the life expectancy for a child with Dravet syndrome?*' whereby *Dravet syndrome* is assigned the Theme role for the Prognosis frame indicated by *life expectancy*.

3.6.1 Ellipsis Resolution

The frame construction step may result in frames with uninstantiated themes or question cues. If a constructed frame includes a question cue but no theme, we attempt to recover the theme argument from prior discourse by ellipsis processing. Consider the question in (4) and the frame in Table 3 extracted from it in previous steps:

(4) *They have diagnosed my niece with Salla disease. ...Can you please let me know what to expect? ...*

Prognosis	*expect*
Theme	-
QCue	*what*

Table 3: Frame with uninstantiated Theme role

In the context of consumer health questions, the main difficulty with resolving such cases is recognizing whether it is indeed a legitimate case of ellipsis. We use the following dependency-based heuristics to determine the presence of ellipsis:

- Check for the presence of a syntactic dependency of one of the types listed in Section 3.5, in which the frame trigger appears as an element. If such a dependency does not exist, consider it a case of ellipsis.
- Otherwise, consider the other element of the dependency:
  - If the other element does not correspond to a term, we cannot make a decision regarding ellipsis, since we do not know the semantics of this other element.
  - If it corresponds to an element that has already been used in creating the frame, the dependency is accounted for.
- If all the dependencies involving the frame trigger are accounted for, consider it a case of ellipsis.

In example (4), the trigger *expect* is found to be in an *xcomp* dependency with the question cue *know*, which has already been used in the frame. Therefore this dependency is accounted for, and we consider this a case of ellipsis. On the other hand, consider the example:

(5) *My child has been diagnosed with pachgyria. What can I expect for my child's future?*

As in the previous example, the Theme role of the Prognosis frame indicated by *expect* is uninstantiated. However, it is not considered an elliptical case, since there is a *prep_for* dependency between *expect* and *future*, a word that is semantically unresolved.

Once the presence of ellipsis is ensured, we fill the Theme role of the frame with the most salient term in the question text, as in anaphora resolution.

In rare cases, the frame may include a theme but not a question cue. This may be due to a lack of explicit question expression (such as in the question *'treatment for Von Hippel-Lindau syndrome.'*) or due to shortcomings in dependency-based linking of frame triggers to question cues. If no fully instantiated frame was extracted from the question, as a last resort, we construct a frame without the question cue in an effort to increase recall.

4 Results and Discussion

We extracted frames from the test questions and compared the results with the annotated target frames. As evaluation metrics, we calculated precision, recall, and F-score. To assess the effect of various components of the system, we evaluated several scenarios:

- Frame extraction without anaphora/ellipsis resolution (indicated as A in Table 4 below)
- Frame extraction with anaphora/ellipsis resolution (B)
- Frame extraction without anaphora/ellipsis resolution but with gold triggers/named entities (C)
- Frame extraction with anaphora/ellipsis resolution and gold triggers/named entities (D)

The evaluation results are provided in Table 4. In the second column, the numbers in parentheses correspond to the numbers of correctly identified frames.

	# of frames	*Recall*	*Precision*	*F-score*
A	14 (13)	0.32	0.93	0.48
B	26 (22)	0.54	0.85	0.66
C	17 (16)	0.39	0.84	0.55
D	35 (33)	0.80	0.94	0.86

Table 4: Evaluation results

The evaluation results show that the dependency-based frame extraction method with dictionary lookup is generally effective; it is precise in identifying frames, even though it misses many relevant frames, typical of most rule-based systems. On the other hand, anaphora/ellipsis resolution helps a great deal in recovering the relevant frames and only has a minor negative effect on precision of the frames, the overall effect being significantly positive. Note also that the increase in recall without gold triggers/named entities is about 40%, while that with gold triggers/named entities is more than double, indicating that accurate term recognition contributes to better anaphora/ellipsis resolution and, in turn, to better question understanding.

The dictionary-based named entity/trigger/ question cue detection is relatively simple, and while it yields good precision, the lack of terms in the corresponding dictionary causes recall errors. An example is given in (6). The named entity *Reed syndrome* was not recognized due to its absence in the dictionary, causing two false negative errors.

(6) *A friend of mine was just told she has Reed syndrome... I was wondering if you could let me know where I can find more information on this topic. I am wondering what treatments there are for this, ...*

Similarly, dependency-based frame construction is straightforward in that it mostly requires direct dependency relations between the trigger and the arguments. While the two additional rules we implemented redress the shortcomings of this straightforward approach, there are cases in which dependency-based mechanism is still lacking. An example is given in (7). The lack of a direct dependency between *treatments* and *this condition* causes a recall error. A more sophisticated mechanism based on dependency chains could recover such frames; however, such chains would also increase the likelihood of precision errors.

(7) *Are people with Lebers hereditary optic neuropathy partially blind for a long period of time .... ?Are there any surgical treatments available to alter this condition or is it permanent for life?*

Anaphora/ellipsis processing clearly benefited our question understanding system. However, we noted several errors due to shortcomings in this processing. For example, from the sentence in (8), the system constructed a General Information frame with the trigger *wonder* and the Theme argument *central core disease*, which caused a false positive error.

(8) *After 34 years of living with central core disease, ... My lower back doesn't seem to work, and I wonder if I will ever be able to walk up stairs or run.*

The system recognized that the trigger *wonder* had an uninstantiated theme argument, which it attempted to recover by ellipsis processing. However, this processing misidentified the case as legitimate ellipsis due to the dependency relations *wonder* is involved in. A more sophisticated approach would take into account specific selectional restrictions of predicates like *wonder;* however, the overall utility of such linguistic knowledge in the context of consumer health questions, which are often ungrammatical and not particularly well-written, remains uncertain.

Our anaphora resolution method was unable to resolve some cases of anaphora. For example, consider the question in (6). The anaphoric mention *this topic* corefers with *Reed syndrome*. However, we miss this anaphora since we did not consider *topic* as a problem hypernym in scenario D, in which gold named entities are used.

5 Conclusions and Future Work

We presented a rule-based approach to consumer health question understanding which relies on lexico-syntactic information and anaphora/ellipsis resolution. We showed that lexico-syntactic information provides a good baseline in understanding such questions and that resolving anaphora and ellipsis has a significant impact on this task.

With regard to question understanding, future work includes generalization of the system to questions on topics other than genetic disorders (e.g., drugs) and aspects (such as complications, prevention, ingredients, location information, etc.) and broader evaluation. We also plan to automate dictionary development to some extent and address misspellings and acronyms in questions. We have been extending our frames to include ancillary keywords (named entities extracted from the question) that are expected to assist the search engine in pinpointing the relevant answer passages, similar to Demner-Fushman and Abhyankar (2012). We will also continue to develop our anaphora/ellipsis processing module, addressing the issues revealed by our evaluation as well as other anaphoric phenomena, such as recognition of pleonastic *it*.

Acknowledgments

This research was supported by the Intramural Research Program of the NIH, National Library of Medicine.

References

Michael A. Bauer and Daniel Berleant. 2012. Usability survey of biomedical question answering systems. *Human Genomics*, 6(1):17.

Alexander Beloborodov, Artem Kuznetsov, Pavel Braslavski. 2013. Characterizing Health-Related Community Question Answering. In *Advances in Information Retrieval*, 680-683.

Brian L. Cairns, Rodney D. Nielsen, James J. Masanz, James H. Martin, Martha S. Palmer, Wayne H. Ward, Guergana K. Savova. 2011. The MiPACQ clinical question answering system. In *AMIA Annual Symposium Proceedings*, pages 171-180.

Sarah Cruchet, Arnaud Gaudinat, Célia Boyer. 2008. Supervised approach to recognize question type in a QA system for health. *Studies in Health Technology and Informatics*, 136:407-412.

Marie-Catherine de Marneffe, Bill MacCartney, Christopher D. Manning. 2006. Generating typed dependency parses from phrase structure parses. In *Proceedings of the 5th International Conference on Language Resources and Evaluation*, pages 449-454.

Dina Demner-Fushman, Swapna Abhyankar, Antonio Jimeno-Yepes, Russell F. Loane, Bastien Rance, François-Michel Lang, Nicholas C. Ide, Emilia Apostolova, Alan R. Aronson. 2011. A Knowledge-Based Approach to Medical Records Retrieval. In *Proceedings of Text Retrieval Conference 2011*.

Dina Demner-Fushman and Swapna Abhyankar. 2012. Syntactic-Semantic Frames for Clinical Cohort Identification Queries. *Lecture Notes in Computer Science, 7348*:100-112.

Charles J. Fillmore and Collin F. Baker. 2001. Frame semantics for text understanding. In *Proceedings of the NAACL'01 Workshop on WordNet and Other Lexical Resources.*

Carol Friedman, Philip O. Alderson, John HM Austin, James J. Cimino, and Stephen B. Johnson. 1994. A general natural-language text processor for clinical radiology. *Journal of the American Medical Informatics Association,* 1(2): 161-174.

Matthew S. Gerber and Joyce Y. Chai. 2012. Semantic Role Labeling of Implicit Arguments for Nominal Predicates. *Computational Linguistics,* 38(4): 755-798.

Aria Haghighi and Dan Klein. 2009. Simple coreference resolution with rich syntactic and semantic features. In *Proceedings of EMNLP 2009*, pages 1152-1161.

Sanda Harabagiu, Dan Moldovan, Christine Clark, Mitchell Bowden, Andrew Hickl, Patrick Wang. 2005. Employing two question answering systems in TREC-2005. In *Proceedings of Text Retrieval Conference 2005.*

Andrew Hickl, John Williams, Jeremy Bensley, Kirk Roberts, Ying Shi, Bryan Rink. 2006. Question Answering with LCC's CHAUCER at TREC 2006. In *Proceedings of Text Retrieval Conference 2006*.

Lawrence Hunter and Kevin B. Cohen. 2006. Biomedical language processing: what's beyond PubMed? *Molecular Cell*. 21(5):589-94.

Halil Kilicoglu and Sabine Bergler 2012. Biological Event Composition. *BMC Bioinformatics*, 13 (Supplement 11):S7.

Jin-Dong Kim, Tomoko Ohta, and Jun'ichi Tsujii. 2008. Corpus annotation for mining biomedical events from literature. *BMC Bioinformatics*, 9:10.

Jin-Dong Kim, Ngan Nguyen, Yue Wang, Jun'ichi Tsujii, Toshihisa Takagi, Akinori Yonezawa. 2012. The Genia Event and Protein Coreference tasks of the BioNLP Shared Task 2011. *BMC Bioinformatics*, 13(Supplement 11):S1.

Adam Lally, John M. Prager, Michael C. McCord, Branimir Boguraev, Siddharth Patwardhan, James Fan, Paul Fodor, Jennifer Chu-Carroll. 2012. Question analysis: How Watson reads a clue. *IBM Journal of Research and Development*, 56(3):2.

Heeyoung Lee, Yves Peirsman, Angel Chang, Nathanael Chambers, Mihai Surdeanu, Dan Jurafsky. 2011. Stanford's Multi-Pass Sieve Coreference Resolution System at the CoNLL-2011 Shared Task. In *Proceedings of the CoNLL-2011 Shared Task*, pages 28-34.

Donald A.B. Lindberg, Betsy L. Humphreys, Alexa T. McCray. 1993. The Unified Medical Language System. *Methods of information in medicine*, 32(4): 281-291.

Feifan Liu, Lamont D. Antieau, Hong Yu. 2011. Toward automated consumer question answering: automatically separating consumer questions from professional questions in the healthcare domain. *Journal of Biomedical Informatics*, 44(6): 1032-1038.

David McClosky, Sebastian Riedel, Mihai Surdeanu, Andrew McCallum, Christopher Manning. 2012. Combining joint models for biomedical event extraction. *BMC Bioinformatics*, 13 (Supplement 11): S9.

Alexa McCray, Russell Loane, Allen Browne, Anantha Bangalore. 1999. Terminology issues in user access to Web-based medical information. In *AMIA Annual Symposium Proceedings*, pages 107–111.

Alexa McCray, Anita Burgun, Olivier Bodenreider. 2001. Aggregating UMLS semantic types for reducing conceptual complexity. In *Proceedings of Medinfo*, 10(Pt1): 216-220.

Makoto Miwa, Paul Thompson, Sophia Ananiadou. 2012. Boosting automatic event extraction from the literature using domain adaptation and coreference resolution. *Bioinformatics*, 28(13):1759-1765.

Yuan Ni, Huijia Zhu, Peng Cai, Lei Zhang, Zhaoming Qui, Feng Cao. 2012. CliniQA: highly reliable clinical question answering system. *Studies in Health Technology and Information*, 180:215-219.

John M. Prager. 2006. Open-domain question answering. *Foundations and Trends in Information Retrieval*, 1(2):91-231.

Sebastian Riedel and Andrew McCallum. 2011. Fast and robust joint models for biomedical event extraction. In *Proceedings of EMNLP 2011*, pages 1-12.

Josef Ruppenhofer, Caroline Sporleder, Roser Morante, Collin Baker, Martha Palmer. 2010. SemEval-2010 Task 10: Linking Events and Their Participants in Discourse. In *Proceedings of the 5th International Workshop on Semantic Evaluation*, pages 45-50.

Matthew S. Simpson and Dina Demner-Fushman. 2012. Biomedical Text Mining: a Survey of Recent Progress. *Mining Text Data 2012*:465-517.

Amanda Spink, Yin Yang, Jim Jansen, Pirrko Nykanen, Daniel P. Lorence, Seda Ozmutlu, H. Cenk Ozmutlu. 2004. A study of medical and health queries to web search engines. *Health Information & Libraries Journal*. 21(1):44-51.

Pontus Stenetorp, Sampo Pyysalo, Goran Topić, Tomoko Ohta, Sophia Ananiadou, Jun'ichi Tsujii. 2012. Brat: a Web-based Tool for NLP-Assisted Text Annotation. In *Proceedings of the Demonstrations Sessions at EACL 2012*, pages 102-107.

Paul Thompson, Syed A. Iqbal, John McNaught, Sophia Ananiadou. 2009. Construction of an annotated corpus to support biomedical information extraction. *BMC Bioinformatics*, 10:349.

José L. Vicedo and Antonio Ferrández. 2000. Importance of pronominal anaphora resolution in question answering systems. In *Proceedings of the 38th Annual Meeting on Association for Computational Linguistics*, pages 555-562.

Katsumasa Yoshikawa, Sebastian Riedel, Tsutomu Hirao, Masayuki Asahara, Yuji Matsumoto. 2011. Coreference Based Event-Argument Relation Extraction on Biomedical Text. *Journal of Biomedical Semantics*, 2 (Supplement 5):S6.

Yan Zhang. 2010. Contextualizing Consumer Health Information Searching: an Analysis of Questions in a Social Q&A Community. In *Proceedings of the 1st ACM International Health Informatics Symposium (IHI'10)*, pages 210-219.

Evaluating large-scale text mining applications beyond the traditional numeric performance measures

Sofie Van Landeghem[1,2], **Suwisa Kaewphan**[3,4], **Filip Ginter**[3], **Yves Van de Peer**[1,2]
1. Dept. of Plant Systems Biology, VIB, Belgium
2. Dept. of Plant Biotechnology and Bioinformatics, Ghent University, Belgium
3. Dept. of Information Technology, University of Turku, Finland
4. Turku Centre for Computer Science (TUCS), Turku, Finland
solan@psb.ugent.be, sukaew@utu.fi
ginter@cs.utu.fi, yvpee@psb.ugent.be

Abstract

Text mining methods for the biomedical domain have matured substantially and are currently being applied on a large scale to support a variety of applications in systems biology, pathway curation, data integration and gene summarization. Community-wide challenges in the BioNLP research field provide gold-standard datasets and rigorous evaluation criteria, allowing for a meaningful comparison between techniques as well as measuring progress within the field. However, such evaluations are typically conducted on relatively small training and test datasets. On a larger scale, systematic erratic behaviour may occur that severely influences hundreds of thousands of predictions. In this work, we perform a critical assessment of a large-scale text mining resource, identifying systematic errors and determining their underlying causes through semi-automated analyses and manual evaluations[1].

1 Introduction

The development and adaptation of natural language processing (NLP) techniques for the biomedical domain are of crucial importance to manage the abundance of available literature. The inherent ambiguity of gene names and complexity of biomolecular interactions present an intriguing challenge both for BioNLP researchers as well as their targeted audience of biologists, geneticists and bioinformaticians. Stimulating such research, various community-wide challenges have been organised and received international participation.

The BioCreative (BC) challenge (Hirschman et al., 2005; Krallinger et al., 2008; Leitner et al., 2010; Arighi et al., 2011) touches upon a variety of extraction targets. The identification of gene and protein mentions ('named entity recognition') is a central task and a prerequisite for any follow-up work in BioNLP. Linking these mentions to their respective gene database identifiers, 'gene normalization', is a crucial step to allow for integration of textual information with authoritative databases and experimental results. Other BC tasks are engaged in finding functional and physical relations between gene products, including Gene Ontology annotations and protein-protein interactions.

Focusing more specifically on the molecular interactions between genes and proteins, the BioNLP Shared Task on Event Extraction (Kim et al., 2009; Kim et al., 2011b; Nedellec and others, 2013) covers a number of detailed molecular event types, including binding and transcription, regulatory control and post-translational modifications. Additionally, separate tracks involve specific applications of event extraction, including infectious diseases, bacterial biotopes and cancer genetics.

Performance of the participants in each of these challenges is measured using numeric metrics such as precision, recall, F-measure, slot error rate, MAP and TAP scores. While such rigorous evaluations allow for a meaningful comparison between different systems, it is often difficult to translate these numeric values into a measurement of practical utility when applied on a large scale. Additionally, infrequent but consistent errors are often not identified through small-scale evaluations, though they may result in hundreds of thousands of wrongly predicted interactions on a larger scale. In this work, we perform an in-depth study of an open-source state-of-the-art event extraction system which was previously applied to the whole of PubMed. Moving beyond the traditional numeric evaluations, we identify a num-

[1] The supplementary data of this study is freely available from http://bioinformatics.psb.ugent.be/supplementary_data/solan/bionlp13/

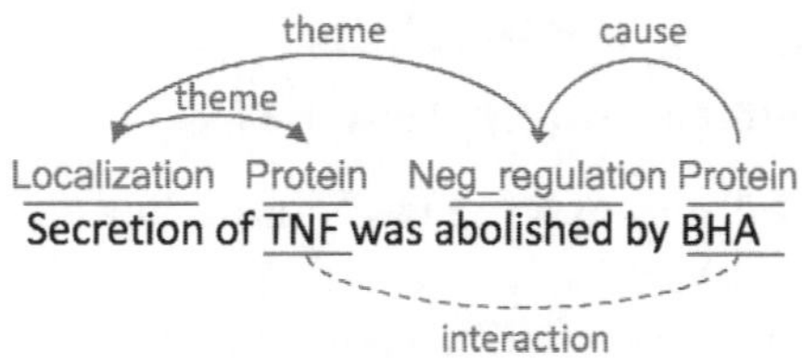

Figure 1: Example event and relation representations, depicted in solid and dotted lines respectively. Picture by Kim et al. (2011a).

ber of systematic errors in the large-scale data, analyse their underlying causes, and design post-processing rules to resolve these errors. We believe these findings to be highly relevant for any practical large-scale implementation of BioNLP techniques, as the presence of obvious mistakes in a text mining resource might undermine the credibility of text mining techniques in general.

2 Data and methods

In this section, we first describe the data and methods used in previous work for the construction of the large-scale text mining resource that is the topic of our error analyses (Section 3).

2.1 Event extraction

Event extraction has become a widely studied topic within the field of BioNLP following the first Shared Task (ST) in 2009. The ST'09 introduced the event formalism as a more detailed representation of the common binary relation annotation (Figure 1). Each event occurrence consists of an event trigger; i.e. one or more consecutive tokens that are linked to a specific event type. While the ST'09 included only 9 event types, among which 3 regulatory event types, the ST'11 further broadened the coverage of event extraction to post-translational modifications and epigenetics (EPI).

To compose a fully correct event, an event trigger needs to be connected to its correct arguments. Within the ST, these arguments are selected from a set of gold-standard gene and gene product annotations (GGPs). The ST guidelines determine an unambiguous formalism to which correct events must adhere: most event types only take one *theme* argument, while *Binding* events can be connected to more than one *theme*. *Regulation* events further have an optional *cause* slot (Figure 1). Connecting the correct arguments to the correct trigger words is denoted as 'edge detection'.

To perform event extraction, we rely on the publicly available Turku Event Extraction System (TEES) (Björne et al., 2012), which was originally developed for the ST'09. The TEES modules for trigger and edge detection are based upon supervised learning principles, employing support vector machines (SVMs) for multi-label classification. TEES has been shown to obtain state-of-the-art performance when measured on the gold-standard datasets of the Shared Tasks of 2009, 2011 and 2013.

2.2 Large-scale processing

Previously, the whole of PubMed has been analysed using a large-scale event extraction pipeline composed of the BANNER named entity recognizer, the McClosky-Charniak parser, and the Turku Event Extraction System (Björne et al., 2010). BANNER identifies gene and protein symbols in text through a machine learning approach based on conditional random fields (Leaman and Gonzalez, 2008). While the resulting large-scale text mining resource EVEX was focused only on abstracts and ST'09 event types (Van Landeghem et al., 2011), it has matured substantially during the past few years and now includes ST'11 EPI event types, full-text processing and gene normalization (Van Landeghem et al., 2013a). In this work, we use the version of EVEX as publicly available on 16 March 2013, containing 40 million event occurrences among 122 thousand gene and protein symbols in 22 million PubMed abstracts and 460 thousand PubMed Central full-text articles. Each event occurrence is linked to a normalized confidence value, automatically derived from the original TEES SVM classification step and the distance to the hyperplane of each prediction.

While this study focuses on the EVEX resource as primary dataset, the findings are also highly relevant for other large-scale text mining resources, especially those based on supervised learning, such as the BioContext (Gerner et al., 2012).

2.3 Cross-domain evaluation

Recently, a plant-specific, application-oriented assessment of the EVEX text mining resource has been conducted by manually evaluating 1,800 event occurrences (Van Landeghem et al., 2013b). In that study, it was established that the general performance rates as measured previously on the ST, are transferrable also to other domains and organisms. Specifically, the 58.5% TEES precision

Event type	Five most frequent trigger words				
Binding	binding	interaction	associated	bind	association
Gene expression	expression	expressed	production	expressing	levels
Localization	secretion	release	localization	secreted	localized
Protein catabolism	degradation	degraded	cleavage	proteolysis	degrade
Transcription	transcription	expression	levels	transcribed	detected
Acetylation	acetylation	acetylated	deacetylation	hyperacetylation	*activation*
Glycosylation	glycosylated	glycosylation	attached	N-linked	*absence*
Hydroxylation	hydroxylation	hydroxylated	hydroxylate	beta-hydroxylation	hydroxylations
Methylation	*radiation*	methylation	methylated	*diffractometer*	trimethylation
DNA methylation	methylation	hypermethylation	methylated	hypermethylated	unmethylated
Phosphorylation	phosphorylation	phosphorylated	dephosphorylation	phosphorylates	phosphorylate
Ubiquitination	ubiquitination	ubiquitinated	ubiquitylation	*ubiquitous*	polyubiquitination
Regulation	effect	regulation	effects	regulated	control
Positive regulation	increased	activation	increase	induced	induction
Negative regulation	reduced	inhibition	decreased	inhibited	inhibitor
Catalysis	mediated	dependent	mediates	removes	induced

Table 1: The top-5 most frequently tagged trigger words per event type in EVEX. The first 5 rows represent fundamental event types, the next 7 post-translational modifications (PTMs), and the last 4 rows are regulatory event types. In this analysis, the PTMs and their reverse types are pooled together. Trigger words that refer to systematic errors are in italic and are discussed further in the text.

rate measured in the ST'09, with the literature data concerning human blood cell transcription factors, corresponded with a 58.6% precision rate for the plant-specific evaluation dataset ('PLEV'). This encouraging result supports the general applicability of large-scale text mining methods trained on relatively small corpora. The findings of this previous study and the resulting data are further interpreted and analysed in more detail in this study.

3 Results

While the text mining pipeline underlying the EVEX resource has been shown to produce state-of-the-art results which are transferrable across domains and organisms, it is conceivable that the mere scale of the resource allows the accumulation of systematic errors. In this section, we perform several targeted semi-automated evaluations to identify, explain and resolve such cases. It is important to note that our main focus is on improving the precision rate of the resource, rather than the recall, aiming to increase the credibility of large-scale text mining resources in general.

3.1 Most common triggers

The trigger detection algorithm of the TEES software is based upon SVM classifiers (Section 2.1), and has been shown to outperform dictionary-based approaches (Kim et al., 2009; Kim et al., 2011c). To investigate its performance in a large-scale application, we first analyse the most frequent trigger words of each event type in EVEX (Table 1). We notice the presence of different inflections of the same word as well as related verbs and nouns, such as 'inhibition', 'inhibited' and 'inhibitor'. The trigger recognition module successfully uses character bigrams and trigrams in its SVM classification algorithm to allow for the identification of such related concepts, even when some of these trigger words were not encountered in the training phase (Björne et al., 2009).

However, occasionally this approach results in confusion between words with small edit distances, such as the trigger word 'ubiquitous' for *Ubiquitination* events. Similarly, the *Acetylation* trigger 'activation' is found within the context of a correct event structure in most cases, but should actually be of the type *Positive regulation*. The implementation of custom post-processing rules to automatically detect and resolve these specific cases would ultimately deal with more than 6,000 false-positive event predictions.

Further, the trigger 'radiation' seems to occur frequently for a *Methylation* event, of which 82% of the instances can be identified in the 'Experimental' subsection of the article. The majority of these articles relate to protein crystallography, and that subsection describes the data from the experimental set-up. Within such sections, phrases like 'Mo Kalpha radiation' are wrongly tagged as *Methylation* events. Similarly, many false-positive *Methylation* predictions refer to the trigger word 'diffractometer'. Removing these instances from the resource would result in the deletion of more

Trigger word s	Most frequent type t_2	Count	Frequency	Infrequent type t_1	Count	Frequency
acetylation	Acetylation	40,291	0.298383	Binding	1,332	0.000216
				Phosphorylation	1,050	0.001045
				Gene expression	969	0.000093
				Localization	1,045	0.000579
secretion	Localization	376,976	0.208888	Acetylation	243	0.001800
glycosylation	Glycosylation	24,226	0.141052	Phosphorylation	389	0.000387
				Gene expression	214	0.000020
phosphorylation	Phosphorylation	589,681	0.586772	Binding	454	0.000074
				DNA methylation	225	0.001297
ubiquitylation	Ubiquitination	4961	0.055976	Binding	128	0.000021
hypermethylation	Methylation	19,501	0.112434	Phosphorylation	365	0.000363
cleavage	Protein catabolism	20,552	0.073728	Gene expression	2,451	0.000234
				Binding	3,011	0.000489
decreased	Negative regulation	374,859	0.062372	Positive regulation	1,721	0.000173
				Binding	855	0.000139
				Gene expression	2,928	0.000280
reduced	Negative regulation	442,400	0.073610	Positive regulation	1,091	0.000110
reduction	Negative regulation	164,736	0.027410	Positive regulation	389	0.000039
absence	Negative regulation	65,180	0.010845	Positive regulation	226	0.000071

Table 2: Examples of trigger words that correspond to the type which has the highest relative frequency (left), but are also found with much lower frequencies in other types (right). The instances corresponding to the right-most column can thus be interpreted as wrong predictions. The full list is available as a machine readible translation table in the supplementary data.

than 82,000 false-positive event predictions.

Finally, we notice that the trigger word 'absence' for *Glycosylation* usually refers to a *Negative regulation*. Similarly, some words appear as most frequent for more than one event type, such as 'levels' (*Gene expression* and *Transcription*). This type of error in trigger type disambiguation is analysed in more detail in the next section.

3.2 Event type disambiguation

While previous work has focused on the disambiguation of event types on a small, gold-standard dataset (Martinez and Baldwin, 2011), the richness of a large-scale text mining resource provides additional opportunities to detect plausible errors. To exploit this large-scale information, we analyse all EVEX trigger words and their corresponding event types, summarizing their raw event occurrence counts as $Occ(t, s)$ where t denotes the trigger type and s the trigger string. As some event types are more abundantly described in literature, we normalize these counts to frequencies ($Freq(t, s)$) depending on the total number of event occurrences per type ($Tot(t)$):

$$Freq(t, s) = \frac{Occ(t, s)}{Tot(t)}$$

with

$$Tot(t) = \sum_{i=1}^{n} Occ(t, s_i)$$

and n the number of different triggers for event type t. We then compare all trigger words and their relative frequencies across different event types.

First, we inspect those cases where a trigger word appears with comparable frequencies for two event types t_1 and t_2:

$$Freq(t_1, s) \leq Freq(t_2, s) \leq 10 \times Freq(t_1, s) \quad (1)$$

A first broad category of these cases are trigger words that refer to both regulatory and non-regulatory events at the same time, such as 'overexpression' (*Gene expression* and *Positive regulation*), or 'ubiquitinates' (*Ubiquitination* and *Catalysis*). The majority of these cases are perfectly valid and are in fact modeled explicitly by the TEES software (Björne et al., 2009).

Further, we find that two broad groups of non-regulatory event types are semantically similar and share common trigger words: *Methylation* and *DNA methylation* (e.g. 'methylation', 'unmethylated', 'hypomethylation'), as well as *Gene expression* and *Transcription* ('expression', 'synthesis', 'levels'), with occasional overlap also with *Localization* ('abundance', 'found'). Similarly, trigger words are often shared among the four regulatory event types ('dependent', 'role', 'regulate'), as the exact type may depend on the broader context within the sentence.

While the previous findings do not necessar-

Curated event type	Predicted event type Localization	Transcription	Expression
Localization	15	0	3
Transcription	0	12	1
Expression	0	2	12
No event	0	2	3
Total	15	16	19

Table 3: Targeted evaluation of 50 mixed events of type *Localization*, *Transcription* and *Gene expression*. The curated event type is compared to the original (hidden) predicted type.

ily refer to wrong predictions, we also notice the usage of punctuation marks as trigger words for various event types. This option was specifically provided in the TEES trigger detection algorithm as the ST'09 training data contains *Binding* instances with '-' as trigger word. However, these punctuation triggers are found to be largely false positives in the PubMed-scale event dataset. Removing them in an additional post-processing step would result in the filtering of more than 130,000 event occurrences, of which the largest part is expected to be incorrect predictions. Similarly, we can easily remove 25,000 events that are related to trigger words that are numeric values.

In a second step, we analyse those cases where

$$k \times Freq(t_1, s) \leq Freq(t_2, s). \quad (2)$$

When this condition holds, it can be hypothesized that trigger predictions of the word s as type t_1 are false positives and should have instead been of type t_2. Automatically generating such lists from the data, we have experimentally determined an optimal value of k = 100 that represents a reasonable trade-off between the amount of false positives that can be identified and the manual work needed for this.

From the resulting list, we can easily identify a number of such cases that are clearly incorrect (Table 2, right column). Specifically, a large number of *Positive regulation* events actually refer to *Negative regulation*, providing an explanation of the lower precision rate of *Positive regulation* predictions in the previous PLEV evaluation (Van Landeghem et al., 2013b). This semi-automated detection procedure can ultimately result in the correction of more than 242,000 events.

The remaining cases for which condition (2) holds are more ambiguous and can not be automatically corrected. However, these cases are more likely to be incorrect and their confidence values could thus be automatically decreased depending on the ratio between $Freq(t_1, s)$ and $Freq(t_2, s)$. A general exception to this rule is formed by the broad groups of semantically similar events, such as *Transcription-Gene expression-Localization*, which we analyse in more detail in the next section.

3.3 Gene expression, Transcription and Localization

Transcription is a sub-process of *Gene expression*, with both event types relating to protein production. However, the distinction between the two in text may not always be straightforward. Additionally, the ST training data for *Transcription* events is significantly smaller than for *Gene expression* events, which may be the reason why not only the TEES performance, but also those of other systems, is considerably lower for *Transcription* than for *Gene expression* (Kim et al., 2011c). Further, cell-type specific gene expression should be captured by additional *site* arguments connected to a *Localization* event, which represents the presence or a change in the location of a protein.

To gain a deeper insight into the interplay between these three different event types, we have performed a manual curation of 50 event occurrences, sampled at random from the *Gene expression*, *Transcription* and *Localization* events available in EVEX. For each event, the trigger word and the corresponding sentence was extracted, but the predicted event type was hidden. An expert annotator subsequently decided on the correct event type of the trigger. Within this evaluation we followed the ST guidelines to only annotate *Gene expression* when there is no evidence for the more detailed *Transcription* type.

Table 3 shows the results. All 15 predicted *Localization* triggers are recorded to be correct. From the 16 predicted *Transcription* events, two involve incorrect event triggers, and two other events refer to the more general *Gene expression* type (75% overall precision). Likewise, only one *Gene expression* event should be of the more spe-

	Curated event type	Error type	Instances	(%)
1	Single-argument Binding	No error	5	10%
2	Single-argument Binding	Edge detection error	0	0%
3	Multiple-argument Binding	Edge detection error	4	8%
4	Single-argument Binding	Entity recognition error	1	2%
5	Multiple-argument Binding	Entity recognition error	19	38%
6	Other	Trigger detection error	21	42%

Table 4: Targeted evaluation of 50 single-argument *Binding* event triggers. Row 1: Fully correct event. Row 2: The correct argument was annotated but not linked. Row 3: At least one correct multiple-argument *Binding* event could have been extracted using the annotated entities in the sentence. Row 4: The correct argument was not annotated. Row 5: No event could be extracted due to missing argument annotations. Row 6: The trigger did not refer to a *Binding* event.

Unannotated entity type	Entity occurrence count	Examples
GGP	10	SPF30, spinal muscular atrophy gene
Generic GGP	9	primary antibodies, peptides, RNA
Chemical compound	10	Ca(2+), iron, manganese(II)

Table 5: Manual inspection of the textual entity types for those *Binding* events where a relevant *theme* argument was not annotated in the entity recognition step.

cific *Transcription* type, three instances should be *Localization*, and three more are considered not to be correct events at all (63% overall precision). In general, we remark that the predicted event type largely corresponds to the curated type (78% of all predictions and 87% of all otherwise correct events).

3.4 Binding

Moving beyond the event type specification as determined by the ST guidelines, the previous PLEV analysis (Section 2.3) has established a remarkable difference between single-argument and multiple-argument *Binding*. In contrast to the regular ST evaluations, this work considered single- and multiple-argument *Binding* as two separate event types, resulting in a precision rate of 93% for multiple-argument *Binding* triggers and only 8% precision for single-argument *Binding* triggers.

As the PLEV study only focused on textual network data, single-argument *Bindings* were not analysed further. In this work however, we further investigate this performance discrepancy and perform an in-depth manual evaluation to try and detect the main causes of this systematic error.

Several hypotheses can be postulated to explain the low precision rate of single-argument *Binding* events. Firstly, a false negative instance of the entity recognition module might result in the absence of annotation for a relevant second interaction partner. Another plausible explanation is an error by the edge detection module of the event extraction mechanism, which would occasionally decide to produce one or several single-argument *Binding* events rather than one multiple-argument *Binding*, even when all involved entities are correctly annotated. Finally, it is conceivable that predicted single-argument triggers simply do not refer to *Binding* events, i.e. they contain false positive predictions of the trigger detection module of the event extraction system.

In some cases, one trigger leads to many different *Binding* events, such as the trigger 'bind' in the sentence *"Sir3 and Sir4 bind preferentially to deacetylated tails of histones H3 and H4"*. In these cases, error types may accumulate: some events could be missed due to unannotated entities, while others may be due to errors in the edge detection step. However, multiple events with the same trigger word are often represented by very similar feature vectors in the classification step, and consequently have almost identical final confidence values. For this reason, we summarize the error as 'Edge detection error' as soon as one pair of entities was correctly annotated but not linked, and as 'Entity recognition error' otherwise.

Table 4 summarizes the results of a curation effort of 50 event triggers linked to a single-argument *Binding* event in EVEX. We notice that in fact, 46% should have been multiple-argument *Binding* events. The main underlying reason for the prediction of an incorrect single-argument *Binding* event, when it should have been a multiple-argument one, is apparently caused by

	Curated event type	Error type	Instances	(%)
1	Phosphorylation	No error	34	68%
2	Phosphorylation	Edge detection error	4	8%
3	Invalid Phosphorylation	Edge detection error	2	4%
4	Phosphorylation	Edge directionality detection error	4	8%
5	Invalid Phosphorylation	Edge directionality detection error	1	2%
6	Phosphorylation	Entity recognition error	3	6%
7	Other	Trigger detection error	2	4%

Table 6: Targeted evaluation of 50 *Phosphorylation* event triggers and their *theme* arguments. Row 1: Fully correct event. Row 2: The correct argument was annotated but not linked. Row 3: An argument was linked but should not have been. Row 4: A causal argument was wrongly annotated as the *theme* argument. Row 5: A causal argument was wrongly annotated as the *theme* argument. Row 6: The correct argument was not annotated. Row 7: The trigger did not refer to a *Phosphorylation* event.

an entity recognition error (19/23 or 83%), while an edge detection error is much less frequent (17%). When we examine these entity recognition errors in more detail, we find that 10 relevant entities are true GGPs in the sense of the Shared Task annotation. However, 9 entities refer to generic GGPs, and 10 instances relate to chemical compounds (Table 5). As these type of entities can not be unambiguously normalized to unique gene identifiers, they fall out-of-scope of the original ST challenge. However, we feel this practice introduces an artificial bias on the classifier and the evaluation. Additionally, this information can prove to be of value within a large-scale text mining resource geared towards practical applications and explorative browsing of textual information.

Finally, we notice that a remarkable 42% of all predicted events contain trigger detection errors. Analysing this subclass in more detail, we found that 5 cases are invalid event triggers, 6 cases refer to other event types such as *Localization* and *Gene expression*, and 10 more cases were considered to be out-of-scope of the ST challenge, such as a factor-disease association.

3.5 Phosphorylation

Within the PLEV evaluation (Section 2.3), it became apparent that *Phosphorylation* is easy to recognise from the sentence (98%) but the full correct event has a much lower precision rate (65%). As we have seen in the previous section, even when a trigger word is correctly predicted, errors may still be generated by the edge detection or entity recognition step. For instance, we might hypothesize that the main underlying reason for the reduced final performance is an error by the entity recognition step, forcing the edge detection mechanism to link an incorrect *theme* due to lack of other options. Other plausible explanations involve genuine errors by the edge detection algorithm when the correct argument is annotated, as well as problems with the identification of causality. As the TEES version applied in this work was developed for the Shared Task 2009 and 2011, it does not predict causal arguments for a *Phosphorylation* event directly, but instead adds *Regulation* events on top of the *Phosphorylations*. Occasionally, we have noticed that the *theme* of a *Phosphorylation* event should in fact have been the *cause* of the embedding *Regulation* association, resulting in a wrongly directed causal relationship.

To investigate these possibilities, we have manually inspected 50 *Phosphorylation* events picked at random from the EVEX resource. Table 6 summarizes the results of this effort. Only two events are found not to be *Phosphorylation* events: one is in fact a *Gene expression* mention, the other involves an incorrect trigger. Additionally, three more events can semantically be regarded as *Phosphorylations*, but do not follow the ST specifications ('Invalid Phosphorylation'), for instance because they only mention causal arguments ('an inhibition of Ca^{2+}/calmodulin-dependent protein phosphorylation'). Among the 45 cases which correctly refer to the *Phosphorylation* type, 34 events are fully correct (68% of the total). Four cases are wrongly extracted by misinterpreting the causal relationship ('Edge directionality detection error') and four more instances refer to genuine mistakes of the edge detection algorithm. Only three other cases can be attributed to a missing entity annotation. In contrast to the previous findings on single-argument *Bindings*, we thus establish that the incorrect *Phosphorylation* events are mainly caused by errors in the edge detection mechanism, which either picks the wrong *theme* from the set of annotated GGPs, or misinterprets the causality direction.

4 Discussion and conclusion

We have performed several semi-automated evaluations and targeted manual curation experiments, identifying and explaining systematic errors in a large-scale event dataset. As a first observation, we notice that a few frequent trigger words are almost always associated to incorrect event predictions, such as the trigger words 'ubiquitous' and 'radiation', or a punctuation symbol. These cases were identified through a large-scale automatic analysis in combination with a limited manual evaluation effort. The results are distributed as a blacklist of event triggers for the implementation or filtering of future large-scale event predictions efforts.

Further, a semi-automated procedure has identified a list of likely incorrect predictions, by comparing the type-specific frequencies of trigger words across all event types. Manual inspection of the most frequent cases allowed us to determine a number of trigger words for which the event type can automatically be corrected. These results are also made publicly available.

Additionally, after removal of the most obvious and frequent errors, a fully automated script can automatically reduce the confidence scores of those event occurrences where the trigger words are found to be much more frequent for another event type. We have established that this procedure should disregard triggers identified within a few specific semantically similar clusters: *DNA methylation/Methylation*, *Regulation/Positive regulation/Negative regulation/Catalysis* and *Gene expression-Transcription/Localization*. An additional targeted evaluation of these last three types revealed that, despite their semantic overlap, the largest fraction of these predictions refers to the correct event type ($78 \pm 11.5\%$).

Finally, we note that trigger detection ($47 \pm 14.6\%$) and entity recognition errors ($44 \pm 14.6\%$) are the main causes of wrongly predicted *Binding* events. The latter causes the event extraction mechanism to artificially produce single-argument *Bindings* instead of multiple-argument *Bindings*. We believe this issue can be resolved by broadening the scope of the entity recognition module to generic GGPs and chemical compounds, and re-applying the TEES algorithm to these entities as if they were normal GGPs as defined in the ST formalism. In contrast, edge detection errors are much more frequently the cause of a wrongly predicted *Phosphorylation* event (statistically significant difference with $p < 0.05$), caused by wrongly identifying the thematic object or the causality of the event. To resolve this issue, we propose future annotation efforts to specifically annotate the protein adding the phosphate group to the target protein as a separate class than the regulation of such a phosphorylation process by other cellular machineries and components (Kim et al., 2013).

In conclusion, we have performed several statistical analyses and targeted manual evaluations on a large-scale event dataset. As a result, we were able to identify a set of rules to automatically delete or correct a number of false positive predictions (supplementary material at `http://bioinformatics.psb.ugent.be/supplementary_data/solan/bionlp13/`). When applying these rules to the winning submission of the recent ST'13 (GE subchallenge), which was based on the TEES classifier (Hakala et al., 2013), 3 false positive predictions could be identified and removed. Even though this procedure only marginally improves the classification results (50.97% to 50.99% F-score), we believe the cleaning procedure to be crucial specifically for the credibility of any large-scale text mining application. For example, applied on the EVEX resource, it would ultimately result in the removal of 242,000 instances and a corrected event type of 230,000 more cases (1.2% of all EVEX events in total). These corrections will be implemented as part of the next big EVEX release. Additionally, the confidence score of more than 120,000 ambiguous cases could be automatically decreased. Alternatively, these cases could be the target of a large-scale re-annotation, for instance using the brat annotation tool (Stenetorp et al., 2012). The resulting dataset could then serve as a new training set to enable active learning on top of existing event extraction approaches.

Acknowledgments

The authors thank Cindy Martens and the anonymous reviewers for a critical reading of the manuscript and constructive feedback. SVL thanks the Research Foundation Flanders (FWO) for funding her research.

References

Cecilia Arighi, Zhiyong Lu, Martin Krallinger, Kevin Cohen, J. Wilbur, Alfonso Valencia, Lynette Hirschman, and Cathy Wu. 2011. Overview of the BioCreative III workshop. *BMC Bioinformatics*, 12(Suppl 8):S1.

Jari Björne, Juho Heimonen, Filip Ginter, Antti Airola, Tapio Pahikkala, and Tapio Salakoski. 2009. Extracting complex biological events with rich graph-based feature sets. In *Proceedings of the BioNLP 2009 Workshop*, pages 10–18.

Jari Björne, Filip Ginter, Sampo Pyysalo, Jun'ichi Tsujii, and Tapio Salakoski. 2010. Scaling up biomedical event extraction to the entire PubMed. In *Proceedings of the BioNLP 2010 Workshop*, pages 28–36.

Jari Björne, Filip Ginter, and Tapio Salakoski. 2012. Generalizing biomedical event extraction. *BMC Bioinformatics*, 13(suppl. 8):S4.

Martin Gerner, Farzaneh Sarafraz, Casey M. Bergman, and Goran Nenadic. 2012. BioContext: an integrated text mining system for large-scale extraction and contextualization of biomolecular events. *Bioinformatics*, 28(16):2154–2161.

Kai Hakala, Sofie Van Landeghem, Tapio Salakoski, Yves Van de Peer, and Filip Ginter. 2013. EVEX in ST13: Application of a large-scale text mining resource to event extraction and network construction. In *Proceedings of the BioNLP Shared Task 2013 Workshop (in press)*.

Lynette Hirschman, Alexander Yeh, Christian Blaschke, and Alfonso Valencia. 2005. Overview of BioCreAtIvE: critical assessment of information extraction for biology. *BMC Bioinformatics*, 6(Suppl 1):S1.

Jin-Dong Kim, Tomoko Ohta, Sampo Pyysalo, Yoshinobu Kano, and Jun'ichi Tsujii. 2009. Overview of BioNLP'09 Shared Task on event extraction. In *Proceedings of the BioNLP 2009 Workshop*, pages 1–9.

Jin-Dong Kim, Tomoko Ohta, Sampo Pyysalo, Yoshinobu Kano, and Junichi Tsujii. 2011a. Extracting bio-molecular events from literature - the BioNLP'09 Shared Task. *Computational Intelligence*, 27(4):513–540.

Jin-Dong Kim, Sampo Pyysalo, Tomoko Ohta, Robert Bossy, Ngan Nguyen, and Jun'ichi Tsujii. 2011b. Overview of BioNLP Shared Task 2011. In *Proceedings of the BioNLP Shared Task 2011 Workshop*, pages 1–6.

Jin-Dong Kim, Yue Wang, Toshihisa Takagi, and Akinori Yonezawa. 2011c. Overview of Genia event task in BioNLP Shared Task 2011. In *Proceedings of the BioNLP Shared Task 2011 Workshop*, BioNLP Shared Task '11, pages 7–15.

Jin-Dong Kim, Yue Wang, Yamamoto Yasunori, Sabine Bergler, Roser Morante, and Kevin Cohen. 2013. The Genia Event Extraction Shared Task, 2013 edition - overview. In *Proceedings of the BioNLP Shared Task 2013 Workshop (in press)*.

Martin Krallinger, Alexander Morgan, Larry Smith, Florian Leitner, Lorraine Tanabe, John Wilbur, Lynette Hirschman, and Alfonso Valencia. 2008. Evaluation of text-mining systems for biology: overview of the second BioCreative community challenge. *Genome Biology*, 9(Suppl 2):S1.

Robert Leaman and Graciela Gonzalez. 2008. BANNER: an executable survey of advances in biomedical named entity recognition. *Pacific Symposium on Biocomputing. Pacific Symposium on Biocomputing*, pages 652–663.

F. Leitner, S.A. Mardis, M. Krallinger, G. Cesareni, L.A. Hirschman, and A. Valencia. 2010. An overview of BioCreative II.5. *Computational Biology and Bioinformatics, IEEE/ACM Transactions on*, 7(3):385–399.

David Martinez and Timothy Baldwin. 2011. Word sense disambiguation for event trigger word detection in biomedicine. *BMC Bioinformatics*, 12(Suppl 2):S4.

Claire Nedellec et al. 2013. Overview of BioNLP Shared Task 2013. In *Proceedings of the BioNLP Shared Task 2013 Workshop (in press)*.

Pontus Stenetorp, Sampo Pyysalo, Goran Topić, Tomoko Ohta, Sophia Ananiadou, and Jun'ichi Tsujii. 2012. brat: a web-based tool for NLP-assisted text annotation. In *Proceedings of the Demonstrations at the 13th Conference of the European Chapter of the Association for Computational Linguistics*, pages 102–107.

Sofie Van Landeghem, Filip Ginter, Yves Van de Peer, and Tapio Salakoski. 2011. EVEX: a PubMed-scale resource for homology-based generalization of text mining predictions. In *Proceedings of the BioNLP 2011 Workshop*, pages 28–37.

Sofie Van Landeghem, Jari Björne, Chih-Hsuan Wei, Kai Hakala, Sampo Pyysalo, Sophia Ananiadou, Hung-Yu Kao, Zhiyong Lu, Tapio Salakoski, Yves Van de Peer, and Filip Ginter. 2013a. Large-scale event extraction from literature with multi-level gene normalization. *PLoS ONE*, 8(4):e55814.

Sofie Van Landeghem, Stefanie De Bodt, Zuzanna J. Drebert, Dirk Inz, and Yves Van de Peer. 2013b. The potential of text mining in data integration and network biology for plant research: A case study on arabidopsis. *The Plant Cell*, 25(3):794–807.

Recognizing sublanguages in scientific journal articles through closure properties

Irina P. Temnikova
Linguistic Modelling Laboratory
Bulgarian Academy of Sciences
irina.temnikova@gmail.com

K. Bretonnel Cohen
Computational Bioscience Program
University of Colorado School of Medicine
Department of Linguistics
University of Colorado at Boulder
kevin.cohen@gmail.com

Abstract

It has long been realized that sublanguages are relevant to natural language processing and text mining. However, practical methods for recognizing or characterizing them have been lacking. This paper describes a publicly available set of tools for sublanguage recognition. Closure properties are used to assess the goodness of fit of two biomedical corpora to the sublanguage model. Scientific journal articles are compared to general English text, and it is shown that the journal articles fit the sublanguage model, while the general English text does not. A number of examples of implications of the sublanguage characteristics for natural language processing are pointed out. The software is made publicly available at [edited for anonymization].

1 Introduction

1.1 Definitions of "sublanguage"

The notion of *sublanguage* has had varied definitions, depending on the aspects of sublanguages on which the authors focused. (Grishman and Kittredge, 1986) focus on syntactic aspects of sublanguages: "...the term suggests a subsystem of language... limited in reference to a specific subject domain. In particular, each sublanguage has a distinctive grammar, which can profitably be described and used to solve specific language-processing problems" (Grishman and Kittredge, 1986).

(Kittredge, 2003) focuses on the spontaneous appearance of sublanguages in restricted domains, where the preconditions for a sublanguage to appear are the sharing of specialized knowledge about a restricted semantic domain and recurrent "situations" (e.g. scientific journal articles, or discharge summaries) in which domain experts communicate. According to (Kittredge, 2003), characteristics of a sublanguage include a restricted lexicon, relatively small number of lexical classes, restricted sentence syntax, deviant sentence syntax, restricted word co-occurrence patterns, and different frequencies of occurrence of words and syntactic patterns from the normal language.

(McDonald, 2000) focuses on the element of restriction in sublanguages—the notion that they are restricted to a specialized semantic domain, a very "focused" audience, and "stipulated content," with the effect that both word choice and syntactic style have reduced options as compared to the normal language.

The notions of restriction that recur in these definitions of "sublanguage" lead directly to (McEnery and Wilson, 2001)'s notion of using the quantification of closure properties to assess whether or not a given sample of a genre of language use fits the sublanguage model. *Closure* refers to the tendency of a genre of language towards finiteness at one or more linguistic levels. For example, a genre of language might or might not use a finite set of lexical items, or have a finite set of sentence structures. Notions of restriction suggest that a sublanguage should tend towards closure on at least some linguistic levels. To quantify closure, we can examine relationships between types and tokens in a corpus of the genre. In particular, we count the number of types that are observed as an increasing number of tokens is examined. If a genre does not exhibit closure, then the number of types will continue to rise continually as the number of tokens increases. On the other hand, closure is demonstrated when the number of types stops growing after some number of tokens has been examined.

1.2 Relevance of sublanguages to natural language processing

The relevance of sublanguages to natural language processing has long been recognized in a variety of fields. (Hirschman and Sager, 1982) and (Friedman, 1986) show how a sublanguage–based approach can be used for information extraction from clinical documents. (Finin, 1986) shows that sublanguage characterization can be used for the notoriously difficult problem of interpretation of nominal compounds. (Sager, 1986) asserts a number of uses for sublanguage–oriented natural language processing, including resolution of syntactic ambiguity, definition of frames for information extraction, and discourse analysis. (Sekine, 1994) describes a prototype application of sublanguages to speech recognition. (Friedman et al., 1994) uses a sublanguage grammar to extract a variety of types of structured data from clinical reports. (McDonald, 2000) points out that modern language generation systems are made effective in large part due to the fact that they are applied to specific sublanguages. (Somers, 2000) discusses the relevance of sublanguages to machine translation, pointing out that many sublanguages can make machine translation easier and some of them can make machine translation harder. (Friedman et al., 2001) uses a sublanguage grammar to extract structured data from scientific journal articles.

1.3 Previous work on sublanguage recognition

Various approaches have been taken to recognizing sublanguages. We posit here two separate tasks—recognizing a sublanguage when one is present, and determining the characteristics of a sublanguage. Information-theoretic approaches have a long history. (Sekine, 1994) clustered documents and then calculated the ratio of the perplexity of the clustered documents to the perplexity of a random collection of words. (Somers, 1998) showed that texts drawn from a sublanguage corpus have low weighted cumulative sums. (Stetson et al., 2002) used relative entropy and squared chi-square distance to identify a sublanguage of cross-coverage notes. (Mihaila et al., 2012) looked at distributions of named entities to identify and differentiate between a wide variety of scientific sublanguages.

Non-information-theoretic, more heuristic methods have been used to identify sublanguages, as well. In addition to the information-theoretic measures described above, (Stetson et al., 2002) also looked at such measures as length, incidence of abbreviations, and ambiguity of abbreviations. (Friedman et al., 2002) use manual analysis to detect and characterize two biomedical sublanguages. (McEnery and Wilson, 2001) examine closure properties; their approach is so central to the topic of this paper that we will describe it in some length separately.

(McEnery and Wilson, 2001) examined the closure properties of three linguistic aspects of their material under study. As materials they used two corpora that were assumed not to meet the sublanguage model—the Canadian Hansard corpus, containing proceedings from the Canadian Parliament, and the American Printing House for the Blind corpus, made up of works of fiction. As a corpus that was suspected to meet the sublanguage model, they used a set of manuals from IBM. All three corpora differed in size, so they were sampled to match the size of the smallest corpus, meaning that all experiments were done on collections 200,000 words in size. The materials under study were evaluated for their closure properties at three linguistic levels. At the most basic level, they looked at lexical items—simple word forms. The hypothesis here was that the non-sublanguage corpora would not tend toward finiteness, i.e. would not reach closure. That is, if the number of word types found was graphed as an increasing number of tokens was examined, the resulting line would grow continually and would show no signs of asymptoting. In contrast, the sublanguage corpus would eventually reach closure, i.e. would stop growing appreciably in size as more tokens were examined.

The next level that they examined was the morphosyntactic level. In particular, they looked at the number of part-of-speech tags per lexical type. Here the intuition was that if the lexicon of the sublanguage is limited, then words might be coerced into a greater number of parts of speech. This would be manifested by a smaller overall number of unique word/part-of-speech tag combinations. Again, we would expect to see that the sublanguage corpus would have a smaller number of word/part-of-speech tag combinations, as compared to the non-sublanguage corpus. Graphing the count of word type/POS tag sets on the y axis and the cumulative number of tokens examined on the x axis, we would see slower growth and lower numbers overall.

The final level that they examined was the syntactic level. In this case, parse tree types were graphed against the number of sentences examined. The intuition here is that if the sublanguage exhibits closure properties on the syntactic level, then the growth of the line will slow and we will see lower numbers overall.

(McEnery and Wilson, 2001) found the hypotheses regarding closure to be substantiated at all levels. We will not reproduce their graphs, but will summarize their findings in terms of ratios. On the lexical level, they found type/token ratios of 1:140 for the IBM manuals (the assumed sublanguage), 1:53 for the Hansard corpus (assumed not to represent a sublanguage), and 1:17 for the American Printing House for the Blind corpus (also assumed not to represent a sublanguage). The IBM manuals consist of a much smaller number of words which are frequently repeated.

At the morphosyntactic level, they found 7,594 type/POS sets in the IBM manuals, 18,817 in the Hansard corpus, and 11,638 in the American Printing House for the Blind corpus–a much smaller number in the apparent sublanguage than in the non-sublanguage corpora. The word/part-of-speech tag averages coincided with the expected findings given these number of types. The averages were 3.19 for the IBM manuals, 2.45 for the Hansard corpus, and 2.34 for the American Printing House for the Blind corpus.

At the syntactic level, they found essentially linear growth in the number of sentence types as the number of sentence tokens increased in the two non-sublanguage corpora—the ratio of sentence types to sentences in these corpora were 1:1.07 for the Hansard corpus and 1:1.02 for the American Printing House for the Blind corpus. In contrast, the growth of sentence types in the IBM manuals was not quite linear. It grew linearly to about 12,000 sentences, asymptoted between 12,000 and 16,000, and then grew essentially linearly but at a somewhat slower rate from 16,000 to 30,000 sentences. The ratio of sentence types to sentence tokens in the IBM manuals was 1:1.66—markedly higher than in the other two corpora.

1.4 Hypotheses tested in the paper

The null hypothesis is that there will be no difference in closure properties between the general English corpus and the two corpora of scientific journal articles that we examine. If the null hypothesis is not supported, then it might be deviated from in three ways. One is that the scientific corpora might show a greater tendency towards closure than the general English corpus. A second is that the general English corpus might show a greater tendency towards closure than the scientific corpora. A third is that there may be no relationship between the closure properties of the two scientific corpora, regardless of the closure properties of the general English corpus—one might show a tendency towards closure, and the other not.

2 Materials and Methods

2.1 Materials

The data under examination was drawn from three sources: the CRAFT corpus (Bada et al., 2012; Verspoor et al., 2012), the GENIA corpus (Kim et al., 2003), and a version of the British National Corpus (Leech et al., 1994) re-tagged with Connexor's Machinese parser (Järvinen et al., 2004). The CRAFT and GENIA corpora are composed of scientific journal articles, while the British National Corpus is a representative corpus comprising many different varieties of spoken and written English.

The CRAFT corpus is a collection of 97 full-text journal articles from the mouse genomics domain. It has been annotated for a variety of linguistic and semantic features; for the purposes of this study, the relevant ones were sentence boundaries, tokenization, and part of speech. We used the 70-document public release subset of the corpus, which comprises about 453,377 words.

The GENIA corpus is a collection of 1,999 abstracts of journal articles about human blood cell transcription factors. Like the CRAFT corpus, it has been annotated for a variety of linguistic and semantic features, again including sentence boundaries, tokenization, and part of speech. In the mid-2000's, the GENIA corpus was shown to be the most popular corpus for research in biomedical natural language processing (Cohen et al., 2005). We used version 3.02 of the corpus, containing about 448,843 words.

The experiment requires a corpus of general English for comparison. For this purpose, we used a subset of the British National Corpus. For purposes of representativeness, we followed the Brown corpus strategy of extracting the first 2,000 words from each article until a total of 453,377 words were reached (to match the size of the CRAFT corpus).

The size of the two data sets is far more than adequate for an experiment of this type—McEnery and Wilson were able to detect closure properties using corpora of only 200,000 words in their experiments.

2.2 Methods

2.2.1 Implementation details

To determine the closure properties of arbitrary corpora, we developed scripts that take a simple input format into which it should be possible to convert any annotated corpus. There are two input file types:

- A file containing one word and its corresponding part-of-speech tag per line. Part of speech tags can consist of multiple tokens, as they do in the BNC tag set, or of single tokens, as they do in most corpora. This file format is used as the input for the lexical closure script and the word type/POS tag script.
- A file containing a sequence of part of speech tags per line, one line per sentence. This file format is used as input for the sentence type closure script. We note that this is an extremely rough representation of "syntax," and arguably is actually asyntactic in that it does not represent constituent or dependency structure at all, but also point out that it has the advantage of being widely applicable and agnostic as to any particular theory of syntactic structure. It also increases the sensitivity of the method to sentence type differences, providing a stronger test of fit to the sublanguage model.

Two separate scripts then process one of these input files to determine lexical, type/POS, and sentence type closure properties. The output of every script is a comma-separated-value file suitable for importing into Excel or other applications for producing plots. The two scripts and our scripts for converting the BNC, CRAFT, and GENIA corpora into the input file formats will be made publicly available at [redacted for anonymization purposes]. To apply the scripts to a new corpus, the

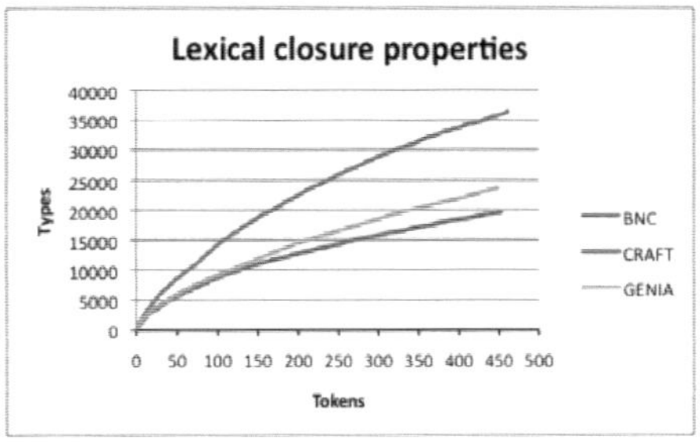

Figure 1: Lexical closure properties. Tick-marks on x axis indicate increments of 50,000 tokens.

only necessary step is to write a script to convert from the corpus's original format to the simple format of the two input file types described above.

2.2.2 Investigating closure properties

In all three cases, the number of types, whether of lexical items, lexical type/part-of-speech pair, or sentence type was counted and graphed on the y axis, versus the number of tokens that had been observed up to that point, which was graphed on the x axis. In the case of the lexical and type/POS graphs, tokens were words, and in the case of the sentence graph, "tokens" were sentences.

We then combined the lines for all three corpora and observed the total size of types, the rate of growth of the line, and whether or not there was a tendency towards asymptoting of the growth of the line, i.e. closure.

Our major deviation from the approach of (McEnery and Wilson, 2001) was that rather than parse trees, we used part-of-speech tag sequences to represent sentence types. This is suboptimal in that it is essentially asyntactic, and in that it obscures the smoothing factor of abstracting away from per-token parts of speech to larger syntactic units. However, as we point out above, it has the advantages of being widely applicable and agnostic as to any particular theory of syntactic structure, as well as more sensitive to sentence type differences.

3 Results

3.1 Lexical closure properties

Figure 1 shows the growth in number of types of lexical items as the number of tokens of lexical items increases. The British National Corpus data is in blue, the CRAFT data is in red, and the GENIA data is in green.

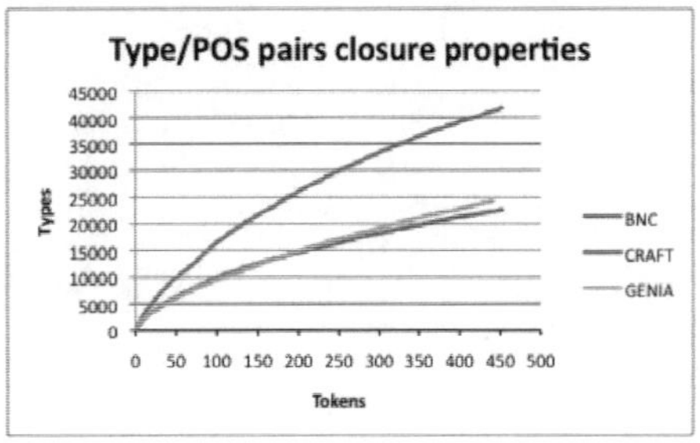

Figure 2: Type-part-of-speech tag closure properties. Tick-marks on x axis indicate increments of 50,000 tokens.

We note a drastic difference between the curve for the BNC and the curves for CRAFT and GENIA. The curves for CRAFT and GENIA are quite similar to each other. Overall, the curve for the BNC climbs faster and much farther, and is still climbing at a fast rate after 453,377 tokens have been examined. In contrast, the curves for CRAFT and GENIA climb more slowly, climb much less, and by the time about 50,000 tokens have been examined the rate of increase is much smaller. The increase in CRAFT and GENIA does not asymptote, as McEnery and Wilson observed for the IBM corpus. However, contrasted with the results for the BNC, there is a clear difference.

The type to token ratios for lexical items for the corpora as a whole are shown in Table 1. As the sublanguage model would predict, CRAFT and GENIA have much higher ratios than BNC.

Corpus name	Ratio
BNC	1: 12.650
CRAFT	1: 23.080
GENIA	1: 19.027

Table 1: Lexical type-to-token ratios.

3.2 Type/POS tag closure properties

Figure 2 shows the growth in number of type-POS tag pairs as the number of tokens of lexical item/POS tag pairs increases. The data from the different corpora corresponds to the same colors as in Figure 1.

Once again, we note a drastic difference between the curve for the BNC and the curves for CRAFT and GENIA. If anything, the differences are more pronounced here than in the case of the lexical closure graph. Again, we do not see an asymptote in the increase of the curves for CRAFT and GENIA, but there is a clear difference when contrasted with the results for the BNC.

The type-to-token sets ratios for the corpora as a whole are shown in Table 2. Again, as the sublanguage model would predict, we see much higher ratios in CRAFT and GENIA than in BNC.

Corpus name	Ratio
BNC	1: 10.80
CRAFT	1: 19.96
GENIA	1: 18.18

Table 2: Type-to-token ratios for type/POS tags.

Because the Machinese Syntax parser was used to obtain the part-of-speech tagging for BNC and the Machinese Syntax parser's tagset is much more granular and therefore larger than the CRAFT and GENIA tag sets, both of which are adaptations of the Penn treebank tag set, we considered the hypothesis that the large size differences of the tag sets were the cause of the differences observed between BNC and the two corpora of scientific journal articles. To test this hypothesis, we manually mapped the BNC tag set to the Penn treebank tag set. The result was a new BNC list of tags, of the same number and granularity as the CRAFT/GENIA ones (35-36 tags). Using this mapping, the BNC part-of-speech tags were converted to the Penn treebank tag set and the experiment was re-run. The results show that there is almost no difference between the results from the first and the second experiments. The resulting graph is omitted for space, but examining it one can observe that the differences between the three corpora in the graph are almost the same in both graphs. The newly calculated type:tokens ratio for BNC are also illustrative. They are highly similar to the type-token ratio for the original tag set—1:10.82 with the mapped data set vs. 1:10.80 with the original, much larger tag set. This supports the original results and demonstrates that differences in tag set sizes do not interfere with the identification of sublanguages.

3.3 Sentence type closure properties

Figure 3 shows the growth in number of sentence types as the number of sentences increases. The data from the different corpora corresponds to the same colors as in Figure 1.

Here we see that all three corpora exhibit sim-

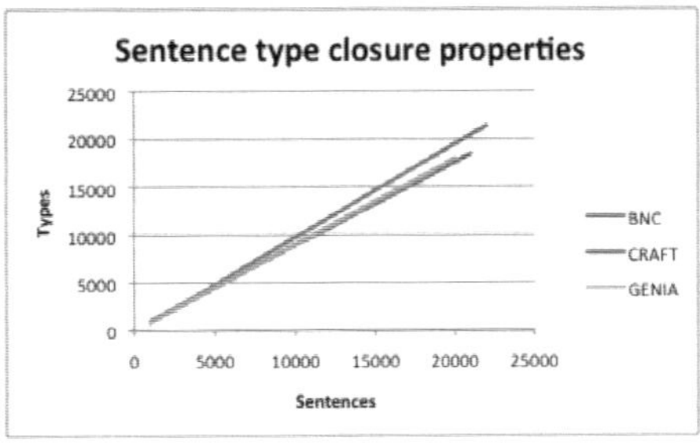

Figure 3: Sentence type closure properties. Tickmarks on x axis indicate increments of 5,000 sentences.

ilar curves—essentially linear, with nearly identical growth rates. This is a strong contrast with the results seen in Figures 1 and 2. We suggest some reasons for this in the Discussion section.

The ratio of sentence types to sentence tokens for the corpora as a whole are given in Table 3. As would be expected from the essentially linear growth observed with token growth for all three corpora, all three ratios are nearly 1:1.

Corpus name	Ratio
BNC	1: 1.03
CRAFT	1: 1.14
GENIA	1: 1.11

Table 3: Sentence type-to-token ratios.

4 Discussion and Conclusions

The most obvious conclusion of this study is that the null hypothesis can be rejected—the scientific corpora show a greater tendency towards closure than the general English corpus. Furthermore, we observe that the two scientific corpora behave quite similarly to each other at all three levels. This second observation is not necessarily a given. If we can consider for a moment the notion that there might be degrees of fit to the sublanguage model, it is clear that from a content perspective the BNC is unlimited; the CRAFT corpus is limited to mouse genomics, but not to any particular area of mouse genomics (indeed, it contains articles about development, disease, physiology, and other topics); and GENIA is more limited than CRAFT, being restricted to the topic of human blood cell transcription factors. If a technique for sublanguage detection were sufficiently precise and granular, it might be possible to show a strict ranking from BNC to CRAFT to GENIA in terms of fit to the sublanguage model (i.e., BNC showing no fit, and GENIA showing a greater fit than CRAFT since its subject matter is even more restricted). However, this does not occur—in our data, CRAFT showed a stronger tendency towards closure at the lexical level, while GENIA shows a stronger tendency towards closure at the morphosyntactic level. It is possible that the small differences at those levels are not significant, and that the two corpora show the same tendencies towards closure overall.

One reason that the IBM manuals in the (McEnery and Wilson, 2001) experiments showed sentence type closure but the CRAFT and GENIA corpora did not in our experiments is almost certainly related to sentence length. The average length of a sentence in the IBM manuals is 11 words, versus 24 in the Hansard corpus and 21 in the American Printing House for the Blind corpus. In this respect, the scientific corpora are much more like the Hansard and American Printing House for the Blind corpora than they are like the IBM manuals—the average length of a sentence in GENIA is 21.47 words, similar to the Hansard and American Printing House for the Blind corpora and about twice the length of sentences in the IBM manuals. Similarly, the average sentence length of the CRAFT corpus is 22.27 words (twice the average sentence length of the IBM manuals), and the average sentence length in the BNC is 20.43 words. Longer sentences imply greater chances for different sentence types.

Another reason for the tendency towards sentence type closure in the IBM manuals, which was not observed in CRAFT and GENIA, is the strong possibility that they were written in a controlled language that specifies the types of syntactic constructions that can be used in writing a manual, e.g. limiting the use of passives, etc., as well as lexical choices and limits on other options (Kuhn, under review). There is no such official controlled language for writing journal articles.

Finally, one reason that the CRAFT and GENIA corpora did not show sentence type closure while the IBM manuals did is that while McEnery and Wilson represented sentence types as parses, we represented them as sequences of part-of-speech tags. Representing sentence types as parse trees has the effect of smoothing out some variability at the leaf node level. For this reason, our representation increases the sensitivity of the method to sentence type differences, providing a stronger test of fit to the sublanguage model.

It has been suggested since Harris's classic work (Harris et al., 1989) that scientific writing forms a sublanguage. However, it is also clear from the work of (Stetson et al., 2002) and (Mihaila et al., 2012) that some putative sublanguages are a better fit to the model than others, and to date there has been no publicly available, repeatable method for assessing the fit of a set of documents to the sublanguage model. This paper presents the first such package of software and uses it to evaluate two corpora of scientific journal articles. Future work will include evaluating the effects of mapping all numbers to a fixed *NUMBER* token, which might affect the tendencies towards lexical closure; evaluating the effect of the size of tag sets on type/part-of-speech ratios, which might affect tendencies towards type/part-of-speech closure; and seeking a way to introduce more syntactic structure into the sentence type analysis without losing the generality of the current approach. We will also apply the technique to other biomedical genres, such as clinical documents. There is also an important next step to take—this work provides a means for recognizing sublanguages, but does not tackle the problem of determining their characteristics. However, despite these limitations, this paper presents a large step towards facilitating the study of sublanguages by providing a quantitative means of assessing their presence.

In analyzing the results of the study, some implications for natural language processing are apparent. Some of these are in accord with the issues for sublanguage natural language processing pointed out in the introduction. Another is that this work highlights the importance of both classic and more recent work on concept recognition for scientific journal articles (and other classes of sublanguages), such as MetaMap (Aronson, 2001; Aronson and Lang, 2010), ConceptMapper (Tanenblatt et al., 2010), and the many extant gene mention systems.

Acknowledgments

Irina Temnikova's work on the research reported in this paper was supported by the project AComIn "Advanced Computing for Innovation", grant 316087, funded by the FP7 Capacity Programme (Research Potential of Convergence Regions). Kevin Bretonnel Cohen's work was supported by grants NIH 5R01 LM009254-07 and NIH 5R01 LM008111-08 to Lawrence E. Hunter, NIH 1R01MH096906-01A1 to Tal Yarkoni, NIH R01 LM011124 to John Pestian, and NSF IIS-1207592 to Lawrence E. Hunter and Barbara Grimpe. The authors thank Tony McEnery and Andrew Wilson for advice on dealing with the tag sets.

References

Alan R. Aronson and Francois-Michel Lang. 2010. An overview of MetaMap: historical perspective and recent advances. *Journal of the American Medical Informatics Association*, 17:229–236.

A. Aronson. 2001. Effective mapping of biomedical text to the UMLS Metathesaurus: The MetaMap program. In *Proc AMIA 2001*, pages 17–21.

Michael Bada, Miriam Eckert, Donald Evans, Kristin Garcia, Krista Shipley, Dmitry Sitnikov, William A. Baumgartner Jr., Kevin Bretonnel Cohen, Karin Verspoor, Judith A. Blake, and Lawrence E. Hunter. 2012. Concept annotation in the craft corpus. *BMC Bioinformatics*, 13(161).

K. B. Cohen, Lynne Fox, Philip V. Ogren, and Lawrence Hunter. 2005. Corpus design for biomedical natural language processing. In *Proceedings of the ACL-ISMB workshop on linking biological literature, ontologies and databases*, pages 38–45. Association for Computational Linguistics.

Timothy W. Finin. 1986. Constraining the interpretation of nominal compounds in a limited context. In Ralph Grishman and Richard Kittredge, editors, *Analyzing language in restricted domains: sublanguage description and processing*, pages 85–102. Lawrence Erlbaum Associates.

Carol Friedman, Philip O. Anderson, John H.M. Austin, James J. Cimino, and Stephen B. Johnson. 1994. A general natural-language text processor for clinical radiology. *Journal of the American Medical Informatics Association*, 1:161–174.

Carol Friedman, Pauline Kra, Hong Yu, Michael Krauthammer, and Andrey Rzhetsky. 2001. GENIES: a natural-language processing system for the extraction of molecular pathways from journal articles. *Bioinformatics*, 17(Suppl. 1):S74–S82.

Carol Friedman, Pauline Kra, and Andrey Rzhetsky. 2002. Two biomedical sublanguages: a description based on the theories of Zellig Harris. *Journal of Biomedical Informatics*, 35:222–235.

Carol Friedman. 1986. Automatic structuring of sublanguage information. In Ralph Grishman and Richard Kittredge, editors, *Analyzing language in restricted domains: sublanguage description and processing*, pages 85–102. Lawrence Erlbaum Associates.

Ralph Grishman and Richard Kittredge. 1986. *Analyzing language in restricted domains: sublanguage description and processing*. Lawrence Erlbaum Associates.

Zellig Harris, Michael Gottfried, Thomas Ryckman, Anne Daladier, Paul Mattick, T.N. Harris, and Susanna Harris. 1989. *The form of information in science: analysis of an immunology sublanguage*. Kluwer Academic Publishers.

Lynette Hirschman and Naomi Sager. 1982. Automatic information formatting of a medical sublanguage. In Richard Kittredge and John Lehrberger, editors, *Sublanguage: studies of language in restricted semantic domains*, pages 27–80. Walter de Gruyter.

Timo Järvinen, Mikko Laari, Timo Lahtinen, Sirkku Paajanen, Pirkko Paljakka, Mirkka Soininen, and Pasi Tapanainen. 2004. Robust language analysis components for practical applications. In *Robust and adaptive information processing for mobile speech interfaces: DUMAS final workshop*, pages 53–56.

Jin-Dong Kim, Tomoko Ohta, Yuka Tateisi, and Jun'ichi Tsujii. 2003. Genia corpus—a semantically annotated corpus for bio-textmining. *Bioinformatics*, 19(Suppl. 1):180–182.

Richard I. Kittredge. 2003. Sublanguages and controlled languages. In Ruslan Mitkov, editor, *The Oxford Handbook of Computational Linguistics*, pages 430–447. Oxford University Press.

Tobias Kuhn. under review. Survey and classification of controlled natural languages. *Computational Linguistics*.

G. Leech, R. Garside, and M. Bryant. 1994. The large-scale grammatical tagging of text: experience with the British National Corpus. In N. Oostdijk and P. de Haan, editors, *Corpus based research into language*.

David D. McDonald. 2000. Natural language generation. In Robert Dale, Hermann Moisl, and Harold Somers, editors, *Handbood of Natural Language Processing*, pages 147–179. Marcel Dekker.

Tony McEnery and Andrew Wilson. 2001. *Corpus Linguistics*. Edinburgh University Press, 2nd edition.

Claudiu Mihaila, Riza Theresa Batista-Navarro, and Sophia Ananiadou. 2012. Analysing entity type variation across biomedical subdomains. In *Third workshop on building and evaluating resources for biomedical text mining*, pages 1–7.

Naomi Sager. 1986. Sublanguage: linguistic phenomenon, computational tool. In Ralph Grishman and Richard Kittredge, editors, *Analyzing language in restricted domains: sublanguage description and processing*, pages 1–17. Lawrence Erlbaum Associates.

Satoshi Sekine. 1994. A new direction for sublanguage nlp. In *Proceedings of the international conference on new methods in natural language processing*, pages 123–129.

Harold Somers. 1998. An attempt to use weighted cusums to identify sublanguages. In *NeMLaP3/CoNLL98: New methods in language processing and computational natural language learning*, pages 131–139.

Harold Somers. 2000. Machine translation. In Robert Dale, Hermann Moisl, and Harold Somers, editors, *Handbook of Natural Language Processing*, pages 329–346. Marcel Dekker.

Peter D. Stetson, Stephen B. Johnson, Matthew Scotch, and George Hripcsak. 2002. The sublanguage of cross-coverage. In *Proc. AMIA 2002 Annual Symposium*, pages 742–746.

Michael Tanenblatt, Anni Coden, and Igor Sominsky. 2010. The ConceptMapper approach to named entity recognition. In *Language Resources and Evaluation Conference*, pages 546–551.

Karin Verspoor, Kevin Bretonnel Cohen, Arrick Lanfranchi, Colin Warner, Helen L. Johnson, Christophe Roeder, Jinho D. Choi, Christopher Funk, Yuriy Malenkiy, Miriam Eckert, Nianwen Xue, William A. Baumgartner Jr., Michael Bada, Martha Palmer, and Lawrence E. Hunter. 2012. A corpus of full-text journal articles is a robust evaluation tool for revealing differences in performance of biomedical natural language processing tools. *BMC Bioinformatics*, 13(207).

BEL networks derived from qualitative translations of BioNLP Shared Task annotations

Juliane Fluck[1*], Alexander Klenner[1], Sumit Madan[1], Sam Ansari[2], Tamara Bobic[1,3], Julia Hoeng[2], Martin Hofmann-Apitius[1,3], Manuel C. Peitsch[2]

[1]Fraunhofer Institute for Algorithms and Scientific Computing, Schloss Birlinghoven, Sankt Augustin, Germany.

[2]Philip Morris International R&D, Philip Morris Products S.A., Quai Jeanrenaud 5, 2000 Neuchâtel, Switzerland.

[3]Bonn-Aachen International Centre for Information Technology, Dahlmannstr. 2, Bonn, Germany

{jfluck, smadan, aklenner, tbobic, mhofmann-apitius}@scai.fraunhofer.de, {sam.ansari, julia.hoeng, manuel.peitsch}@pmi.com

Abstract

Interpreting the rapidly increasing amount of experimental data requires the availability and representation of biological knowledge in a computable form. The Biological expression language (BEL) encodes the data in form of causal relationships, which describe the association between biological events. BEL can successfully be applied to large data and support causal reasoning and hypothesis generation.

With the rapid growth of biomedical literature, automated methods are a crucial prerequisite for handling and encoding the available knowledge. The BioNLP shared tasks support the development of such tools and provide a linguistically motivated format for the annotation of relations. On the other hand, BEL statements and the corresponding evidence sentences might be a valuable resource for future BioNLP shared task training data generation.

In this paper, we briefly introduce BEL and investigate how far BioNLP-shared task annotations could be converted to BEL statements and in such a way directly support BEL statement generation. We present the first results of the automatic BEL statement generation and emphasize the need for more training data that captures the underlying biological meaning.

1 Introduction

Currently a lot of effort is made to extract information from scientific articles and encode the relevant parts in machine-readable language. In order to tackle these tasks, curators must be experts in both biological domain and computational representation of knowledge.

With the introduction of BEL, a new knowledge coding convention was made available, thus simplifying the curation process and ensuring machine readability[1]. BEL was initially designed and used in 2003 by Selventa (operating as Genstruct® Inc. at the time) to capture relationships between biological entities in scientific literature (Slater and Song 2012). It is flexible enough to store content from multiple knowledge layers and a broad range of analytical and decision-supporting applications. Knowledge bases encoded in BEL are suitable for querying, interpreting, reasoning and visualising of networks.

BEL represents scientific findings by capturing causal and correlative relationships in a given context, including information about the biological system and experimental conditions. The supporting evidences are captured and linked to the publication references. It is specifically designed to adopt external vocabularies and ontologies, and therefore represents life-science knowledge in language and schema known by the community. Entities in BEL statements are mapped to widely accepted namespaces, which specify a set of domain entities (e.g., HGNC[2], CHEBI[3]). Continuous development and commercial use in more than 80 life science projects in the last ten years qualify BEL as suitable for displaying causal networks for both humans and computers. Various networks built in BEL were mainly focusing on disease mechanisms (Schlage

[1]http://wiki.openbel.org/display/BLD/BEL+Language+Documentation+v1.0+-+Current

[2] http://www.genenames.org/

[3] http://www.ebi.ac.uk/chebi/

et al., 2011) and are used for causal reasoning (Chindelevitch et al., 2012, Huang et al., 2012 and Selventa 2012). Since 2012, BEL is also available in the public domain through the OpenBEL consortium. The OpenBel portal[4] defines the BEL language standard and provides formatted content and compatible tools for research.

The necessary information to develop a BEL knowledge base is currently harvested mainly by manual translation of literature into BEL statements. To support automated extraction of statements by text mining techniques, additional efforts and adaptations of existing text mining platforms are necessary.

The BioNLP community has developed various approaches, which may already support the automated extraction of BEL statements. To estimate how far current tools can generate BEL relationships, we focused on the BioNLP shared tasks series[5]. The BioNLP-shared tasks specify fine-grained information extraction tasks for biologically relevant targets, mainly centred on proteins and genes. In the two previous events, BioNLP-ST 2009 and 2011, more than 30 teams participated with their systems, a number of which are available as open source. In BioNLP-ST 2013 series, additional training data for pathway curation including chemical entities is available.

The organizers develop a linguistically based event representation and provide annotated training and test data to the participants. The annotated events in training data can directly be used for comparison with BEL definitions and available BEL statements. If the conversion of said event annotations to BEL statements (and vice versa) is successful on the semantic level, we have a promising opportunity to support both domains. Information encoded in the BEL statements in combination with corresponding evidence sentences could be used as training data to support further tool development.

2 Related Network Representations

For pathway representations there exist two widely adopted machine readable representations: Systems Biology Markup Language (SBML)[6] (Hucka et al., 2003) and Biological Pathway Exchange (BioPAX) (Demir et al., 2010). SBML is an XML-based data exchange format that supports a formal mathematical representation of chemical reactions including kinetic parameters. BioPAX is an RDF/OWL-based standard language enabling integration, exchange, visualization, and analysis of biological pathway data. Pathway representations in BioPax were already compared to the BioNLP-ST representations (Ohta et al., (1) 2011) and let to the introduction of the Pathway curation task in 2013[7]. For this task additional entity types and event types were proposed and resulted in a set of new annotations (Ohta et al., (2) 2011). A comparison between BEL and BioPax can be found at the OpenBEL Portal[8]. BioPAX focuses on pathway construction and partly may require more information than available in most publications. BEL's design enables the representation of causal relationships across a wide range of mechanistic detail and between the levels of molecular event, cellular process, and organism-scale phenotype. BEL is designed to represent discrete scientific findings and their relevant contextual information as qualitative causal relationships that can drive knowledge-based analytics. BEL enables biological interference by applications but furthermore is intended as an intuitive language of discourse for biologists. In such a way BEL is well aligned to the communications done in publications. The condensed representation of BEL statements and human as well as machine readability are great advantages of the BEL language.

3 Overview of basic concepts in BEL

BEL defines semantic triples that are stored in structured human readable BEL document files. A semantic triple is defined as a subject – predicate – object triple, where subject is always a BEL term, object either a BEL term or a BEL statement (recursive nature of BEL) and the predicate one of the BEL relationship types. A BEL term is composed of a BEL function, a corresponding entity and a referencing namespace. The two main classes of BEL terms define abundance of an entity (e.g., gene) or a biological process (e.g., disease).

Optionally, statements can be enriched by con-

[4] http://www.openbel.org/
[5] http://2013.bionlp-st.org/
[6] http://sbml.org

[7] https://sites.google.com/site/bionlpst2013/tasks/pathway-curation
[8] Comparison of BEL V1.0 and BioPAX Level3.pdf http://www.openbel.org/content/bel-lang-resource-documents

text information annotations like the evidence sentences, tissue type, species or cell line. Two annotation types are reserved, i.e., 'Citation' and 'Evidence'. 'Evidence' should state the exact sentence that holds the statement's information, where 'Citation' is the source of this knowledge.

Predefined namespaces cover a variety of biological entities: genes, proteins, chemicals, diseases and biological processes. For a complete definition of BEL we refer to the BEL Language documentation.

BEL Expression	Explanation
p(HGNC:AKT1)	Term: Protein Abundance function p(Ns:entity)
r(HGNC:AKT1)	Term: RNA Abundance function r(Ns:entity)
a(CHEBI:phosphoenolpyruvate)	Term: Chemical Abundance function a(Ns:entity)
p(HGNC:AKT1, sub(V,243,P))	Term: Protein Abundance function with substitution modification p(Ns:entity, sub(Aai,Pos,Aaj))
p(HGNC:AKT1, pmod(P,S,21))	Term: Protein Abundance function with phosphorylation modification p(Ns:entity,pmod(P,Aa,Pos))
kin (p(HGNC:AKT1))	Term: Protein Abundance function with kinase modification kin(p(Ns:entity))
complex (p(HGNC:CHUK), p(HGNC:IKBKB), p(HGNC:IKBKG))	Term: Complex Abundance function complex (p(Ns:entity)i,..., p(Ns:entity)n)
tloc(p(HGNC:EGFR), MESHCL: "Cell Membrane", MESCL:Endosomes)	Term: Translocation function for Protein Abundance specifying the original and target location Tloc(p(Ns:entity), Ns:entity, Ns:entity)
deg(p(HGNC:AKT1))	Term: Degradation function for protein abundance deg(p(nNs:protein))
Reaction: rxn(reactants(a(CHEBI: phosphoenolpyruvate), a(CHEBI:ADP)), products (a(CHEBI:pyruvate), a(CHEBI:ATP)))	Statement: reaction expressing the transformation of products into reactants, each defined by a list of abundances rxn(reactants(a(Ns:entity)...), products(a(Ns:entity)...)
p(HGNC:IL6) -> r(HGNC:ENO1)	Statement: increase Term ->Term or Term -> Statement
p(HGNC:TNF) -| r(HGNC:NOS3)	Statement: decrease Term -|Term or Term -| Statement
p(HGNC:TNF) -- r(HGNC:NOS3)	Statement: association Term --Term or Term --Statement

Table 1: Example BEL terms and statements. Abbreviations: Ns=namespace, Aa=amino acid, Pos=position

In this work we focus mainly on protein-protein relationships (for simplification 'protein' refers to the corresponding gene, the RNA intermediate and the gene product itself[9]). Protein-protein relationships are a main focus of the BioNLP shared tasks and cover core relationships of BEL. An overview of possible statements is given in Table 1 and shortly described below. Protein entities are represented by BEL terms, consisting of the abundance function, the normalized entity and optionally modifications expressed as additional arguments within the abundance function:

BEL statement: *p(HGNC:AKT1, pmod(P, S, 21))*
Entity: *AKT1*
Namespace: *HGNC*
Optional modification: *pmod(P,S,21)*

The used namespace denotes the approved symbol of HUGO Gene Nomenclature Committee[10]. An overview of currently used namespaces is given at the OpenBEL portal. The pmod() function explicitly denotes the modification type (here *P*=phosphorylation), the 1-letter code for the corresponding amino acid (*S*=Serin) and the position in the protein sequence. Other modifications are represented with different codes, e.g., M=methylation or U=ubiquitination.

BEL terms may contain protein activity information such as kinase or transcription factor activity or certain functions like complex, degradation, translocation or reaction in addition.

```
SET Citation = {"PubMed","Cell","16962653","2006-10-07","Jacinto E|Facchinetti V|Liu D|Soto N|Wei S|Jung SY|Huang Q|Qin J|Su B",""}
SET Cell = "Fibroblasts"
SET Species = "10090"
SET Evidence = "We next examined the Akt T-loop Thr308 phosphorylation in wild-type and SIN1−/− cells. We found that although Ser473 phosphorylation was completely abolished in the SIN1−/− cells, Thr308 phosphorylation of Akt was not blocked (Figure 3A)."

p(MGI:Mapkap1) -> p(MGI:Akt1,pmod(P,S,473))
p(MGI:Mapkap1) causesNoChange
p(MGI:Akt1,pmod(P,T,308))
```

Figure 1: Example of enriched BEL Statement

By default (but not mandatory) 'Evidence' and 'Citation' annotations are provided for each

[9] according to BioNLP shared tasks annotations
[10] http://www.genenames.org/data/hgnc_data.php?hgnc_id=391

statement. In case of extraction from literature the reference source and the evidence sentences are given. Alternative evidences may be derived from tables, figures, supplementary material or other knowledge sources. Optionally, the BEL statements can be annotated with specified information about experimental methods, the biological system in which the facts are represented, or even information in which part of the full text the evidence has been found. An example of such a BEL statement from a small sample set at the OpenBEL portal[11] is shown in Figure 1. Such detailed information from literature, in combination with the BEL statements, could serve as ideal source for the generation of training data for text mining purposes to facilitate the development of future automated extraction algorithms.

4 Analysis of basic concepts in the BioNLP shared task annotations

In the main BioNLP shared task (GE12) nine event types are defined (cf Table 2). 'Gene expression', 'Transcription', 'Protein catabolism', 'Phosphorylation' and 'Localization' are simple events, having one protein as *Theme* argument.

Event	Primary Arg.	Secondary Arg.
Gene Expression	Theme(Protein)	
Transcription	Theme(Protein)	
Protein Catabolism	Theme(Protein)	
Phosphorylation	Theme(Protein)	Site
Localization	Theme(Protein)	AtLoc, ToLoc
Binding	Theme(Protein)+	Site+
Regulation, Positive Regulation, Negative Regulation	Theme(Protein/Event) ,Cause(Protein/Event)	Cause, Site, CSite

Table 2: Event types defined in the BioNLP competitions (adapted from (Kim et al., 2012). A '+' sign indicates multiple occurrences allowed.

Events 'Phosphorylation' and 'Localization' may have additional secondary arguments, like the phosphorylation site or the localization arguments ToLoc and AtLoc. 'Binding' events can have an arbitrary number of proteins as *Themes*. Events 'Positive regulation', 'Negative regulation' and 'Regulation' are *Regulation Events* and have a primary *Theme* argument and an optional *Cause* argument, both being either a protein or an event. The trigger is always the textual representation of the entities. Table 3 depicts an example annotation for the following sentences[13]:

S1) E1-4: "RFLAT-1: a new zinc finger transcription factor that activates RANTES gene expression in T lymphocytes."

S2) E5-9: "In this study we hypothesized that the phosphorylation of TRAF2 inhibits binding to the CD40 cytoplasmic domain."

ID	Theme Type	Trigger	Theme	Cause
T1	Protein	RFLAT-1		
T2	Protein	RANTES		
E3	Gene Expression	gene expression	T2	
E4	Positive Regulation	activates	E3	T1
T5	Protein	TRAF-2		
T6	Protein	CD40		
E7	Phosphorylation	phosphorylation	T5	
E8	Binding	binding	T6	T5
E9	Negative Regulation	inhibits	E8	E7

Table 3: Example BioNLP 09 shared task annotation. The gene/protein entities with the Ids T1, T2, T5, and T6 were already provided. The task was to detect the events E3, E4, E7, E8 and E9.

5 Syntactic mapping from BioNLP annotation to BEL statements

For mapping of the BEL statements and the output of the BioNLP shared tasks systems we compared the training data for the GENIA BioNLP task with the BEL statements found in the small corpus at the OpenBEL website. The BioNLP shared task provides no normalization of the entities to namespaces. Since we are mainly interested in the transformation of the event, we ignore the normalization aspect in the conversion process. For most Shared Task events we could

[11] https://github.com/OpenBEL/openbel-framework-resources/blob/master/knowledge/small_corpus.bel

[12] https://sites.google.com/site/bionlpst/home/genia-event-extraction-genia

[13] Examples taken from http://www.nactem.ac.uk/tsujii/GENIA/SharedTask/detail.shtml

generate BEL Terms which are summarized with the rule set in Table 4 and Table 5.
Standard translation for all protein Themes is protein abundance *p(namespace:entity)*. In a later network generation step within the BEL framework RNA abundance and gene abundance are added automatically to the network of statements for all protein abundances. Due to this reason, we only consider RNA or gene abundance if we detect strong evidences for those states. For Gene_expression, the protein abundance is only converted to RNA abundance (r(namespace:entity)) if the trigger word is 'gene expression'.

1.1	GeneExpression(Theme(protein)) → p(Ns:protein) If the GeneExpression trigger word is stemmed to 'express'
1.2	GeneExpression(Theme(protein)) → r(Ns:protein) For all other GeneExpression trigger words.
2	Transcription(Theme(protein)) → r(Ns:entity)
3	Phosphorylation(Theme(protein), <Site>) → p(Ns:protein, <pmod(P,*Aa, Pos*)>)
4	ProteinCatabolism(Theme(protein))→ deg(p(Ns:protein))
5.1	Localization(Theme(protein)) → *sec* (p(Ns:protein)) If the Localization trigger is stemmed to 'secrete'
5.2	Localization(Theme(protein),AtLoc) → *surf*(p(Ns:protein)) If the Localization trigger is stemmed to 'express' and If AtLoc is 'cell surface' or 'surface'
5.3	Localization(Theme(protein),AtLoc, ToLoc) → *tloc* (p(Ns:protein),Ns:AtLoc,Ns:ToLoc) In BEL statements it is necessary to have AtLoc and ToLoc; for some cases the missing information can be inferred otherwise artificial location information is given.
6	Binding(Theme(protein)+,Site+) → complex(p(ns:protein),+) The site information will be ignored.

Table 4: Rule set 1 to map BioNLP annotations to BEL statements.

If the trigger word 'expression' is used, both RNA and protein expression might be meant by the authors, hence we keep the protein abundance in those cases. Similarly for Transcription, the abundance is changed to RNA abundance. All complexes are translated to protein abundance and chemical names are directly translated into abundance (a(ns:chemical names)). Protein modification events such as Phosphorylation can be directly converted to BEL terms. The different modification events are translated to a single letter code in BEL. If the position information is given in the site expression it can directly be converted to the amino acid single letter code (Aa) and the position information (Pos). For the simple events Protein degradation and Binding, the translation is straightforward given their similar representation. The site information of the Binding event is omitted in the BEL statement conversion. It would only be included if there is an experiment showing that a mutation of the site would lead to a suppression of the complex building.

In the case of 'Localization', depending on the localisation trigger different BEL functions are possible. Given the localization trigger 'secrete' the BEL annotation is converted to the secretion (sec) function. If trigger words 'surface' or 'cell surface' are identified, the cellSurface (surf) function is assigned. For other Atloc and ToLoc triggers the function translocation (tloc) is used. This function always needs two arguments of location. If one of the arguments (AtLoc or ToLoc) is missing, a general annotation of MESHCL:"Intracellular Space" is proposed as unknown intracellular location.

Activity status like gtp(p(protein)), kin (p(protein)), tscript(p(protein)), cat(p(protein)), phos(p(protein)) are often found in the BEL example corpus. This information might be partly inferred through the evidence information. In the first example sentence from Table 2, RFLAT-1 might be directly translated into tscript (p(RFLAT-1)). In other cases if a protein phosphorylates another protein directly, the kin(p(protein)) annotation can be added as well. However, in most cases the information cannot directly be inferred from the sentences (cf. Figure 1). The annotators obviously use their background knowledge to include this information. In the actual status of the Shared Task to BEL conversion we omitted those functions.

Looking at the rule-set for transferring Shared-Task events to BEL statements, it is observed that for most events (six out of nine) only *BEL terms* are generated, i.e., only the left or right hand side of a complete statement. Three rules generate complete BEL statements out of the following events: *Regulation*, *Positive Regulation* and *Negative Regulation*. Analysis of the distribution of Events in Shared-Tasked training set (BioNLP ST 2011) reveals that approximately half of the events are Regulation events and thus, could lead to a set of complete statements. In Table 5, we describe the rules which generate complete BEL statements.

7	PositiveRegulation(Theme(Protein/Event), Cause(Protein/Event)) → p(ns:protein)/B(Event) -> p(ns:protein)/B(Event)
8	NegativeRegulation(Theme(Protein/Event), Cause(Protein/Event)) → p(ns:protein)/B(Event) -| p(ns:protein)/B(Event)
9	Regulation(Theme(Protein/Event), Cause(Protein/Event)) → p(ns:protein)/B(Event) -- p(ns:protein)/B(Event)

Table 5: Rule set 2 to map BioNLP annotations to BEL statements.

For all 'Regulation' events the *Theme* is translated to the object of the BEL statement and might be a protein or another BEL statement (B(Event)). The *Cause* is integrated as subject within the statement and can be a protein or a statement. All 'Positive Regulation' events in the Shared Task annotations are converted to 'increase' statements of BEL. We do not differentiate between 'increase' and 'directly increase' in the conversion process. Similarly, all 'Negative Regulation' events are converted to a 'decrease' statement ignoring 'directly decrease'. In the BEL annotations those two statement groups are the most frequent statements in both corpora. In the Shared Tasks relations we have the additional relation Regulation. There is no directly corresponding BEL relation for a general regulation event, since it restricts the impact for causal reasoning. The event which has the most similar meaning is the statement 'association'. It is used for associations of proteins but also for associations of proteins and diseases when no further information is available in the text. The additional annotations Site and CSite are currently ignored since there is no structure in BEL to include this information directly.

In all three regulation events the Cause is an optional argument and might be missing. Out of the 7574 regulation events 2152 events contain a cause and thus can be converted to a complete BEL statements. For all other events the left hand side of the statement is missing.

For obtaining an overview of the conversion process we converted the event annotations from the GENIA training corpus to BEL statements (all relations containing a speculation or a negation were omitted). The automatically generated BEL documents were checked for syntactical errors with the OpenBEL framework parser and validator. Several adaptations were necessary in the automatic conversion process to generate syntactically correct BEL statements.

Since we have no namespaces available we designed an artificial namespace to generate correct statements. Furthermore incomplete statements with missing subjects (Causes) were not accepted by the BEL framework. An example of such an incomplete BEL statement is the following (converted form the shared task annotation depicted in Figure 2):

-| p(BioNLP:STAT4) -| p(BioNLP:IL10)

For all missing *Causes* we included an artificial *Cause* resulting in the following statement for the given example:

p(BioNLP:FIXME)-| p(BioNLP:STAT4) -| p(BioNLP:IL10)

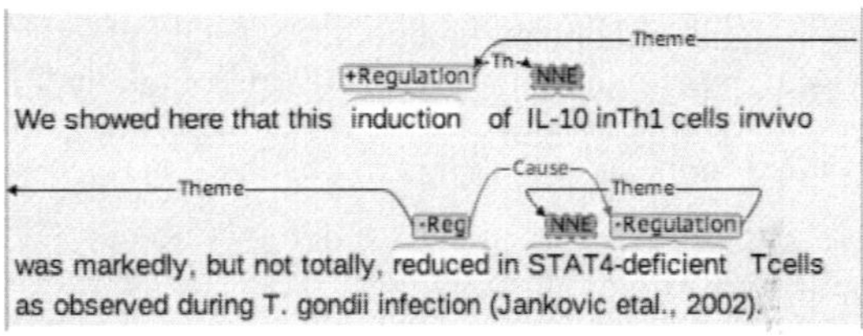

Figure 2: An example sentence from BioNLP-ST 2011 GE train corpus, visualized using brat. [14]

Overall 5333 BEL statements were generated resulting in 588 full statements, 3057 incomplete statements (where the CAUSE is missing and FIXME was introduced) and 1688 BEL terms without any relation. Remaining syntactic errors were caused through BEL statements containing more than two relations (118 statements), which could not be handled by the BEL framework. A first version of the converted corpus is available under: http://www.scai.fraunhofer.de/ge2011-to-bel.html.

6 Preliminary comparison of converted statements with BEL knowledge resources

In the BioNLP shared tasks all possible events that fulfill the guidelines are annotated. In real life use-cases irrelevant or unproven interactions are omitted and biological experts extract BEL statements when they are in focus of their interest. Furthermore experimental evidence for the relation should be should be given in the text.

[14] http://brat.nlplab.org

In addition biologists are able to do a semantic interpretation of the experimental results and generate inferred statements. To find solutions for semantic interpretation for a number of incomplete statements in the direct conversion for the BioNLP-ST annotations we compared sentences such as annotated in figure 2 with evidence sentences in the BEL sample set. In the following examples we show how an expert curator conversely infers BEL statements by interpreting experiment readouts.

Example 1:
Evidence = "PI 3- kinase/PKCξ, but not PI 3-kinase/Akt signaling pathway, is inhibited in IRS-2-deficient brown adipocytes upon insulin stimulation"

p(HGNC:IRS2)-> kinase(p(HGNC:PRKCZ))
p(HGNC:IRS2) causesNoChange kin(p(HGNC:AKT1))

Example 2:
Evidence = "transient transfection of primary brown adipocytes with a dominant negative form of p21 Ras completely abolished insulin-induced UCP-1-CAT transactivation."

p(PFH:"RAS Family") -> (p(HGNC:INS) -> r(HGNC:UCP1))

Example 3:
Evidence = "We next examined the Akt T-loop Thr308 phosphorylation in wild-type and SIN1−/− cells. We found that Thr308 phosphorylation was completely abolished in the SIN1−/− cells."

p(MGI:Mapkap1) -> p(MGI:Akt1,pmod(P,T,308))

The examples given above demonstrate a standard experimental setting. In most cases the functionality of a gene is abolished and the effect (e.g. increase, decrease or no effect) on the corresponding interaction targets is observed. Sometimes, observed effects are compared to cell systems where the normal form (wild type or control) is transfected as well (cf. Example 3).

All examples share the readout: The BEL statement is not describing the experiment (given in the sentence), but the observed implication inferred from the experiment (cf. Example 2). Instead of encoding that a dysfunctional p21 RAS leads to an abolishment of insulin induced UCP1 transactivation, the final BEL statement represents the resulting implication, i.e. wild-type p21 RAS increases INS, which subsequently increases UCP1:

p(PFH:"RAS Family") -> (p(HGNC:INS) -> r(HGNC:UCP1))

Similarly, in Example 3 from the abolishment of a function, the converse argument is derived, i.e. Mapkap 1 increases the phosphorylation of Akt1 at T308. This example shows another main issue in deriving BEL statements: two or more sentences are needed to get all information necessary to create a valid BEL statement. Human curators use multiple sentences as evidence and do additional interpretation of the provided information. In Example 3, the AKT phosphorylation is given in the first sentence and the phosphorylation event is given in the following sentence only in referring to the site and not to the protein. BioNLP-ST already includes annotation spanning several sentences but interpretation and merging of those annotations is not trivial. To complete such statements two different relations have to be combined and that is true for many modification relations. Especially in the case of phosphorylation, which is a regular activating signal in kinase pathways, we need solutions including information from different sentences. The BEL corpus has a high number of phosphorylation events and can serve as a base for the generation of further training data.

Another commonly observed experiment uses luciferase and CAT vectors. Those systems are used to analyze transcriptional activity of promoters in dependence of stimuli. The result of such an experiment is oftentimes given only as a relation to CAT or luciferase like in the following example:

Example 4:
Evidence = "introduction of miR-145, but not miR-143, with the luciferase vector in Cos cells resulted in relief of the repression and an ~150-fold increase in luciferase activity compared to the CMV-luciferase- Myocd 3' UTR-luciferase vector alone."

miR(HGNC:MIR145) -> p(HGNC:MYOCD)
miR(HGNC:MIR143) causesNoChange p(HGNC:MYOCD)

BioNLP shared task annotation would capture positive regulation of luciferase activity with the cause miR-145. The derived statement however does not state an abundance function for luciferase but the originally tested protein (indirectly via its promotor) i.e., Myocd. Here, the inserted promoter information is given at the end of the sentence, although it is often provided in a separate sentence.

The second BEL statement in Example 4 provides another relation type, which is not directly captured by the shared task annotations. Negative results are annotated in BEL statements with the relation causesNoChange and are valuable relations in causal reasoning. They might be interpreted using the negation annotation in shared task to capture this type of event.

Those examples are only a few out of numerous others. For the development of suitable systems, annotated training corpora are crucial. The BEL documents might be a good starting point to generate further training corpora containing a high number of such evidence examples. However, the conversion of the BEL statements to BioNLP shared task annotation is not trivial, since position information is completely missing. Nevertheless, it might reduce the annotation effort, give good examples and serve as a basis for biological interpretation of the relations. For initial automatic systems it might be even sufficient to offer such experimental evidence sentences in addition to the extracted relations to users.

7 Discussion and Conclusions

Generally, a syntactic conversion of BioNLP shared task annotations to BEL terms and statements is possible and in most cases without information loss. Tools developed or adapted for the BioNLP shared task are principally suited for the generation of causal BEL networks. However, the analysis of the automatically converted BEL statements from the BioNLP shared tasks shows that in a number of cases incomplete BEL statements were generated. Part of the reason is the need for an additional interpretation layer that would help in generating biologically meaningful statements. Another reason for the failure to extract full statements is the distribution of the relation over more than one sentence.

The properties of BEL statements and the additional information coded in the BEL documents represent a valuable resource for generating further training data for the development of more real-world oriented systems. Unfortunately, the information of the BEL documents cannot directly be converted back to textual annotation. The main reason is that the position information of entities within the relation is missing. Reverse engineering is also challenging because the trigger words are not given. Furthermore, normalization to namespaces used in BEL statements makes the direct mapping difficult.

Nevertheless, the text mining community can learn from the BEL documents what are relevant statements for causal reasoning and from which evidence sentences humans extract the information. The example BEL statements given show that humans use a number of experimental systems such as inactive versions of proteins or reporter genes to prove existing relationships. It might be a realistic task to use BEL documents as a starting point to generate training corpora for the automatic classification of such sentences and for information extraction systems to extract relations from those sentences. For some relations like the phosphorylation or the reporter genes, we might be even able to extract relations over sentences when enough training data is available.

Another problem not tackled by the BioNLP shared tasks is the mapping to the name spaces. There are already systems available combining BioNLP based relation extraction systems and named entity recognition (NER) systems allowing for normalization and (eg. Björne et al., 2012 and Van Landeghem et al., 2013). Future systems have to combine relation extraction and NER systems allowing for normalization. Gene and protein names have already been in the focus of the BioCreative assessments during the last years (cf. Morgan et al., 2008 and Lu et al., 2011). In addition, chemical entities are coming more and more into the focus of the community (e.g., in the BioCreative 2013 task[15]). In the examples from the BEL corpus we see additional problems coming from the area of engineered genes. Name variants are often used (e.g., Sin-/- or CMV-luciferase- Myocd 3' UTR-luciferase), which causes further problems in the normalization task.

Bridging the BEL and the BioNLP-ST community offers benefits for both sides. The BioNLP shared tasks are a considerable start for the automatic generation of causal networks. Moreover, already available BEL documents can support the generation of the huge amount of additional training data, which is necessary for further relation extraction development.

[15] http://www.biocreative.org/events/biocreative-iv/CFP/

Acknowledgments

We would like to thank Natalie Catlett and Ted Slater of Selventa for providing their time and expertise in helping us understand BEL. We acknowledge support of our research from Philip Morris International.

References

Jari Björne, Sofie Van Landeghem, Sampo Pyysalo, Tomoko Ohta, Filip Ginter, Yves Van de Peer, Sophia Ananiadou and Tapio Salakoski. 2012. PubMed-Scale Event Extraction for Post-Translational Modifications, Epigenetics and Protein Structural Relations. *Proceedings of BioNLP 2012, 82-90*

Leonid Chindelevitch, Daniel Ziemek, Ahmed Enayetallah, Ranjit Randhawa, Ben Sidders, Christoph Brockel and Enoch Huang. 2012. Causal reasoning on biological networks: interpreting transcriptional changes. *Bioinformatics. 28(8):1114-21.*

Emek Demir et al. 2010. The BioPAX community standard for pathway data sharing. *Nature biotechnology , 28(9):935–942.*

Chia-Ling Huang, John Lamb, Leonid Chindelevitch, Jarek Kostrowicki, Justin Guinney, Charles DeLisi and Daniel Ziemek. 2012. Correlation set analysis: detecting active regulators in disease populations using prior causal knowledge. *BMC Bioinformatics. 2012 13:46.*

Michael Hucka et al. 2003. The systems biology markup language (SBML): a medium for representation and exchange of biochemical network models. *Bioinformatics , 19(4):524–531.*

Jim-Dong Kim, Ngan Nguyen, Yue Wang, Jun'ichi Tsujii, Toshihisa Takagi and Akinori Yonezawa. 2012. The Genia Event and Protein Coreference tasks of the BioNLP Shared Task 2011. *BMC Bioinformatics. 13 Suppl 11:S1.*

Zhiyong Lu et al. 2011. The gene normalization task in BioCreative III. *BMC Bioinformatics , 12(Suppl 8):S2.*

Alexander A Morgan et al. 2008. Overview of BioCreative II gene normalization. *Genome Biol. 9 Suppl 2:S3.*

Tomoko Ohta,_ Sampo Pyysalo, Sophia Ananiadou and Jun'ichi Tsujii. 2011. Pathway Curation Support as an Information Extraction Task. *Proceedings of the Fourth International Symposium on Languages in Biology and Medicine (LBM 2011).*

Tomoko Ohta, Sampo Pyysalo and_Jun'ichi Tsujii. 2011. From Pathways to Biomolecular Events: Opportunities and Challenges. *Proceedings of the 2011 Workshop on Biomedical Natural Language Processing , ACL-HLT 2011, pages 105–113.*

Walter K. Schlage, et al. 2011. A computable cellular stress network model for non-diseased pulmonary and cardiovascular tissue. *BMC Syst Biol. 5:168.*

Ted Slater and Diana H. Song. 2012. Saved by the BEL: ringing in a common language for the life sciences. *Drug Discovery World Fall 2012 75:80*

Selventa 2012 Reverse Causal Reasoning Methods Whitepaper http://www.selventa.com/publications/white-papers

Sofia Van Landeghem, Jari Björne, Chih H Wei, Kai Hakala , Sampo Pyysalo, Sophia Ananiadou,

Hung-Yu Kao, Zhiyong Lu, Tapio Salakoski, Yves Van de Peer, and Filip Ginter. 2013. Large-Scale Event Extraction from Literature with Multi-Level Gene Normalization. *PLoS ONE 8(4): e55814.*

Exploring word class n-grams to measure language development in children

Gabriela Ramírez de la Rosa and **Thamar Solorio**
University of Alabama at Birmingham
Birmingham, AL 35294, USA
gabyrr,solorio@cis.uab.edu

Manuel Montes-y-Gómez
INAOE
Sta. Maria Tonantzintla, Puebla, Mexico
mmontesg@ccc.inaoep.mx

Yang Liu
The University of Texas at Dallas
Richardson, TX 75080, USA
yangl@hlt.utdallas.edu

Aquiles Iglesias
Temple University
Philadelphia, PA 19140, USA
iglesias@temple.edu

Lisa Bedore and **Elizabeth Peña**
The University of Texas at Austin
Austin, TX 78712, USA
lbedore,lizp@mail.utexas.edu

Abstract

We present a set of new measures designed to reveal latent information of language use in children at the lexico-syntactic level. We used these metrics to analyze linguistic patterns in spontaneous narratives from children developing typically and children identified as having a language impairment. We observed significant differences in the z-scores of both populations for most of the metrics. These findings suggest we can use these metrics to aid in the task of language assessment in children.

1 Introduction

The analysis of spontaneous language samples is an important task across a variety of fields. For instance, in language assessment this task can help to extract information regarding language proficiency (e.g. is the child typically developing or language impaired). In second language acquisition, language samples can help determine if a child's proficiency is similar to that of native speakers.

In recent years, we have started seeing a growing interest in the exploration of NLP techniques for the analysis of language samples in the clinical setting. For example, Sahakian and Snyder (2012) propose a set of linguistic measures for age prediction in children that combines three traditional measures from language assessment with a set of five data-driven measures from language samples of 7 children. A common theme in this emerging line of research is the study of the syntax in those language samples. For instance, to annotate data to be used in the study of language development (Sagae et al., 2005), or to build models to map utterances to their meaning, similar to what children do during the language acquisition stage (Kwiatkowski et al., 2012). In addition, language samples are also used for neurological assessment, as for example in (Roark et al., 2007; Roark et al., 2011) where they explored features such as Yngve and Frazier scores, together with features derived from automated parse trees to model syntactic complexity and surprisal. Similar features are used in the classification of language samples to discriminate between children developing typically and children suffering from autism or language impairment (Prud'hommeaux et al., 2011). In a similar line of research, machine learning and features inspired by NLP have been explored for the prediction of language status in bilingual children (Gabani et al., 2009; Solorio et al., 2011). More recent work has looked at the feasibility of scoring coherence in story narratives (Hassanali et al., 2012a) and also on the inclusion of coherence as an additional feature to boost prediction accuracy of language status (Hassanali et al., 2012b).

The contribution of our work consists on new metrics based on n-grams of Part of Speech (POS) tags for assessing language development in children that combine information at the lexical and syntactic levels. These metrics are designed to capture the lexical variability of specific syntactic constructions and thus could help to describe the level of language maturity in children. For instance, given two lists of examples of the use of determiner + noun: ⟨the dog, the frog, the tree⟩ and ⟨this dog, a frog, these trees⟩ we want to be able to say that the second one has more lexical variability than the first one for that grammatical pattern.

Our approach to compute these new metrics does not require any special treatment on the transcripts or special purpose parsers beyond a POS tagger. On the contrary, we provide a set of measures that in addition to being easy to interpret by practitioners, are also easy to compute.

2 Background and Motivation

To establish language proficiency, clinical researchers and practitioners rely on a variety of measures, such as number of different words, type-token ratio, distribution of part-of-speech tags, and mean length of sentences and words per minute (Lu, 2012; Yoon and Bhat, 2012; Chen and Zechner, 2011; Yang, 2011; Miller et al., 2006), to name a few. Most of these metrics can be categorized as low-level metrics since they only consider rates of different characteristics at the lexical level. These measures are helpful in the solution of several problems, for example, building automatic scoring models to evaluate non-native speech (Chen and Zechner, 2011). They can also be used as predictors of the rate of growth of English acquisition in specific populations, for instance, in typically developing (TD) and language impaired (LI) bilingual children (Rojas and Iglesias, 2012; Gutiérrez-Clellen et al., 2012). Among the most widely used metrics are mean length of utterance (MLU), a measure of syntactic complexity (Bedore et al., 2010), and measures of lexical productivity, such as the number of different words (NDW) and the child's ratio of functional words to content words (F/C) (Sahakian and Snyder, 2012).

MLU, NDW, F/C and some other low-level measures have demonstrated to be valuable in the assessment of language ability considering that practitioners often only need to focus on productivity, diversity of vocabulary, and sentence organization. Although useful, these metrics only provide superficial measures of the children's language skills that fail to capture detailed lexico-syntactic information. For example, in addition to knowing that a child is able to use specific verb forms in the right context, such as, third person singular present tense or regular past tense, knowledge about what are the most common patterns used by a child, or how many different lexical forms for *noun* + *verb* are present in the child's speech is needed because answering these questions provides more detailed information about the status of grammatical development. To fill in this need, we propose a set of measures that aim to capture language proficiency as a function of lexical variability in syntactic patterns. We analyze the information provided by our proposed metrics on a set of spontaneous story retells and evaluate empirically their potential use in language status prediction.

3 Proposed measures

To present the different metrics we propose in this study we begin with the definition of the following concepts:

A *syntactic pattern* p is an n-gram of part-of-speech tags denoted as $p = \langle t_1\ t_2\ ...\ t_n \rangle$, where t_i indicates the part-of-speech tag corresponding to the word at position i. For simplicity we use t_i^p to indicate the tag at position i from pattern p. Two examples of syntactic patterns of length two are 'DT NN' and 'DT JJ' [1].

A *lexical form* f is an n-gram of words. It is defined as $f = \langle w_1\ w_2\ ...\ w_n \rangle$, where w_i is the word at position i. Similarly to the previous definition, we use w_i^f to indicate the word at position i in a lexical form f.

A lexical form f corresponds to a syntactic pattern p if and only if $|f|$ is equal to $|p|$ and $\forall_k tag(w_k^f) = t_k^p$, where $tag()$ is a function that returns the part-of-speech of its argument. The set of lexical forms in a given transcript corresponding to a syntactic pattern p is denoted by LF^p. Two examples of lexical forms from the syntactic pattern 'DT NN' are 'the cat' and 'the frog'.

[1] We use the Penn Treebank POS tagset

DT	the (62), a (17), all (8), no(2), that (1)
NN	frog (16), boy(7), dog (6), boat (4), name (3), place (2), house (2), water (2), rabbit (2), noise (2), stick (1), tree (1), bye(1), floor (1), um (1), baby (1), forest (1), room (1), foot (1), rock (1), squirrel (1), back (1), rabb (1), card (1), one (1), present (1), dress (1), box (1), family (1)
VBD	saw (7), dropped (4), said (4), started (4), looked (3), kicked (3), called (3), found (2), took (2), got (2), jumped (2), heard (2), thought (1), turned (1), fell (1), waked (1), stood (1), wa (1), touched (1), told (1), scared (1), tur (1), haded (1), opened (1), shh (1)
DT NN	the frog (3), the dog (2), the place (2), the water (2), the boat (2), a noise (2), the forest (1), the rock (1), a tree (1), a present (1), a um (1), the card (1), the box (1), the rabb (1), the floor (1), the back (1), no one (1)
DT VBD	all started (2), all heard (1)

Table 1: Example of 5 syntactic patterns with their lists of lexical forms and the number of repetitions of each of them. This information corresponds to an excerpt of an example transcript. DT is the part-of-speech tag for determiner, NN for noun, and VBD for verb in past tense.

The *bag-of-words* associated to a syntactic pattern p is denoted as W^p. This set is composed of all the words from the lexical forms that correspond to the syntactic pattern p. It is formally defined as follows: $W^p = \{w | w \in f, f \in LF^p\}$. For example, the bag-of-words of the syntactic pattern 'DT NN' with lexical forms 'the cat' and 'the frog' is $\{the, cat, frog\}$.

Table 1 shows five syntactic patterns of a transcript's fragment. For each syntactic pattern in the transcript we show the list of its lexical forms and their frequency. We will use this example in the description of the measures in the following subsections.

3.1 Number of different lexical forms (NDLF)

Analogous to the number of different words (NDW), where words in the transcript are considered atomic units, we propose a metric where the atomic units are lexical forms. Then, we measure the number of different lexical forms used for each syntactic pattern in the transcript. Formally, given a syntactic pattern p and its set of lexical forms LF^p, the *number of different lexical forms* is computed as follows:

$$NDLF(p) = |LF^p| \quad (1)$$

This measure gives information about the number of different ways the child can combine words in order to construct a fragment of a speech that corresponds to a specific grammatical pattern. Research in language assessment has shown that when children are in the early acquisition stages of certain grammatical constructions they will use the patterns as "fixed expressions". As children master these constructions they are able to use these grammatical devices in different contexts, but also with different surface forms. Thereby, we could use this measure to discriminate the syntactic patterns the child has better command of from those that might still be problematic and used infrequently or with a limited combination of surface forms. For example, from the information on Table 1 we see that $NDLF(DT\ NN) = 17$, and $NDLF(DT\ VBD) = 2$. This seems to indicate that the child has a better command of the grammatical construction *determiner* + *noun* (DT NN) and can thus produce more different lexical forms of this pattern than *determiner* + *verb* (DT + VBD). But also, we may use this measure to identify rare patterns, that are unlikely to be found in a typically developing population.

3.2 Lexical forms distribution (LFdist)

Following the idea of lexical forms as atomic units, *NDLF* allows to know the different lexical forms present in the transcripts. But we do not know the distribution of use of each lexical form for a specific syntactic pattern. In other words, NDLF tells us the different surface forms observed for each syntactic pattern, but it does not measure the frequency of use of each of these lexical forms, nor whether each of these forms are used at similar rates. We propose to use LFdist to provide information about the distribution of use for LF^p, the set of lexical forms observed for the syntactic pattern p. We believe that uniform distributions can be indicative of syntactic structures that the child has mastered, while uneven distributions can reveal structures that the child has only memorized (i.e. the child uses a fixed and small set of lexical forms). To measure this distribution we use the entropy of each syntactic pattern. In particular, given a syntactic pattern p and its set of lexical forms LF^p, the *lexical form distribution* is computed as follows:

$$LFdist(p) = - \sum_{f_i \in LF^p} prob(f_i) \log prob(f_i) \quad (2)$$

where

$$prob(f_i) = \frac{count(f_i)}{\sum_{f_k \in LF^p} count(f_k)} \quad (3)$$

and $count()$ is a function that returns the frequency of its argument. Larger values of *LFdist* indicate a greater difficulty in the prediction of the lexical form that is being used under a specific grammatical pattern. For instance, in the example of Table 1, $LFdist(DT\ VBD) = 0.91$ and $LFdist(DT\ NN) = 3.97$. This indicates that the distribution in the use of lexical forms for *determiner + noun* is more uniform than the use of lexical forms for *determiner + verb*, which implies that for *determiner + verb* there are some lexical forms that are more frequently used than others[2]. Syntactic patterns with small values of *LFdist* could flag grammatical constructions the child does not feel comfortable manipulating and thus might still be in the acquisition stage of language learning.

3.3 Lexical variation (LEX)

Until now we are considering lexical forms as atomic units. This could lead to overestimating the real lexical richness in the sample, in particular for syntactic patterns of length greater than 1. To illustrate this consider the syntactic pattern $p = \langle DT\ NN \rangle$ and suppose we have the following set of lexical forms for $p = \{$'the frog', 'a frog', 'a dog', 'the dog'$\}$. The value for $NDLF(p) = 4$. But how many of these eight words are in fact different? That is the type of distinction we want to make with the next proposed measure: LEX, that is also an adaptation of type-token ratio (Lu, 2012) used in the area of communication disorders but computed over each grammatical pattern. For this example, we want to be able to find that the lexical variation of $\langle DT\ NN \rangle$ is 0.5 (because there are only four different words out of eight). Formally, given a syntactic pattern p, its set of lexical forms LF^p, and the bag-of-words W^p, the *lexical variation* is defined as shown in Equation 4.

[2]We recognize that this is an oversimplification of the entropy measure since the number of outcomes will most likely be different for each syntactic pattern.

$$LEX(p) = \frac{|W^p|}{|LF^p| * n} \quad (4)$$

Note that $|LF^p| = NDLF(p)$, and n is the length of the syntactic pattern p. In Table 1 the lexical variation of the pattern *'determiner + noun'* (DT+NN) is equal to 0.58 ($\frac{20}{17*2}$), and for *determiner + verb* (DT+VBD) is equal to 0.75 ($\frac{3}{2*2}$). That means 58% of total words used under the pattern 'DT+NN' are different, in comparison with the 75% for 'DT+VBD'. In general, the closer the value of *LEX* is to 1, there is less overlap between the words in the lexical forms for that pattern. Our hypothesis behind this measure is that for the same syntactic pattern TD children may have less overlap of words than children with LI, e.g. less overlap indicates the use of a more diverse set of words.

3.4 Lexical use of syntactic knowledge (LexSyn)

With LEX we hope to accomplish the characterization of lexical richness of syntactic patterns assuming that each part-of-speech has a similar number of possible lexical forms. We assume as well that less overlap in the words used for the same grammatical pattern represents a more developed language than that with more overlap. However the definition of LEX overlooks a well known fact about language: different word classes have a different range of possibilities as their lexical forms. Consider open class items, such as nouns and verbs, where the lexicon is large and keeps growing. In contrast, closed class items, such as prepositions and determiners are fixed and have a very small number of lexical forms. Therefore it seems unfair to assign equal weight to the overlap of words for these different classes. To account for this phenomenon, we propose a new measure that includes the information about the syntactic knowledge that the child shows for each part of speech. That is, we weigh the level of overlap for specific grammatical constructions according to the lexicon for the specific word classes involved. Since we limit our analysis to the language sample at hand, we define the ceiling of the lexical richness of a specific word class to be the total number of different surface forms found in the transcript. In particular, given a syntactic pattern $p = \langle t_1\ t_2\ ...\ t_n \rangle$, with its set of lexical forms LF^p, the lexical use of syntactic knowledge is defined as:

$$LexSyn(p) = \frac{1}{n}\sum_{i=1}^{n}\frac{|w_i^f|f \in LF^p|}{NDLF(t_i^p)} \quad (5)$$

where the numerator is the size of the set of words in the i-th position in all the lexical forms. Note that this measure does not make sense for syntactic patterns of length < 2. Instead, syntactic patterns of length 1 were used to identify the syntactic knowledge of the child by using the NDLF of each POS in p. In the example of Table 1, $LexSyn(DT\ NN) = 0.59$. This value corresponds to the sum of the number of different determiners used in position 1 for LF^p divided by the total number of different determiners that this child produced in the sample (for this case, the number of determiners that this child produced is given by *NDLF*(*DT*), that is 5), plus the number of different nouns used under this syntactic pattern over the total number of nouns produced by the child (*NDLF*(*NN*)=29). The complete calculation of $LexSyn(DT\ NN) = \frac{1}{2} * (\frac{3}{5} + \frac{17}{29}) = 0.59$. This contrasts with the value of *LexSyn* for the pattern '*determiner + verb*', $LexSyn(DT\ VBD) = \frac{1}{2} * (\frac{1}{5} + \frac{2}{25}) = 0.14$ that seems to indicate that the child has more experience combining determiners and nouns than determiners and verbs. Perhaps this child has had limited exposure to other patterns combining determiner and verb, or this pattern is at a less mature stage in the linguistic repertoire of the child.

Children with LI tend to exhibit a less developed command of syntax than their TD cohorts. Syntactic patterns with large values of LexSyn show a high versatility in the use of those syntactic patterns. However, since the syntactic reference is taken from the same child, this versatility is relative only to what is observed in that single transcript. For instance, suppose that the total number of different determiners observed in the child's transcript is 1. Then any time the child uses that determiner in a syntactic pattern, the knowledge of this class, according to our metric, will be 100%, which is correct, but this might not be enough to determine if the syntactic knowledge of the child for this grammatical class corresponds to age expectations for a typically developing child. In order to improve the measurement of the lexical use of syntactic knowledge we propose the measure **LexSynEx**, that instead of using the information of the same child to define the coverage of use for a specific word class, it uses the information observed for a held out set of transcripts from TD children. This variation allows the option of moving the point of reference to a specific cohort, according to what is needed.

4 Data set

The data used in this research is part of an ongoing study of language impairment in Spanish-English speaking children (Peña et al., 2003). From this study we used a set of 175 children with a mean age of about 70 months. Language status of these children was determined via expert judgment by three bilingual certified speech-language pathologists. At the end of the data collection period, the experts reviewed child records in both languages including language samples, tests protocols, and parent and teacher questionnaire data. They made independent judgments about children's lexical, morphosyntactic, and narrative performance in each language. Finally, they made an overall judgment about children's language ability using a 6 point scale (severely language impaired to above normal impairment). If at least two examiners rated children's language ability with mild, moderate or severe impairment they were assigned to the LI group. Percent agreement among the three examiners was 90%. As a result of this process, 20 children were identified by the clinical researchers as having LI, while the remaining 155 were identified as typically developing (TD).

The transcripts were gathered following standard procedures for collection of spontaneous language samples in the field of communication disorders. Using a wordless picture book, the children were asked to narrate the story. The two books used were 'A boy, a dog, and a frog' (Mayer, 1967) and 'Frog, where are you?' (Mayer, 1969). For each child in the sample, 4 transcripts of story narratives were collected, 2 in each language. In this study we use only the transcripts where English was the target language.

5 Procedure

The purpose of the following analysis is to investigate the different aspects in the child's language that can be revealed by the proposed metrics. All our measures are based on POS tags. We used the Charniak parser (Charniak, 2000) to generate the POS tags of the transcripts. For all the results reported here we removed the utterances from the interrogators and use all utterances by the children. From the 155 TD instances, we randomly selected 20, that together with the 20 instances with LI form the test set. The remaining 135 TD instances were used as the normative population, our training set.

After the POS tagging process, we extracted the set of syntactic patterns with length equal to 1, 2, 3 and 4 that appear in at least 80% of the transcripts in the training set. The 80% threshold was chosen with the goal of preserving the content that is most likely to represent the TD population.

6 Analysis of the proposed measures and implications

Figure 1 shows 5 plots corresponding to each of our proposed measures. Each graph shows a comparison between the average values of the TD and the LI populations. The x-axis in the graphs represents all the syntactic patterns gathered from the training set that appeared on the test data, and the y-axis represents the difference in the z-score values of each measure from the test set. The x-axis is sorted in descending order according to the z-score differences between values of TD and LI.

The most relevant discovery is that *NDFL*, *LFdist*, *LexSyn* and *LexSynEx* show a wider gap in the z-scores between the TD and LI populations for most of the syntactic patterns analyzed. This difference is easy to note visually as most of the TD patterns tend to have larger values, while the ones for children with LI have lower scores. Therefore, it seems our measures are indeed capturing relevant information that characterizes the language of the TD population.

Analyzing *LEX* from Figure 1, we see that most of the *LEX* values are positive, for both TD and LI instances, and we cannot observe marked differences between them. That might be a consequence of assuming all word classes can have an equivalent number of different lexical forms. Once we weigh each POS tag in the pattern by the word forms the child has used (as in *LexSyn* and *LexSynEx*), noticeable differences across the two groups emerge. When we include syntactic knowledge of a group of children (as in *LexSynEx*), those similarities disappear. This behavior highlights the need for a combined lexico-syntactic measure that can describe latent information about language usage in children.

For building an intervention plan that helps to improve child language skills, practitioners could

LFdist
verb (3rd person singular present)
verb (past tense) + personal pronoun
personal pronoun + auxiliary verb + adverb
verb (gerund)
NDLF
there + auxiliary verb
personal pronoun + auxiliary verb + adverb
adjective + noun
verb (3rd person singular present)
LexSyn
verb (past tense) + personal pronoun
personal pronoun + verb (past tense) + personal pronoun
personal pronoun + auxiliary verb + adverb
there + auxiliary verb
LexSynEx
personal pronoun + auxiliary verb + adverb
personal pronoun + verb (past tense) + personal pronoun
verb (past tense) + personal pronoun
there + auxiliary verb

Table 2: List of syntactic patterns with the biggest difference between LI and TD in 4 measures: *LFdist*, *NDLF*, and *LexSyn* and *LexSynEx*.

use the knowledge of specific grammatical constructions that need to be emphasized –those that seem to be problematic for the LI group. These structures can be identified by pulling the syntactic patterns with the largest difference in z-scores from the TD population. Table 2 shows a list of syntactic patterns with small values for LI and the largest differences between LI and TD instances in the test set. As the table indicates, most of the syntactic patterns have length greater than 1. This is not surprising since we aimed for developing measures of higher-order analysis that can complement the level of information provided by commonly used metrics in language assessment (as in the case of MLU, NDW or F/C). The table also shows that while each measure identifies a different subset of syntactic patterns as relevant, some syntactic patterns emerge in all the metrics. For instance, *personal pronoun + auxiliary verb + adverb* and *there + auxiliary verb*. This repetition highlights the importance of those grammatical constructions. But the differences also show that the metrics complement each other. In general, the syntactic patterns in the list represent complex grammatical constructions where children with LI are showing a less advanced command of language use.

Table 3 shows some statistics about the lexical forms present under *pronoun + verb (3rd person singular present) + verb (gerund or present participle)* (PP VBZ VBG) in all our data set. The last

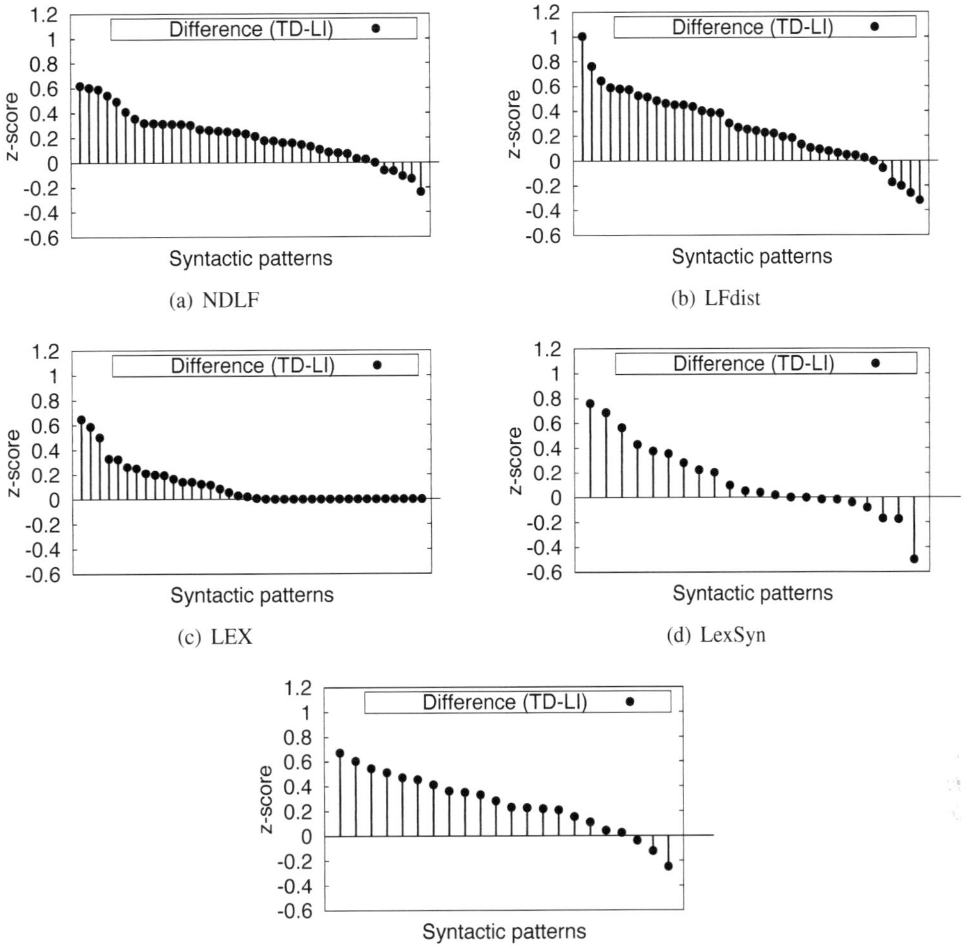

(a) NDLF

(b) LFdist

(c) LEX

(d) LexSyn

(e) LexSynEx

Figure 1: Performance comparison of the proposed measures for the TD and LI groups. Each data point represents the difference in z-scores between the average values of the TD and LI instances in the test set.

row in that table presents an example of the lexical forms used by two children. Note that for the child with LI, there is only one lexical form: *he is touching*. On the other hand, the TD child is using the grammatical pattern with six different surface forms. Clinical practitioners can take this information and design language tasks that emphasize the use of 'PP VBZ VBG' constructions.

	TD	LI
number of PP	6	5
number of VBZ	3	2
number of VBG	7	4
Example (instances: td-0156 and li-3022)	she is putting she is going he is pushing she is looking she is carrying she is playing	he is touching

Table 3: Statistics of the surface forms for the grammatical pattern *PP VBZ VBG*.

6.1 Analysis of correlations among measures

To analyze the level of overlap between our measures we computed correlation coefficients among them. The results are shown in Table 4.

The results from the correlation analysis are not that surprising. They show that closely related measures are highly to moderately correlated. For instance, LEX and *eLEX* have a correlation of 0.69, and *LexSynEx* and *LexSyn* have a correlation of 0.61. *NDLF* and *LFdist* showed a positive correlation score of 0.81. This high correlation hints to the fact that as the number of lexical forms increases, so does the gap between their fre-

	LFdist	NDLF	LEX	eLEX	LexSyn	LexSynEx
LFdist	1.00					
NDLF	0.81	1.00				
LEX	-0.53	-0.31	1.00			
eLEX	-0.54	-0.43	0.69	1.00		
LexSyn	0.07	0.02	-0.23	-0.10	1.00	
LexSynEx	-0.02	-0.03	-0.08	-0.03	0.61	1.00

Table 4: Correlation matrix for the proposed metrics.

quency of use. While this may be a common phenomenon of language use, it does not have a negative effect since the same effect will be observed in both groups of children and we care to see the differences in performance between a TD and an LI population.

For all other pairs of measures, the correlation scores were in the range of $[-0.5, 0.1]$. It was interesting to note that *LexSyn* showed the lowest correlation with the rest of the measures (between $[-0.11, 0.01]$).

Correlation coefficients between our metrics and MLU, NDW, and F/C were computed separately for syntactic patterns of different lengths. However all the different matrices showed the same correlation patterns. We found a *high* correlation between MLU and NDW, but low correlation with all our proposed measures, except for one case: NDW and LexSyn seemed to be highly correlated ($\sim$-0.7). Interestingly, we noted that despite the high correlation between MLU and NDW, MLU and LexSyn showed weak correlation ($\sim$-0.4). Overall, the findings from this analysis support the use of our metrics as complimentary measures for child language assessment.

7 Conclusions and future work

We proposed a set of new measures that were developed to characterize the lexico-syntactic variability of child language. Each measure aims to find information that is not captured by traditional measures used in communication disorders.

Our study is still preliminary in nature and requires an in depth evaluation and analysis with a larger pool of subjects. However the results presented are encouraging. The set of experiments we discussed showed that TD and LI children have significant differences in performance according to our metrics and thus these metrics can be used to enrich models of language trajectories in child language acquisition. Another potential use of metrics similar to those proposed here is the design of targeted intervention practices.

The scripts to compute the metrics as described in this paper are available to the research community by contacting the authors. However, the simplicity of the metrics makes it easy for anyone to implement, and it certainly makes it easy for clinical researchers to interpret.

Our proposed metrics are a contribution to the set of already known metrics for language assessment. The goal of these new metrics is not to replace existing ones, but to complement what is already available with concise information about higher-order syntactic constructions in the repertoire of TD children.

We are interested in evaluating the use of our metrics in a longitudinal study. We believe they are a promising framework to represent language acquisition trajectories.

Acknowledgments

This research was partially funded by NSF under awards 1018124 and 1017190. The first author also received partial funding from CONACyT.

References

Lisa M. Bedore, Elizabeth D. Peña, Ronald B. Gillam, and Tsung-Han Ho. 2010. Language sample measures and language ability in Spanish-English bilingual kindergarteners. *Journal of Communication Disorders*, 43:498–510.

Eugene Charniak. 2000. A maximum-entropy-inspired parser. In *Proceedings of the 1st North American chapter of the Association for Computational Linguistics conference*, NAACL 2000, pages 132–139, Stroudsburg, PA, USA. Association for Computational Linguistics.

Miao Chen and Klaus Zechner. 2011. Computing and evaluating syntactic complexity features for automated scoring of spontaneous non-native speech. In *Proceedings of the 49th Annual Meeting of the Association for Computational Linguistics: Human Language Technologies - Volume 1*, HLT '11, pages 722–731, Stroudsburg, PA, USA. Association for Computational Linguistics.

Keyur Gabani, Melissa Sherman, Thamar Solorio, Yang Liu, Lisa M. Bedore, and Elizabeth D. Peña. 2009. A corpus-based approach for the prediction of language impairment in monolingual English and Spanish-English bilingual children. In *Proceedings of Human Language Technologies: The 2009 Annual Conference of the North American Chapter of the Association for Computational Linguistics*, NAACL '09, pages 46–55, Stroudsburg, PA, USA. Association for Computational Linguistics.

V. Gutiérrez-Clellen, G. Simon-Cereijido, and M. Sweet. 2012. Predictors of second language acquisition in Latino children with specific language impairment. *American Journal of Speech Language Pathology*, 21(1):64–77.

Khairun-nisa Hassanali, Yang Liu, and Thamar Solorio. 2012a. Coherence in child language narratives: A case study of annotation and automatic prediction of coherence. In *Proceedings of 3rd Workshop on Child, Computer and Interaction (WOCCI 2012)*.

Khairun-nisa Hassanali, Yang Liu, and Thamar Solorio. 2012b. Evaluating NLP features for automatic prediction of language impairment using child speech transcripts. In *Interspeech*.

Tom Kwiatkowski, Sharon Goldwater, Luke Zettelmoyer, and Mark Steedman. 2012. A probabilistic model of syntactic and semantic acquisition from child-directed utterances and their meanings. In *Proceedings of the 13th Conference of the European Chapter of the Association for Computational Linguistics*, pages 234–244, Avignon, France. Association for Computational Linguistics.

Xiaofei Lu. 2012. The relationship of lexical richness to the quality of ESL learners' oral narratives. *The Modern Language Journal*, 96(2):190–208.

Mercer Mayer. 1967. *A boy, a dog, and a frog*. Dial Press.

Mercer Mayer. 1969. *Frog, where are you?* Dial Press.

Jon F. Miller, John Heilmann, Ann Nockerts, Aquiles Iglesias, Leah Fabiano, and David J. Francis. 2006. Oral language and reading in bilingual children. *Learning Disabilities Research and Practice*, 21:30–43.

Elizabeth D. Peña, Lisa M. Bedore, Ronald B. Gillam, and Thomas Bohman. 2003. Diagnostic markers of language impairment in bilingual children. Grant awarded by the NIDCH, NIH.

Emily T. Prud'hommeaux, Brian Roark, Lois M. Black, and Jan van Santen. 2011. Classification of atypical language in autism. In *Proceedings of the 2nd Workshop on Cognitive Modeling and Computational Linguistics*, pages 88–96, Portland, Oregon, USA, June. Association for Computational Linguistics.

Brian Roark, Margaret Mitchell, and Kristy Hollingshead. 2007. Syntactic complexity measures for detecting mild cognitive impairment. In *Biological, translational, and clinical language processing*, pages 1–8, Prague, Czech Republic, June. Association for Computational Linguistics.

Brian Roark, Margaret Mitchell, John-Paul Hosom, Kristy Hollingshead, and Jeffrey Kaye. 2011. Spoken language derived measures for detecting mild cognitive impairment. *IEEE Transcations on Audio, Speech, and Language Processing*, 19(7):2081–2090, September.

Raúl Rojas and Aquiles Iglesias. 2012. The language growth of Spanish-speaking English language learners. *Child Development*.

Kenji Sagae, Alon Lavie, and Brian MacWhinney. 2005. Automatic measurement of syntactic development in child language. In *Proceedings of the 43rd Annual Meeting of the Association for Computational Linguistics*, ACL '05, pages 197–204, Stroudsburg, PA, USA. Association for Computational Linguistics.

Sam Sahakian and Benjamin Snyder. 2012. Automatically learning measures of child language development. In *ACL*, pages 95–99. The Association for Computational Linguistics.

Thamar Solorio, Melissa Sherman, Y. Liu, Lisa Bedore, Elizabeth Peña, and A. Iglesias. 2011. Analyzing language samples of Spanish-English bilingual children for the automated prediction of language dominance. *Natural Language Engineering*, pages 367–395.

Charles Yang. 2011. A statistical test for grammar. In *Proceedings of the 2nd Workshop on Cognitive Modeling and Computational Linguistics*, pages 30–38, Portland, Oregon, USA, June. Association for Computational Linguistics.

Su-Youn Yoon and Suma Bhat. 2012. Assessment of ESL learners' syntactic competence based on similarity measures. In *EMNLP-CoNLL*, pages 600–608. Association for Computational Linguistics.

Adapting a parser to clinical text by simple pre-processing rules

Maria Skeppstedt
Dept. of Computer and Systems Sciences (DSV)
Stockholm University, Forum 100, 164 40 Kista, Sweden
mariask@dsv.su.se

Abstract

Sentence types typical to Swedish clinical text were extracted by comparing sentence part-of-speech tag sequences in clinical and in standard Swedish text. Parsings by a syntactic dependency parser, trained on standard Swedish, were manually analysed for the 33 sentence types most typical to clinical text. This analysis resulted in the identification of eight error types, and for two of these error types, pre-processing rules were constructed to improve the performance of the parser. For all but one of the ten sentence types affected by these two rules, the parsing was improved by pre-processing.

1 Introduction

Input speed is often prioritised over completeness and grammatical correctness in health record narratives. This has the effect that lower results are achieved when parsers trained on standard text are applied on clinical text (Hassel et al., 2011).

Syntactic annotations to use for training a parser on clinical text are, however, expensive (Albright et al., 2013) and treebanking large clinical corpora is therefore not always an option for smaller languages (Haverinen et al., 2009). There are studies on adaptation of standard parsers to the biomedical domain, focusing on overcoming difficulties due to different vocabulary use (Candito et al., 2011). How to overcome difficulties due to syntactic differences between standard and clinical language is, however, less studied. The aim of this study was therefore to explore syntactic differences between clinical language and standard language and to analyse errors made by the parser on sentence types typical to the clinical domain. To exemplify how this knowledge can be used, two simple pre-processing rules for improving parser performance on these typical sentences were developed.

2 Method

To find sentence types typical to the clinical domain, a comparison to standard text was conducted. The used clinical corpus was: free-text entries from assessment sections, thus mostly containing diagnostic reasoning, that were randomly selected from the Stockholm EPR corpus[1] (Dalianis et al., 2009); and the used standard corpus was: Läkartidningen (Kokkinakis, 2012), a journal from the Swedish Medical Association.

The comparison was carried out on part-of-speech sequences on a sentence level. The part-of-speech tagger Granska (Carlberger and Kann, 1999), having an accuracy of 92% on clinical text (Hassel et al., 2011), was applied on both corpora, and the proportion of each sentence tag sequence was calculated. 'Sentence tag sequence' refers here to the parts-of-speech corresponding to each token in the sentence, combined to one unit, e.g. '*dt nn vb nn mad*' for the sentence '*The patient has headache.*'. Pronouns, nouns and proper names were collapsed into one class, as they often play the same role in the sentence, and as terms specific to the clinical domain are tagged inconsistently as either nouns or proper names (Hassel et al., 2011). As sentences from Läkartidningen not ending with a full stop or a question mark are less likely to be full sentences, they were not included, in order to obtain a more contrasting corpus.

A 95% confidence interval for the proportion of each sentence combination was computed using the Wilson score interval, and the difference between the minimum frequency in the clinical corpus and the maximum frequency in the standard language corpus was calculated. Thereby, statistics for the minimum difference between the two domains was achieved.

[1]This research has been approved by the Regional Ethical Review Board in Stockholm (Etikprövningsnämnden i Stockholm), permission number 2012/834-31/5.

A total of 458 436 sentence types were found in the clinical corpus. Of these, there were 1 736 types significantly more frequent in the clinical corpus than in the standard corpus, not having overlapping confidence interval for the proportions. 33 sentence types, to which 10% of the sentences in the corpus belonged, had more than 0.1 percentage points difference between minimum frequency in the clinical corpus and maximum frequency in the standard language corpus. For each of these 33 sentence types, 30 sentences were randomly extracted and the dependency parser MaltParser (Nivre et al., 2009), pre-trained on Talbanken (Nivre et al., 2006) using the algorithm *stacklazy* (Nivre et al., 2009), was applied to these part-of-speech tagged sentences. Error categories were manually identified, using MaltEval (Nilsson and Nivre, 2008) for visualisation.

Given the identified error categories, two pre-processing rules were constructed. These were then evaluated by applying the same pre-trained parser model on pre-processed sentences as on original sentences. A manual analysis was performed on a subset of the sentences that were differently parsed after pre-processing.

3 Results

Although only one sentence type was a full sentence (*nn vb pp nn mad*), most sentences were correctly parsed. Omitted words could be inferred from context, and therefore also the intended syntax. Eight error types, to which most errors belonged, were identified: 1) Abbreviated words ending with a full stop interpreted as the last word in a sentence, resulting in an incorrect sentence splitting. 2) Abbreviations incorrectly labelled as nouns by Granska, resulting in sentences exclusively containing nouns. 3) Adjectives not recognised as such (often because they were abbreviated), resulting in AT relations being labelled as DT relations. 4) A general adverbial relation incorrectly assigned an adverb of place or time relation or vice versa. 5) The first word in compound expressions parsed as a determiner to the second. 6) *nn pp nn pp nn mad* sentences for which a preposition had been incorrectly attributed. 7) The sentence type *nn jj* (noun adjective), for which most evaluated sentences were incorrectly parsed. 8) An omitted initial subject, resulting in the object incorrectly being parsed as the subject of the sentence.

Pre-processing rules were constructed for error types 7) and 8). As a verb in the middle of *nn jj*-sentences (in most cases copula) was left out, the first pre-processing rule added copula in the middle of these sentences. The second rule added the pronoun *I* as the first word in sentences starting with a verb, as this was the most frequently left out subject, along with the slightly less frequent omission, *patient*. The rules were not applied on sentences ending with a question mark.

10 (out of 33) sentence types were affected by the two rules. The proportion of those receiving a different parsing after pre-processing is shown in the column *Changed* in Table 1. A subset of these sentences, for which the parsing was changed, was manually classified as either incorrect (= containing at least one parsing or labelling error) or completely correct.

For sentences classified as incorrect, a more granular comparison between the original and the modified parsing was carried out. For these sentences, the difference in average unlabelled (*UAS*) and labelled (*LAS*) attachment score between the pre-processed and the original parsing was computed. A positive value indicates that although the pre-processing resulted in some incorrectly parsed sentences, these sentences were improved by pre-processing. The sentence types *vb pp nn nn mad* and *vb pp nn pp nn mad* were thus slightly improved by the pre-processing, although they had a low proportion of correctly parsed sentences.

A negative value for attachment score difference, on the other hand, indicates that parsing for the incorrectly parsed sentences was impaired by pre-processing. As these figures only apply to sentences incorrectly parsed after pre-processing, this means that although e.g. the type *vb ab nn mad* has negative UAS and LAS difference, this only applies to the 3 sentences that were incorrectly parsed by the pre-processed version.

With one important exception, sentences modified by pre-processing, were either a) given a completely correct parsing and labelling in between 64% and 100% of the cases, or were b) slightly improved by pre-processing. A reasonable simplification in this case is that there can only be one correct parsing of a sentence, as although there might be occurrences of syntactically ambiguous sentences, it is unlikely that their interpretation is not given by the context in the closed domain of language used for diagnostic reasoning.

Given this simplification, this means that a sentence was transformed from an incorrectly parsed sentence to a correctly parsed sentence in 64% or more of the cases, when pre-processing was applied. The difference in attachment score shows that the parsing is not drastically degraded for the rest of the sentences, although it mostly changed to a worse parsing. The overall effect of applying pre-processing is therefore positive. Sentences of the type *vb nn pp nn mad* is the important exception to this positive effect, important as 54% of the sentences belonging to this type received a different parsing after pre-processing and as 0.39% of the sentences in the corpus belong to this type. Only 61% of the pre-processed sentences of this type had a correct unlabelled parsing and only 32% had a correct labelled parsing. Many of these sentences were similar to *Writes a prescription of Trombyl*, for which *of Trombyl* incorrectly is given the word *write* as the head after pre-processing.

Almost all of the sentences of the type *nn jj mad* were correctly parsed when a copula was inserted between the noun and the adjective. Of the other types of sentences that improved, many improved by an incorrectly labelled subject relation being changed to an object relation. There were, however, also improvements because some adverbs of place and time were correctly labelled after the pre-processing rules had been applied.

4 Discussion

Even if quantitative data is given in Table 1, the core of this study has been to use a qualitative approach: searching for different categories of errors rather than determining accuracy figures, and investigating whether pre-processing has a positive effect, rather than determining the final accuracy.

The next step is to apply the findings of this study for developing a small treebank of clinical text. A possible method for facilitating syntactic annotation is to present pre-annotated data to the annotator (Brants and Plaehn, 2000) for correction or for selection among several alternatives. As the overall effect of applying pre-processing were improved parsings, the pre-annotation could be carried out by applying a model trained on standard language and improve it with the pre-processing rules investigated here. The other identified error types also give suggestions of how to improve the parser, improvements that should be attempted before using a parser trained on standard language for pre-annotation. Error types 1), 2) and partly 3) were due to abbreviations negatively affecting part-of-speech tagging and sentence splitting. Therefore, abbreviation expansion would be a possible way of improving the parser. That available medical vocabularies also could be useful is shown by error type 5), which was due to the parser failing to recognise compound expressions.

Of the sentences in the corpus, only 10% belonged to the analysed sentence types, and even fewer were affected by the evaluated pre-processing rules. It is, however, likely that the two developed pre-processing rules have effects on all sentence types lacking a verb or starting with a verb, thus effecting more sentence type than those included in this study. This is worth studying, as is also syntactic differences for shorter part-of-speech sequences than sentence level sequences.

Another possible method for domain adaptation would be to adapt the training data to construct a model more suitable for parsing clinical text. Instead of applying pre-processing, sentences in the training data could be modified to more closely resemble sentences in clinical text, e.g. by removing words in the treebank corpus to achieve the incomplete sentences typical to clinical text. Differences in vocabulary has not been included in this study, but methods from previous studies for bridging differences in vocabulary between the general and medical domain could also be applied for improving parser performance.

For supplementing a treebank to also include sentences typical to clinical text, some of the methods investigated here for extracting such sentence types, could be employed

5 Conclusion

Sentence types typical to clinical text were extracted, and eight categories of error types were identified. For two of these error types, pre-processing rules were devised and evaluated. For four additional error types, techniques for text-normalisation were suggested. As the pre-processing rules had an overall positive effect on the parser performance, it was suggested that a model for syntactic pre-annotation of clinical text should employ the evaluated text pre-processing.

Acknowledgements

Many thanks to Joakim Nivre and to the four reviewers for their many valuable comments.

Sentence type	# In test	% Changed	# Manually classified	% Correct unlabelled (labelled)	# Incorrect unlabelled (labelled)	pp UAS(LAS) difference among incorrect
a) vb nn mad	1181	30%	40	100 (100)%	0 (0)	
vb jj nn mad	317	13%	32	100 (94) %	0 (2)	
nn jj mad	316	100%	200	94 (94) %	12 (12)	
vb ab nn mad	256	33%	31	90 (90) %	3 (3)	-25 (-25) pp
vb pp nn mad	674	5%	27	100 (85) %	0 (4)	(-19) pp
vb ab pp nn mad	222	21%	30	100 (70) %	0 (9)	(+7) pp
vb pp jj nn mad	207	7%	14	100 (64) %	0 (5)	(-16) pp
b) vb pp nn nn mad	197	5%	9	22 (11) %	7 (8)	0 (+10) pp
vb pp nn pp nn mad	232	5%	12	75 (4) %	3 (12)	0 (+2) pp
c) vb nn pp nn mad	813	54%	28	61 (32) %	11 (19)	-20 (-15) pp

Table 1: *In test*: Number of sentences in test set of this type. *Changed*: Proportion of sentences that received a different parsing after pre-processing had been applied. *Manually classified*: Number of manually classified sentences. *Correct*: Proportion of sentences that were correctly parsed (and labelled) after pre-processing had been applied. *# Incorrect:* Number of incorrectly parsed (and labelled) sentences after pre-processing. *UAS (LAS) difference*: For these incorrect sentences: The difference in UAS, unlabelled attachment score, (and LAS, labelled attachment score) before and after pre-processing. (For sentence types with more than 90% correct sentences, this difference was not calculated.)

References

Daniel Albright, Arrick Lanfranchi, Anwen Fredriksen, William F Styler, 4th, Colin Warner, Jena D Hwang, Jinho D Choi, Dmitriy Dligach, Rodney D Nielsen, James Martin, Wayne Ward, Martha Palmer, and Guergana K Savova. 2013. Towards comprehensive syntactic and semantic annotations of the clinical narrative. *J Am Med Inform Assoc*, Jan.

Thorsten Brants and Oliver Plaehn. 2000. Interactive corpus annotation. In *LREC*. European Language Resources Association.

Marie Candito, Enrique H. Anguiano, and Djamé Seddah. 2011. A Word Clustering Approach to Domain Adaptation: Effective Parsing of Biomedical Texts. In *Proceedings of the 12th International Conference on Parsing Technologies*, pages 37–42, Dublin, Ireland, October. Association for Computational Linguistics.

Johan Carlberger and Viggo Kann. 1999. Implementing an efficient part-of-speech tagger. *Software–Practice and Experience*, 29:815–832.

Hercules Dalianis, Martin Hassel, and Sumithra Velupillai. 2009. The Stockholm EPR Corpus - Characteristics and Some Initial Findings. In *Proceedings of ISHIMR 2009, Evaluation and implementation of e-health and health information initiatives: international perspectives. 14th International Symposium for Health Information Management Research, Kalmar, Sweden*, pages 243–249.

Martin Hassel, Aron Henriksson, and Sumithra Velupillai. 2011. Something Old, Something New - Applying a Pre-trained Parsing Model to Clinical Swedish. In *Proceedings of NODALIDA'11 - 18th Nordic Conference on Computational Linguistics*, Riga, Latvia, May 11-13.

Katri Haverinen, Filip Ginter, Veronika Laippala, and Tapio Salakoski. 2009. Parsing Clinical Finnish: Experiments with Rule-Based and Statistical Dependency Parsers. In Kristiina Jokinen and Eckhard Bick, editors, *Proceedings of NODALIDA'09, Odense, Denmark*, pages 65–72.

Dimitrios Kokkinakis. 2012. The journal of the Swedish medical association - a corpus resource for biomedical text mining in Swedish. In *The Third Workshop on Building and Evaluating Resources for Biomedical Text Mining (BioTxtM), an LREC Workshop. Turkey*.

Jens Nilsson and Joakim Nivre. 2008. Malteval: An evaluation and visualization tool for dependency parsing. In *Proceedings of the Sixth International Language Resources and Evaluation. LREC*, pages 161–166.

Joakim Nivre, Jens Nilsson, and Johan Hall. 2006. Talbanken05: A Swedish treebank with phrase structure and dependency annotation. In *Proceedings of the fifth international conference on Language Resources and Evaluation (LREC 2006)*, pages 24–26.

Joakim Nivre, Marco Kuhlmann, and Johan Hall. 2009. An improved oracle for dependency parsing with online reordering. In *Proceedings of the 11th International Conference on Parsing Technologies*, IWPT '09, pages 73–76, Stroudsburg, PA, USA. Association for Computational Linguistics.

Using the argumentative structure of scientific literature to improve information access

Antonio Jimeno Yepes
National ICT Australia
Victoria Research Laboratory
Melbourne, Australia
antonio.jimeno@gmail.com

James G. Mork
National Library of Medicine
8600 Rockville Pike
Bethesda, 20894, MD, USA
mork@nlm.nih.gov

Alan R. Aronson
National Library of Medicine
8600 Rockville Pike
Bethesda, 20894, MD, USA
alan@nlm.nih.gov

Abstract

MEDLINE/PubMed contains structured abstracts that can provide argumentative labels. Selection of abstract sentences based on the argumentative label has shown to improve the performance of information retrieval tasks. These abstracts make up less than one quarter of all the abstracts in MEDLINE/PubMed, so it is worthwhile to learn how to automatically label the non-structured ones.

We have compared several machine learning algorithms trained on structured abstracts to identify argumentative labels. We have performed an intrinsic evaluation on predicting argumentative labels for non-structured abstracts and an extrinsic evaluation to predict argumentative labels on abstracts relevant to Gene Reference Into Function (GeneRIF) indexing.

Intrinsic evaluation shows that argumentative labels can be assigned effectively to structured abstracts. Algorithms that model the argumentative structure seem to perform better than other algorithms. Extrinsic results show that assigning argumentative labels to non-structured abstracts improves the performance on GeneRIF indexing. On the other hand, the algorithms that model the argumentative structure of the abstracts obtain lower performance in the extrinsic evaluation.

1 Introduction

MEDLINE®/PubMed® is the largest repository of biomedical abstracts. The large quantity of unstructured information available from MEDLINE/PubMed prevents finding information efficiently. Reducing the information that users need to process could improve information access and support database curation. It has been suggested that identifying the argumentative label of the abstract sentences could provide better information through information retrieval (Ruch et al., 2003; Jonnalagadda et al., 2012) and/or information extraction (Mizuta et al., 2006).

Some journals indexed in MEDLINE/PubMed already provide the abstracts in a structured format (Ripple et al., 2012). A structured abstract[1] is an abstract with distinct labeled sections (e.g., Introduction, Background, or Results). In the MEDLINE/PubMed data, these labels usually appear in all uppercase letters and are followed by a colon (e.g., *MATERIALS AND METHODS:*). Structured abstracts are becoming an increasingly larger segment of the MEDLINE/PubMed database with almost a quarter of all abstracts added to the MEDLINE/PubMed database each year being structured abstracts. A recent PubMed query (April 22, 2013) shows 1,050,748 citations from 2012, and 249,196 (23.72%)[2] of these are considered structured abstracts.

On August 16, 2010, PubMed began displaying structured abstracts formatted to highlight the various sections within the structured abstracts to help readers identify areas of interest[3]. The XML formatted abstract from MEDLINE/PubMed separates each label in the structured abstract and includes a mapping to one of five U.S. National Library of Medicine (NLM) assigned categories as shown in the example below:

<AbstractText Label="MATERIALS AND METHODS" NlmCategory="METHODS">

The five NLM categories that all labels are mapped to are OBJECTIVE, CONCLUSIONS, RESULTS, METHODS, and BACKGROUND (Ripple et al., 2011). If a label is new

[1]http://www.nlm.nih.gov/bsd/policy/structured_abstracts.html
[2]hasstructuredabstract AND 2012[pdat]
[3]http://www.nlm.nih.gov/pubs/techbull/ja10/ja10_structured_abstracts.html

or not in the list of reviewed structured abstract labels, it will receive a category of *UNASSIGNED*. There are multiple criteria for deciding what abstracts are considered structured abstracts or not. One simple definition would be that an abstract contains one or more author defined labels. A more rigid criterion which is followed by NLM[4] is that an abstract must contain three or more unique valid labels (previously identified and categorized), and one of the labels must be an ending type label (e.g., *CONCLUSIONS*). The five NLM categories are normally manually reviewed and assigned once a year to as many new labels as possible. Currently, NLM has identified 1,949 (August 31, 2012) unique labels and categorized them into one of the five categories. These 1,949 labels make up approximately 98% of all labels and label variations found in the structured abstracts in MEDLINE/PubMed[3]. An example of structured abstract is presented in Table 1.

Several studies have shown that the labels of the structured abstracts can be reassigned effectively based on a Conditional Random Field (CRF) models (Hirohata et al., 2008). On the other hand, it is unclear if these models are as effective on non-structured abstracts (Agarwal and Yu, 2009).

In this paper, we compare several learning algorithms trained on structured abstract data to assign argumentative labels to non-structured abstracts. We performed comparison tests of the trained models both intrinsically on a held out set of the structured abstracts and extrinsically on a set of non-structured abstracts.

The intrinsic evaluation is performed on a data set of held out structured abstracts that have had their label identification removed to model non-structured abstracts. Argumentative labels are assigned to the sentences based on the trained models and used to identify label categorization.

The extrinsic evaluation is performed on a data set of non-structured abstracts on the task of identifying GeneRIF (Gene Into Function) sentences. Argumentative labels are assigned to the sentences based on the trained models and used to perform the selection of relevant GeneRIF sentences.

Intrinsic evaluation shows that argumentative labels can be assigned effectively to structured abstracts. Algorithms that model the argumentative structure, like Conditional Random Field (CRF), seem to perform better than other algorithms. Results show that using the argumentative labels assigned by the learning algorithms improves the performance in GeneRIF sentence selection. On the other hand, models like CRF, which better model the argumentative structure of the structured abstracts, tend to perform below other learning algorithms on the extrinsic evaluation. This shows that non-structured abstracts do not have the same layout compared to structured ones.

2 Related work

As presented in the introduction, one of the objectives of our work is to assign structured abstract labels to abstracts without these labels. The idea is to help in the curation process of existing databases and to improve the efficiency of information access. Previous work on MEDLINE/PubMed abstracts has focused on learning to identify these labels mainly in the Randomized Control Trials (RCT) domain. (McKnight and Srinivasan, 2003) used a Support Vector Machine (SVM) and a linear classifier and tried to predict the labels of MEDLINE structured abstracts. Their work finds that it is possible to learn a model to label the abstract with modest results. Further studies have been conducted by (Ruch et al., 2003; Tbahriti et al., 2005; Ruch et al., 2007) to use the argumentative model of the abstracts. They have used this to improve retrieval and indexing of MEDLINE citations, respectively. In their work, they have used a multi-class Naïve Bayes classifier.

(Hirohata et al., 2008) have shown that the labels in structured abstracts follow a certain argumentative structure. Using the current set of labels used at the NLM, a typical argumentative structure consists of OBJECTIVE, METHODS, RESULTS and CONCLUSION. This notion is somewhat already explored by (McKnight and Srinivasan, 2003) by using the position of the sentence.

More advanced approaches have been used that train a model that considers the sequence of labels in the structured abstracts. (Lin et al., 2006) used a generative model, comparing them to discriminative ones. More recent work has been dealing with Conditional Random Fields (Hirohata et al., 2008) with good performance.

(Agarwal and Yu, 2009) used similar approaches and evaluated the labeling of full text articles with the trained model on structured abstracts. Their evaluation included as well a set of

[4]http://structuredabstracts.nlm.nih.gov/Implementation.shtml

```
<Abstract> <AbstractText Label="PURPOSE" NlmCategory="OBJECTIVE">To explore the effects of cervical loop electrosurgical excision procedure (LEEP) or cold knife conization (CKC) on pregnancy outcomes.</AbstractText>
<AbstractText Label="MATERIALS AND METHODS" NlmCategory="METHODS">Patients with cervical intraepithelial neoplasia (CIN) who wanted to become pregnant and received LEEP or CKC were considered as the treatment groups. Women who wanted to become pregnant and only underwent colposcopic biopsy without any treatments were considered as the control group. The pregnancy outcomes were observed and compared in the three groups.</AbstractText>
<AbstractText Label="RESULTS" NlmCategory="RESULTS">Premature delivery rate was higher (p = 0.048) in the CKC group (14/36, 38.88%) than in control group (14/68, 20.5%) with a odds ratio (OR) of 2.455 (1.007 - 5.985); and premature delivery was related to cone depth, OR was significantly increased when the cone depth was more than 15 mm. There was no significant difference in premature delivery between LEEP (10 / 48, 20.83%) and the control groups. The average gestational weeks were shorter (p = 0.049) in the CKC group (36.9 +/- 2.4) than in the control group (37.8 +/- 2.6), but similar in LEEP (38.1 +/- 2.4) and control groups. There were no significant differences in cesarean sections between the three groups. The ratio of neonatal birth weight less than 2,500 g was significantly higher (p = 0.005) in the CKC group (15/36) than in the control group (10/68), but similar in the LEEP and control groups.</AbstractText>
<AbstractText Label="CONCLUSION" NlmCategory="CONCLUSIONS">Compared with CKC, LEEP is relatively safe. LEEP should be a priority in the treatment of patients with CIN who want to become pregnant.</AbstractText>
</Abstract>
```


Table 1: XML example for PMID 23590007

abstracts manually annotated. They found that the performance on full-text was below what was expected. A similar result was found in the manually annotated set. They found, as well, that the abstract sentences are noisy and sometimes the sentences from structured abstracts did not belong with the label they were assigned to.

A large number of abstracts in MEDLINE are not structured; thus intrinsic evaluation of the algorithms trained to predict the argumentative labels on structured abstracts is not completely realistic. Extrinsic evaluation has been previously performed by (Ruch et al., 2003; Tbahriti et al., 2005; Ruch et al., 2007) in information retrieval results evaluating a Naïve Bayes classifier. We have extended this work by evaluating a larger set of algorithms and heuristics on a data set developed to tune and evaluate a system for GeneRIF indexing on a data set containing mostly non-structured abstracts. The idea is that GeneRIF relevant sentences will be assigned distinctive argumentative labels.

A Gene Reference Into Function (GeneRIF) describes novel functionality of genes. The creation of GeneRIF entries involves the identification of the genes mentioned in MEDLINE citations and the citation sentences describing a novel function. GeneRIFs are available from the NCBI (National Center for Biotechnology Information) Gene database[5]. An example sentence is shown below linked to the BRCA1 gene with gene id 672 from the citation with PubMed® identifier (PMID) 22093627:

FISH-positive EGFR expression is associated with gender and smoking status, but not correlated with the expression of ERCC1 and BRCA1 proteins in non-small cell lung cancer.

There is limited previous work related to GeneRIF span extraction. Most of the available publications are related to the TREC Genomics Track in 2003 (Hersh and Bhupatiraju, 2003). There were two main tasks in this track, the first one consisted of identifying relevant citations to be considered for GeneRIF annotation.

In the second task, the participants had to provide spans of text that would correspond to relevant GeneRIF annotations for a set of citations. Considering this second task, the participants were not provided with a training data set. The Dice coefficient was used to measure the similarity between the submitted span of text from the title and abstract of the citation and the official GeneRIF text in the test set.

Surprisingly, one of the main conclusions was that a very competitive system could be obtained by simply delivering the title of the citation as the best GeneRIF span of text. Few teams (EMC (Jelier et al., 2003) and Berkley (Bhalotia et al., 2003) being exceptions), achieved results better than that simple strategy. Another conclusion of the Genomics Track was that the sentence position in the citation is a good indicator for GeneRIF sentence identification: either the title or sentences close to the end of the citation were found to be the best candidates.

Subsequent to the 2003 Genomics Track, there has been some further work related to GeneRIF

[5]http://www.ncbi.nlm.nih.gov/sites/entrez?db=gene

sentence selection. (Lu et al., 2006; Lu et al., 2007) sought to reproduce the results already available from Entrez Gene (former name for the NCBI Gene database). In their approach, a set of features is identified from the sentences and used in the algorithm: Gene Ontology (GO) token matches, cue words and sentence position in the abstract. (Gobeill et al., 2008) combined argumentative features using discourse-analysis models (LASt) and an automatic text categorizer to estimate the density of Gene Ontology categories (GOEx). The combination of these two feature sets produced results comparable to the best 2003 Genomics Track system.

3 Methods

As in previous work, we approach the problem of learning to label sentences in abstracts using machine learning methods on structured abstracts. We have compared a large range of machine learning algorithms, including Conditional Random Field. The evaluation is performed intrinsically on a held out set of structured abstracts and then evaluated extrinsically on a dataset developed for the evaluation of algorithms for GeneRIF indexing.

3.1 Structured abstracts data set

This data set is used to train the machine learning algorithms and to peform the intrinsic evaluation of structured abstracts. The abstracts have been collected from PubMed using the query *hasstructuredabstract*, selecting the top 100k citations satifying the query.

The abstract defined within the Abstract attribute is split into several AbstractText tags. Each AbstractText tag has the label *Label* that shows the original label as provided by the journal while the *NlmCategory* represents the category as added by the NLM.

From this set, 2/3 of the citations (66,666) are considered for training the machine learning algorithms while 1/3 of the citations (33,334) are reserved for testing. The abstract paragraphs have been split into sentences and the structured abstract label has been transferred to them. For instance, all the sentences in the INTRODUCTION section are labeled as INTRODUCTION.

An analysis of the abstracts has shown that there are cases in which the article keywords were included as part of the abstract in a *BACKGROUND* section. These were easily recognized by the original label *KEYWORD*. We have removed these paragraphs since they are not typical sentences in MEDLINE but a list of keywords. We find that there are sections like OBJECTIVE where the number of sentences is very low, with less than 2 sentences on average, while RESULTS is the section with the largest number of sentences on average with over 4.5 sentences.

There are five candidate labels identified from the structured abstracts, presented in Table 2. The distribution of labels shows that some labels like CONCLUSIONS, METHODS and RESULTS are very frequent. CONCLUSIONS and METHODS are assigned to more than one paragraph since the number is bigger compared to the number of citations in each set. This seems to happen when more than one journal label in the same citation map to METHODS or CONCLUSION, e.g. PMID: 23538919.

Label	Paragraphs	Sentences
BACKGROUND	53,348	132,890
CONCLUSIONS	101,830	205,394
METHODS	107,227	304,487
OBJECTIVE	60,846	95,547
RESULTS	95,824	436,653

Table 2: Structured abstracts data set statistics

We have compared the performance of several learning algorithms. Among other classifiers, we use Naïve Bayes and Linear Regression, which might be seen as a generative learner versus discriminative (Jordan, 2002) learner. We have used the implementation available from the Mallet package (McCallum, 2002).

In addition to these two classifiers, we have used AdaBoostM1 and SVM. SVM has been trained using stochastic gradient descent (Zhang, 2004), which is very efficient for linear kernels. Table 2 shows a large imbalance between the labels, so we have used the modified Huber Loss (Zhang, 2004), which has already been used in the context of MeSH indexing (Yeganova et al., 2011). Both algorithms were trained based on the one-versus-all approach. We have turned the algorithms into multi-class classifiers by selecting the prediction with the highest confidence by the classifiers (Tsoumakas and Katakis, 2007). We have used the implementation of these algorithms available from the MTI ML package[6], previously used in the task of MeSH indexing (Jimeno-Yepes et al., 2012).

The learning algorithms have been trained on the text of the paragraph or sentences from the data set presented above. The text is lowercased and tokenized. In addition to the textual features, the position of the sentence or paragraph from the beginning of the abstract is used as well.

As we have seen, argumentative structure of the abstract labels has been previously modeled using a linear chain CRF (Lafferty et al., 2001). CRF is trained using the text features from sentences or paragraphs in conjunction of the abstract labels to perform the label assignment. In our experiments, we have used the implementation available from the Mallet package, using only an order 1 model.

3.2 GeneRIF data set

We have developed a data set to compare and evaluate GeneRIF indexing approaches (Jimeno-Yepes et al., 2013) as part of the Gene Indexing Assistant project at the NLM[7]. The current scope of our work is limited to the human species. The development is performed in two steps described below. The first step consists of selecting citations from journals typically associated with human species. During the second step, we apply Index Section rules for citation filtering plus additional rules to further focus the set of selected citations. Since there was no GeneRIF indexing before 2002, only articles from 2002 through 2011 from the 2011 MEDLINE Baseline [8] (11/19/2010) were used to build the data set.

A subset of the filtered citations was collected for annotation. The annotations were performed by two annotators. Guidelines were prepared and tested on a small set by the two annotators and refined before annotating the entire set.

The data set has been annotated with GeneRIF categories of the sentences. The categories are: Expression, Function, Isolation, Non-GeneRIF, Other, Reference, and Structure. We assigned the GeneRIF category to all the categories that did not belong to Non-GeneRIF. The indexing task is then to categorize the sentences into GeneRIF sentences and Non-GeneRIF ones. Based on their annotation work on the data set, the F-measure for the annotators is 0.81. We have used this annotation for the extrinsic evaluation of GeneRIF indexing.

This data set has been further split into training and testing subsets. Table 3 shows the distribution between GeneRIF and Non-GeneRIF sentences.

Set	Total	GeneRIF	Non-GeneRIF
Training	1987	829 (42%)	1158 (58%)
Testing	999	433 (43%)	566 (57%)

Table 3: GeneRIF sentence distribution

In previous work, the indexing of GeneRIF sentences, on our data set, was performed based on a trained classifier on a set of features that performed well on the GeneRIF testing set (Jimeno-Yepes et al., 2013). Naïve Bayes was the learning algorithm that performed the best compared to the other methods and has been selected in this work as the method to be used to combine the features of the argumentative labeling algorithms.

The set of features in the baseline experiments include the position of the sentence from the beginning of the abstract, the position of the sentence counting from the end of the abstract, the sentence text, the annotation of disease terms, based on MetaMap (Aronson and Lang, 2010), and gene terms, based on a dictionary approach, and the Gene Ontology term density (Gobeill et al., 2008).

4 Results

As mentioned before, we have performed the evaluation of the algorithms intrinsically, given a set of structured abstracts, and extrinsically based on their performance on GeneRIF sentence indexing.

4.1 Intrinsic evaluation (structured abstracts)

Tables 4 and 5 show the results of the intrinsic evaluation for paragraph and sentence experiments respectively. The algorithms are trained to label the paragraphs or sentences from the structured abstracts. The precision (P), recall (R) and F_1 (F) values are presented for each argumentative label. The methods evaluated include Naïve Bayes (NB), Logistic Regression (LR), SVM based on modified Huber Loss (Huber) and AdaBoostM1 (ADA). These methods have been trained on the text of either the sentence or the paragraph, and might include their position feature, indicated with the letter P (e.g. NB P for Naïve Bayes trained

[6]http://ii.nlm.nih.gov/MTI_ML/index.shtml

[7]http://www.lhncbc.nlm.nih.gov/project/automated-indexing-research

[8]http://mbr.nlm.nih.gov

Label		NB	NB P	LR	LR P	ADA	ADA P	Huber	HuberP	CRF
BACKGROUND	P	0.6047	0.6853	0.6374	**0.7369**	0.6098	0.7308	0.5862	0.7166	0.7357
	R	0.5672	0.7190	0.5868	**0.7207**	0.3676	0.7337	0.4984	0.6694	0.7093
	F	0.5854	0.7017	0.6110	**0.7287**	0.4587	0.7323	0.5387	0.6922	0.7223
CONCLUSIONS	P	0.7532	0.8626	0.8365	0.9413	0.6975	0.8862	0.7578	0.9051	**0.9769**
	R	0.8606	0.9366	0.8675	0.9552	0.8246	0.9404	0.7987	0.9340	**0.9784**
	F	0.8033	0.8981	0.8517	0.9482	0.7557	0.9125	0.7777	0.9193	**0.9776**
METHODS	P	0.9002	0.9278	0.9113	0.9396	0.8256	0.9041	0.8668	0.9116	**0.9684**
	R	0.9040	0.9126	0.9294	0.9493	0.8955	0.9250	0.9012	0.9237	**0.9675**
	F	0.9021	0.9201	0.9203	0.9444	0.8591	0.9144	0.8837	0.9176	**0.9680**
OBJECTIVE	P	0.7294	0.7650	0.7167	0.7531	0.6763	0.7565	0.6788	0.7160	**0.7608**
	R	0.6453	0.7190	0.7255	0.7549	0.6937	0.7228	0.6733	0.7365	**0.7759**
	F	0.6848	0.7413	0.7210	0.7540	0.6849	0.7393	0.6761	0.7261	**0.7683**
RESULTS	P	0.8841	0.9106	0.9086	0.9372	0.8554	0.9157	0.8560	0.9122	**0.9692**
	R	0.8414	0.8542	0.8857	0.9216	0.7842	0.8564	0.8447	0.8846	**0.9758**
	F	0.8622	0.8815	0.8970	0.9294	0.8182	0.8851	0.8503	0.8981	**0.9725**
Average	P	0.7743	0.8303	0.8021	0.8616	0.7329	0.8387	0.7491	0.8323	**0.8822**
	R	0.7637	0.8283	0.7990	0.8604	0.7131	0.8357	0.7433	0.8296	**0.8814**
	F	0.7690	0.8293	0.8005	0.8610	0.7229	0.8372	0.7462	0.8310	**0.8818**

Table 4: Intrinsic evaluation of paragraph based labeling

Label		NB	NB P	LR	LR P	ADA	ADA P	Huber	HuberP	CRF
BACKGROUND	P	0.4983	0.6313	0.5558	**0.6862**	0.4779	0.6417	0.5153	0.6495	0.6738
	R	0.4980	0.6921	0.5084	**0.7139**	0.3207	0.6993	0.3372	0.6554	0.7104
	F	0.4981	0.6603	0.5311	**0.6998**	0.3838	0.6693	0.4076	0.6524	0.6916
CONCLUSIONS	P	0.5876	0.7270	0.6794	0.8431	0.5672	0.7651	0.6153	0.7767	**0.8977**
	R	0.7103	0.8388	0.6788	0.8187	0.4998	0.6816	0.5163	0.7213	**0.8671**
	F	0.6431	0.7789	0.6791	0.8307	0.5314	0.7209	0.5615	0.7480	**0.8821**
METHODS	P	0.7857	0.8206	0.8193	0.8549	0.7224	0.7793	0.7343	0.7894	**0.8931**
	R	0.8084	0.8366	0.8427	0.8696	0.7789	0.8152	0.7828	0.8250	**0.8988**
	F	0.7969	0.8285	0.8308	0.8622	0.7496	0.7968	0.7578	0.8068	**0.8960**
OBJECTIVE	P	0.5522	0.6237	0.6032	**0.6696**	0.5497	0.6671	0.5525	0.6259	0.6258
	R	0.4894	0.5530	0.4995	**0.5534**	0.4082	0.4518	0.4479	0.5036	0.5779
	F	0.5189	0.5862	0.5465	**0.6060**	0.4685	0.5388	0.4947	0.5581	0.6009
RESULTS	P	0.8294	0.8517	0.8071	0.8449	0.6903	0.7665	0.6957	0.7877	**0.8892**
	R	0.7517	0.7743	0.8429	0.8679	0.7998	0.8143	0.6957	0.8208	**0.8995**
	F	0.7886	0.8112	0.8246	0.8563	0.7410	0.7897	0.6957	0.8039	**0.8943**
Average	P	0.6506	0.7309	0.6930	0.7797	0.6015	0.7239	0.6226	0.7258	**0.7959**
	R	0.6516	0.7390	0.6745	0.7647	0.5615	0.6924	0.5560	0.7052	**0.7907**
	F	0.6511	0.7349	0.6836	0.7721	0.5808	0.7078	0.5874	0.7154	**0.7933**

Table 5: Intrinsic evaluation of sentence based labeling

with the features from text and the position). The results include those based on CRF trained on the text of either the sentence or the paragraph taking into account the labeling sequence.

CRF has the best performance in both tables, with the differences being more dramatic on the paragraph results. These results are comparable to (Hirohata et al., 2008), even though we are working with a different set of labels. Comparing the remaining learning algorithms, LR performs better than the other classifiers. Both AdaBoostM1 and SVM perform not as well as NB and LR; this could be due to the noise referred to by (Agarwal and Yu, 2009) that appears in the structured abstract sentences. Considering either the paragraph or the sentence text, the position information helps improve their performance.

CONCLUSIONS, METHODS and RESULTS labels have the best performance, which matches the most frequent labels in the dataset (see Table 2). BACKGROUND and OBJECTIVE have worse performance compared to the other labels. These two labels have the largest imbalance compared to the other labels, which seems to negatively impact the classifiers performance.

The results based on the paragraphs outperform the ones based on the sentences. Argumentative structure of the paragraphs seems to be easier, probably due to the fact that individual sentences have been shown to be noisy (Agarwal and Yu, 2009), and this could explain this behaviour.

4.2 Extrinsic evaluation (GeneRIFs)

Extrinsic evaluation is performed on the GeneRIF data set presented in the Methods section. The idea of the evaluation is to assign one of the argumentative labels to the sentences, based on the models trained on structured abstracts, and evaluate the impact of this assignment in the selection of GeneRIF sentences. From the set of machine learning algorithms intrinsically evaluated, we have selected the LR models trained with and without position information (Pos) and the CRF model. The LR and CRF models are used to label the GeneRIF training and testing data with the argumentative labels.

Table 6 shows the results of the extrinsic evaluation. Results obtained with the argumentative label feature and with or without the set of features used in the baseline are compared to the baseline model, i.e. NB and the set of features presented in the Methods section. In all the cases, precision (P), recall (R) and F_1 using the argumentative features improve over the baseline.

The intrinsic evaluation was performed either on sentences or paragraphs. The sentence models perform better than the paragraph based models. We find as well that LR with sentence position performs slightly better than when combined with the baseline features, with higher recall but lower precision. Contrary to the intrinsic results, LR performs better than CRF, even though both outperform the baseline. This means that non-structured sentences do not necessarily follow the same argumentative structure as the structured abstracts.

Label	P	R	F
Baseline	0.6210	0.6605	0.6405
LR Par	**0.7235**	0.6767	0.6993
LR Par + Base	0.7184	0.8014	**0.7576**
LR Par Pos	0.5978	**0.8891**	0.7149
LR Par Pos + Base	0.6883	0.8060	0.7426
LR Sen	0.7039	0.7852	0.7424
LR Sen + Base	**0.7325**	0.7968	0.7633
LR Sen Pos	0.7014	**0.9007**	**0.7887**
LR Sen Pos + Base	0.7222	0.8406	0.7769
CRF Par	0.6682	0.6744	0.6713
CRF Par + Base	**0.7036**	**0.8060**	**0.7513**
CRF Sen	0.6536	**0.8499**	0.7390
CRF Sen + Base	**0.7134**	0.7875	**0.7486**

Table 6: GeneRIF extrinsic evaluation

5 Discussion

Results show that it is possible to automatically predict the argumentative label of the structured abstracts and to improve the performance for GeneRIF annotation. Intrinsic evaluation shows that paragraph labeling is easier compared to sentence labeling, which might be partly due to the noise in the sentences as identified by (Agarwal and Yu, 2009). The excellent performance for paragraph labeling was already shown by previous work (Hirohata et al., 2008) while sentence labeling issues for structured abstracts was previously introduced by (Agarwal and Yu, 2009). In both intrinsic tasks, adding the position of the paragraph or sentence improves the performance of the learning algorithms.

Extrinsic evaluation shows that, compared to the baseline features for GeneRIF annotation, adding argumentative labeling using the trained models improves its performance, which is close to the human performance reported in the Methods section. On the other hand, we find that the CRF models show lower performance compared to the LR models. From the LR models, the position of the sentence or paragraph seems to have better performance.

In addition, the LR model trained on the sentences performs better compared to the model trained on the paragraphs. This might be partly due to the fact that sentence based models seem to be better suited than the paragraph based ones as might have been expected. The fact that the CRF models performance is below the LR models denotes that the structured abstracts seem to follow a pattern that is different in the case of non-structured abstracts. Looking closer at the assigned labels, the LR models tend to assign more CONCLUSIONS and RESULTS labels to the GeneRIF sentences compared to the CRF ones.

6 Conclusions and Future Work

We have presented an evaluation of several learning algorithms to label abstract text in MEDLINE/PubMed with argumentative labels, based on MEDLINE/PubMed structured abstracts. The results show that this task can be achieved with high performance in the case of labeling the paragraphs but this is not the same in the case of sentences. This intrinsic evaluation was performed on structured abstracts, and in this set the CRF models seem to perform much better compared to the other models that do not use the labeling sequence.

On the other hand, when applying the trained models to MEDLINE/PubMed non-structured abstracts, we find that the extrinsic evaluation of these labeling on the GeneRIF task shows lower performance for the CRF models. This indicates that the structured abstracts follow a pattern that non-structured ones do not follow. The extrinsic evaluation shows that labeling the sentences with argumentative labels improves the indexing of GeneRIF sentences. The argumentative labels help identifying target sentences for the GeneRIF indexing, but more refined labels learned from non-structured abstracts could provide better performance. An idea to extend this research would be evaluating the latent discovery of section labels and to apply this labeling to the proposed GeneRIF task and to other tasks, e.g. MeSH indexing. Latent labels might accommodate better the argumentative structure of non-structured abstracts.

As shown in this work, the argumentative layout of non-structured abstracts and structured abstracts is not the same. There is still the open question if there is any layout regularity in the non-structured abstracts that could be exploited to improve information access.

7 Acknowledgements

NICTA is funded by the Australian Government as represented by the Department of Broadband, Communications and the Digital Economy and the Australian Research Council through the ICT Centre of Excellence program.

This work was also supported in part by the Intramural Research Program of the NIH, National Library of Medicine.

References

S Agarwal and H Yu. 2009. Automatically classifying sentences in full-text biomedical articles into Introduction, Methods, Results and Discussion. *Bioinformatics*, 25(23):3174–3180.

A R Aronson and F M Lang. 2010. An overview of MetaMap: historical perspective and recent advances. *Journal of the American Medical Informatics Association*, 17(3):229–236.

G. Bhalotia, PI Nakov, A S Schwartz, and M A Hearst. 2003. BioText team report for the TREC 2003 genomics track. In *Proceedings of TREC*. Citeseer.

J Gobeill, I Tbahriti, F Ehrler, A Mottaz, A Veuthey, and P Ruch. 2008. Gene Ontology density estimation and discourse analysis for automatic GeneRiF extraction. *BMC Bioinformatics*, 9(Suppl 3):S9.

W Hersh and R T Bhupatiraju. 2003. TREC genomics track overview. In *TREC 2003*, pages 14–23.

K Hirohata, Naoaki Okazaki, Sophia Ananiadou, Mitsuru Ishizuka, and Manchester Interdisciplinary Biocentre. 2008. Identifying sections in scientific abstracts using conditional random fields. In *Proc. of 3rd International Joint Conference on Natural Language Processing*, pages 381–388.

R Jelier, M Schuemie, C Eijk, M Weeber, E Mulligen, B Schijvenaars, B Mons, and J Kors. 2003. Searching for GeneRIFs: concept-based query expansion and Bayes classification. In *Proceedings of TREC*, pages 167–174.

A Jimeno-Yepes, J G Mork, D Demner-Fushman, and A R Aronson. 2012. A One-Size-Fits-All Indexing Method Does Not Exist: Automatic Selection Based on Meta-Learning. *Journal of Computing Science and Engineering*, 6(2):151–160.

A Jimeno-Yepes, J C Sticco, J G Mork, and A R Aronson. 2013. GeneRIF indexing: sentence selection based on machine learning. *BMC Bioinformatics*, 14(1):147.

S Jonnalagadda, G D Fiol, R Medlin, C Weir, M Fiszman, J Mostafa, and H Liu. 2012. Automatically extracting sentences from medline citations to support clinicians' information needs. In *Healthcare Informatics, Imaging and Systems Biology (HISB), 2012 IEEE Second International Conference on*, pages 72–72. IEEE.

A Jordan. 2002. On discriminative vs. generative classifiers: A comparison of logistic regression and naive bayes. *Advances in neural information processing systems*, 14:841.

J D Lafferty, A McCallum, and F Pereira. 2001. Conditional random fields: Probabilistic models for segmenting and labeling sequence data. In *Proceedings of the Eighteenth International Conference on Machine Learning*, ICML '01, pages 282–289, San Francisco, CA, USA. Morgan Kaufmann Publishers Inc.

J Lin, D Karakos, D Demner-Fushman, and S Khudanpur. 2006. Generative content models for structural analysis of medical abstracts. In *Proceedings of the HLT-NAACL BioNLP Workshop on Linking Natural Language and Biology*, pages 65–72. Association for Computational Linguistics.

Z Lu, K B Cohen, and L Hunter. 2006. Finding GeneRIFs via gene ontology annotations. In *Pacific Symposium on Biocomputing. Pacific Symposium on Biocomputing*, page 52. NIH Public Access.

Z Lu, K B Cohen, and L Hunter. 2007. GeneRIF quality assurance as summary revision. In *Pacific Symposium on Biocomputing*, page 269. NIH Public Access.

A McCallum. 2002. Mallet: A machine learning for language toolkit. *URL http://mallet.cs.umass.edu.*

L McKnight and P Srinivasan. 2003. Categorization of sentence types in medical abstracts. In *AMIA Annual Symposium Proceedings*, volume 2003, page 440. American Medical Informatics Association.

Y Mizuta, A Korhonen, T Mullen, and N Collier. 2006. Zone analysis in biology articles as a basis for information extraction. *International journal of medical informatics*, 75(6):468–487.

A M Ripple, J G Mork, L S Knecht, and B L Humphreys. 2011. A retrospective cohort study of structured abstracts in MEDLINE, 1992–2006. *Journal of the Medical Library Association: JMLA*, 99(2):160.

A M Ripple, J G Mork, J M Rozier, and L S Knecht. 2012. Structured Abstracts in MEDLINE: Twenty-Five Years Later.

P Ruch, C Chichester, G Cohen, G Coray, F Ehrler, H Ghorbel, and V Müller, Hand Pallotta. 2003. Report on the TREC 2003 experiment: Genomic track. *TREC-03*.

P Ruch, A Geissbuhler, J Gobeill, F Lisacek, I Tbahriti, A Veuthey, and A R Aronson. 2007. Using discourse analysis to improve text categorization in MEDLINE. *Studies in health technology and informatics*, 129(1):710.

I Tbahriti, C Chichester, F Lisacek, and P Ruch. 2005. Using argumentation to retrieve articles with similar citations: An inquiry into improving related articles search in the MEDLINE digital library. In *International Journal of Medical Informatics*. Citeseer.

G Tsoumakas and I Katakis. 2007. Multi-label classification: An overview. *International Journal of Data Warehousing and Mining (IJDWM)*, 3(3):1–13.

L Yeganova, Donald C Comeau, W Kim, and J Wilbur. 2011. Text mining techniques for leveraging positively labeled data. In *Proceedings of BioNLP 2011 Workshop*, pages 155–163. Association for Computational Linguistics.

T Zhang. 2004. Solving large scale linear prediction problems using stochastic gradient descent algorithms. In *Proceedings of the twenty-first international conference on Machine learning*, page 116. ACM.

Using Latent Dirichlet Allocation for Child Narrative Analysis

Khairun-nisa Hassanali and **Yang Liu**
The University of Texas at Dallas
Richardson, TX, USA
nisa,yangl@hlt.utdallas.edu

Thamar Solorio
University of Alabama at Birmingham
Birmingham, AL, USA
solorio@uab.edu

Abstract

Child language narratives are used for language analysis, measurement of language development, and the detection of language impairment. In this paper, we explore the use of Latent Dirichlet Allocation (LDA) for detecting topics from narratives, and use the topics derived from LDA in two classification tasks: automatic prediction of coherence and language impairment. Our experiments show LDA is useful for detecting the topics that correspond to the narrative structure. We also observed improved performance for the automatic prediction of coherence and language impairment when we use features derived from the topic words provided by LDA.

1 Introduction

Language sample analysis is a common technique used by speech language researchers to measure various aspects of language development. These include speech fluency, syntax, semantics, and coherence. For such analysis, spontaneous narratives have been widely used. Narrating a story or a personal experience requires the narrator to build a mental model of the story and use the knowledge of semantics and syntax to produce a coherent narrative. Children learn from a very early age to narrate stories. The different processes involved in generating a narrative have been shown to provide insights into the language status of children.

There has been some prior work on child language sample analysis using NLP techniques. Sahakian and Snyder (2012) used a set of linguistic features computed on child speech samples to create language metrics that included age prediction. Gabani et al. (2011) combined commonly used measurements in communication disorders with several NLP based features for the prediction of Language Impairment (LI) vs. Typically Developing (TD) children. The features they used included measures of language productivity, morphosyntactic skills, vocabulary knowledge, sentence complexity, probabilities from language models, standard scores, and error patterns. In their work, they explored the use of language models and machine learning methods for the prediction of LI on two types of child language data: spontaneous and narrative data.

Hassanali et al. (2012a) analyzed the use of coherence in child language and performed automatic detection of coherence from child language transcripts using features derived from narrative structure such as the presence of critical narrative components and the use of narrative elements such as cognitive inferences and social engagement devices. In another study, Hassanali et al. (2012b) used several coherence related features to automatically detect language impairment.

LDA has been used in the field of narrative analysis. Wallace et al. (2012) adapted LDA to the task of multiple narrative disentanglement, in which the aim was to tease apart narratives by assigning passages from a text to the subnarratives that they belong to. They achieved strong empirical results.

In this paper, we explore the use of LDA for child narrative analysis. We aim to answer two questions: Can we apply LDA to children narratives to identify meaningful topics? Can we represent these topics automatically and use them for other tasks, such as coherence detection and language impairment prediction? Our results are promising. We found that using LDA topic modeling can infer useful topics, and incorporating features derived from such automatic topics improves the performance of coherence classification and language impairment detection over the previously reported results.

Coherence Scale	TD	LI	Total
Coherent	81	6	87
Incoherent	18	13	31
Total	**99**	**19**	**118**

Table 1: Number of TD and LI children on a 2-scale coherence level

2 Data

For the purpose of the experiments, we used the Conti-Ramsden dataset (Wetherell et al., 2007a; Wetherell et al., 2007b) from the CHILDES database (MacWhinney, 2000). This dataset consists of transcripts belonging to 118 adolescents aged 14 years. The adolescents were given the wordless picture story book "Frog, where are you?" and asked to narrate the story based on the pictures. The storybook is about the adventures of a boy who goes searching for his missing pet frog. Even though our goal is to perform child narrative analysis, we used this dataset from adoloscents since it was publicly available, and was annotated for language impairment and coherence. Of the 118 adolescents, 99 adolescents belonged to the TD group and 19 adolescents belonged to the language impaired group. Hassanali et al. (2012a) annotated this dataset for coherence. A transcript was annotated as coherent, as long as there was no difficulty in understanding the narrative, and incoherent otherwise. Table 1 gives the TD and LI distribution on a 2-scale coherence level. Figure 1 shows an example of a transcript produced by a TD child.

```
um the boy had the frog.
and he's playing with it.
and then he went to sleep and forgot to put a lid or anything on it.
and then in the middle of the night, the frog went out.
and in the morning he got really worried.
he was looking for his frog.
and he was like ignoring his dog like if it did  if it
he's just ignoring to him  ignoring him.
and he was looking around everywhere for the frog.
and then he looked up on a big rock.
and saw  and he fell on a  like a deer.
and then the deer went running and chucked him like in a pond.
and he heard the frog.
and then he saw the frog.
and then it was with like s and diff  another
and then the frogs gave him like a baby frog to have.
~
```

Figure 1: Sample transcript from a TD child

3 Narrative Topic Analysis Using LDA

Latent Dirichlet Allocation (LDA) (Blei et al., 2003) has been used in NLP to model topics within a collection of documents. In this study, we use LDA to detect topics in narratives. Upon examining the transcripts, we observed that each topic was described in about 3 to 4 utterances. We therefore segmented the narratives into chunks of 3 utterances, with the assumption that each segment corresponds roughly to one topic.

We used the software by Blei et al.[1] to perform LDA. Prior to performing LDA, we removed the stop words from the transcripts. We chose α to be 0.8 and K to be 20, where α is the parameter of the Dirichlet prior on the per-document topic distributions and K denotes the number of topics considered in the model.

We chose to use the transcripts of TD children for generating the topics, because the transcripts of TD children have fewer disfluencies, incomplete utterances, and false starts. As we can observe from Table 1, a higher percentage of TD children produced coherent narratives when compared to children with LI.

Table 2 gives the topic words for the top 10 topics extracted using LDA. The topics in Table 2 were manually labeled after examination of the topic words extracted using LDA. We found that some of the topics extracted by LDA corresponded to subtopics. For example, searching for the frog in the house has subtopics of the boy searching for the frog in room and the dog falling out of the window, which were part of the topics covered by LDA. The subtopics are marked in italics in Table 2.

The following narrative components were identified as important features for the automatic prediction of coherence by Hassanali et al. (2012a).

1. Instantiation: introduce the main characters of the story: the boy, the frog, and the dog, and the frog goes missing
2. 1st episode: search for the frog in the house
3. 2nd episode: search for the frog in the tree
4. 3rd episode: search for the frog in the hole in the ground
5. 4th episode: search for the frog near the rock
6. 5th episode: search for the frog behind the log
7. Resolution: boy finds the frog in the river and takes a frog home

Upon examining the topics extracted by LDA, we observed that all the components mentioned above

[1] http://www.cs.princeton.edu/ blei/lda-c/index.html

Topic No	Topic Words Used by TD Population	Topic Described
1	went,frog,sleep,glass,put,caught,jar,yesterday,out,house	Introduction
2	frog,up,woke,morning,called,gone,escaped,next,kept,realized	Frog goes missing
3	window,out,fell,dog,falls,broke,quickly,opened,told,breaking	*Dog falls out of window*
4	tree,bees,knocked,running,popped,chase,dog,inside,now,flying	Dog chases the bees
5	deer,rock,top,onto,sort,big,up,behind,rocks,picked	Deer behind the rock
6	searched,boots,room,bedroom,under,billy,even, floor,tilly,tried	*Search for frog in room*
7	dog,chased,owl,tree,bees,boy,came,hole,up,more	Boy is chased by owl from a tree with beehives
8	jar,gone,woke,escaped,night,sleep,asleep,dressed,morning,frog	Frog goes missing
9	deer,top,onto,running,ways,up,rocks,popped,suddenly,know	Boy runs into the deer
10	looking,still,dog,quite,cross,obviously,smashes,have,annoyed	*Displeasure of boy with dog*

Table 2: Top 10 topic words extracted by LDA on the story telling task. Subtopics are shown in italics.

were present in these topics. Many of the LDA topics corresponded to a picture or two in the storybook.

4 Using LDA Topics for Coherence and Language Impairment Classification

We extended the use of LDA for two tasks, namely: the automatic evaluation of coherence and the automatic evaluation of language impairment. For the experiments below, we used the WEKA toolkit (Hall et al., 2009) and built several models using the naive Bayes, Bayesian net classifier, Logistic Regression, and Support Vector Machine (SVM) classifier. Of all these classifiers, the naive Bayes classifier performed the best, and we report the results using the naive Bayes classifier in Tables 3 and 4. We performed all the experiments using leave-one-out cross-validation, wherein we excluded the test transcript that belonged to a TD child from the training set when generating topics using LDA.

4.1 Automatic Evaluation of Coherence

We treat the automatic evaluation of coherence as a classification task. A transcript could either be classified as coherent or incoherent. We use the results of Hassanali et al. (2012a) as a baseline. They used the presence of narrative episodes, and the counts of narrative quality elements such as cognitive inferences and social engagement devices as features in the automatic prediction of coherence. We add the features that we automatically extracted using LDA.

We checked for the presence of at least six of the ten topic words or their synonyms per topic in a window of 3 utterances. If the topic words were present, we took this as a presence of a topic; otherwise we denoted it as an absence of a topic. In total, there were 20 topics that we extracted using LDA, which is higher compared to the 8 narrative structure topics that were annotated for by Hassanali et al. (2012a).

Table 3 gives the results for the automatic classification of coherence. As we observe in Table 3, there is an improvement in performance over the baseline. We attribute this to the inclusion of subtopics that were extracted using LDA.

4.2 Automatic Evaluation of Language Impairment

We extended the use of LDA to create a summary of the narratives. For the purpose of generating the summary, we considered only the narratives generated by TD children in the training set. We generated a summary, by choosing 5 utterances corresponding to each topic that was generated using LDA, thereby yielding a summary that consisted of 100 utterances.

We observed that different words were used to represent the same concept. For example, "look" and "search" were used to represent the concept of searching for the frog. Since the narration was based on a picture storybook, many of the children used different terms to refer to the same animal. For example, "the deer" in the story has been interpreted to be "deer", "reindeer", "moose", "stag", "antelope" by different children. We created an extended topic vocabulary using Wordnet to include words that were semantically similiar to the topic keywords. In addition, for an utterance to be

Feature Set	Coherent			Incoherent			Accuracy
	Precision	Recall	F-1	Precision	Recall	F-1	(%)
Narrative (Hassanali et al., 2012a) (baseline)	0.869	0.839	0.854	0.588	0.645	0.615	78.814
Narrative + automatic topic features	**0.895**	**0.885**	**0.89**	**0.688**	**0.71**	**0.699**	**83.898**

Table 3: Automatic classification of coherence on a 2-scale coherence level

in the summary, we put in the additional constraint that neighbouring utterances within a window of 3 utterances also talk about the same topic. We used this summary for constructing unigram and bigram word features for the automatic prediction of LI.

The features we constructed for the prediction of LI were as follows:

1. Bigrams of the words in the summary
2. Presence or absence of the words in the summary regardless of the position
3. Presence or absence of the topics detected by LDA in the narratives
4. Presence or absence of the topic words that were detected using LDA

We used both the topics detected and the presence/absence of topic words as features since the same topic word could be used across several topics. For example, the words "frog", "dog", "boy", and "search" are common across several topics. We refer to the above features as "new features".

Table 4 gives the results for the automatic prediction of LI using different features. As we can observe, the performance improves to 0.872 when we add the new features to Gabani's and the narrative structure features. When we use the new features by themselves to predict language impairment, the performance is the worst. We attribute this to the fact that other feature sets are richer since these features take into account aspects such as syntax and narrative structure.

We performed feature analysis on the new features to see what features contributed the most. The top scoring features were the presence or absence of the topics detected by LDA that corresponded to the introduction of the narrative, the resolution of the narrative, the search for the frog in the room, and the search for the frog behind the log. The following bigram features generated from the summary contributed the most: "deer rock", "lost frog", and "boy hole". Using a subset of these best features did not improve the performance when we added them to the narrative features and Gabani's features.

Feature	P	R	F-1
Gabani's (Gabani et al., 2011)	0.824	0.737	0.778
Narrative (Hassanali et al., 2012a)	0.385	0.263	0.313
New features	0.308	0.211	0.25
Narrative + Gabani's	0.889	0.842	0.865
Narrative + Gabani's + new features	**0.85**	**0.895**	**0.872**

Table 4: Automatic classification of language impairment

5 Conclusions

In this paper, we explored the use of LDA in the context of child language analysis. We used LDA to extract topics from child language narratives and used these topic keywords to create a summary of the narrative and an extended vocabulary. The topics extracted using LDA not only covered the main components of the narrative but also covered subtopics too. We then used the LDA topic words and the summary to create features for the automatic prediction of coherence and language impairment. Due to higher coverage of the LDA topics as compared to manual annotation, we found an increase in performance of both automatic prediction of coherence and language impairment with the addition of the new features. We conclude that the use of LDA to model topics and extract summaries is promising for child language analysis.

Acknowledgements

This research is supported by NSF awards IIS-1017190 and 1018124.

References

David M. Blei, Andrew Y. Ng, and Michael I. Jordan. 2003. Latent dirichlet allocation. *the Journal of machine Learning research*, 3:993–1022.

Keyur Gabani, Thamar Solorio, Yang Liu, Khairun-nisa Hassanali, and Christine A. Dollaghan. 2011. Exploring a corpus-based approach for detecting language impairment in monolingual English-speaking children. *Artificial Intelligence in Medicine*, 53(3):161–170.

Mark Hall, Eibe Frank, Geoffrey Holmes, Bernhard Pfahringer, Peter Reutemann, and Ian H. Witten. 2009. The WEKA data mining software: An update. *ACM SIGKDD Explorations Newsletter*, 11(1):10–18.

Khairun-nisa Hassanali, Yang Liu, and Thamar Solorio. 2012a. Coherence in child language narratives: A case study of annotation and automatic prediction of coherence. In *Proceedings of WOCCI 2012 - 3rd Workshop on Child, Computer and Interaction*.

Khairun-nisa Hassanali, Yang Liu, and Thamar Solorio. 2012b. Evaluating NLP features for automatic prediction of language impairment using child speech transcripts. In *Proceedings of INTERSPEECH*.

Brian MacWhinney. 2000. *The CHILDES project: Tools for analyzing talk, Volume I: Transcription format and programs*. Lawrence Erlbaum Associates.

Sam Sahakian and Benjamin Snyder. 2012. Automatically learning measures of child language development. In *Proceedings of the 50th Annual Meeting of the Association for Computational Linguistics: Short Papers-Volume 2*, pages 95–99. Association for Computational Linguistics.

Bryon C. Wallace. 2012. Multiple narrative disentanglement: Unraveling infinite jest. In *Proceeding of the 2012 Conference of the North American Chapter of the Association for Computational Linguistics: Human Language Technologies*, pages 1–10.

Danielle Wetherell, Nicola Botting, and Gina Conti-Ramsden. 2007a. Narrative in adolescent specific language impairment (SLI): a comparison with peers across two different narrative genres. *International Journal of Language & Communication Disorders*, 42(5):583–605.

Danielle Wetherell, Nicola Botting, and Gina Conti-Ramsden. 2007b. Narrative skills in adolescents with a history of SLI in relation to non-verbal IQ scores. *Child Language Teaching and Therapy*, 23(1):95.

Effect of Out Of Vocabulary terms on inferring eligibility criteria for a retrospective study in Hebrew EHR

Raphael Cohen*
Computer Science Dept.
Ben-Gurion University in the Negev
cohenrap@bgu.ac.il

Michael Elhadad
Computer Science Dept.
Ben-Gurion University in the Negev
elhadad@cs.bgu.ac.il

1 Background

The Electronic Health Record (EHR) contains information useful for clinical, epidemiological and genetic studies. This information of patient symptoms, history, medication and treatment is not completely captured in the structured part of the EHR but is often found in the form of free-text narrative.

A major obstacle for clinical studies is finding patients that fit the eligibility criteria of the study. Using EHR in order to automatically identify relevant cohorts can help speed up both clinical trials and retrospective studies (Restificar, Korkontzelos et al. 2013).

While the clinical criteria for inclusion and exclusion from the study are explicitly stated in most studies, automating the process using the EHR database of the hospital is often impossible as the structured part of the database (age, gender, ICD9/10 medical codes, etc.') rarely covers all of the criteria.

Many resources such as UMLS (Bodenreider 2004), cTakes (Savova, Masanz et al. 2010), MetaMap (Aronson and Lang 2010) and recently richly annotated corpora and treebanks (Albright, Lanfranchi et al. 2013) are available for processing and representing medical texts in English. Resource poor languages, however, suffer from lack in NLP tools and medical resources. Dictionaries exhaustively mapping medical terms to the UMLS medical meta-thesaurus are only available in a limited number of languages besides English. NLP annotation tools, when they exist for resource poor languages, suffer from heavy loss of accuracy when used outside the domain on which they were trained, as is well documented for English (Tsuruoka, Tateishi et al. 2005; Tateisi, Tsuruoka et al. 2006).

In this work we focus on the problem of classifying patient eligibility for inclusion in retrospective study of the epidemiology of epilepsy in Southern Israel. Israel has a centralized structure of medical services which include advanced EHR systems. However, the free text sections of these EHR are written in Hebrew, a resource poor language in both NLP tools and handcrafted medical vocabularies.

Epilepsy is a common chronic neurologic disorder characterized by seizures. These seizures are transient signs and/or symptoms of abnormal, excessive, or hyper synchronous neuronal activity in the brain. Epilepsy is one of the most common of the serious neurological disorders (Hirtz, Thurman et al. 2007).

2 Corpus

We collected a corpus of patient notes from the Pediatric Epilepsy Unit, an outpatient clinic for neurology problems, not limited to epilepsy, in Soroka Hospital. This clinic is the only available pediatric neurology clinic in southern Israel and at the time of the study was staffed by a single expert serving approximately 225,000 children. The clinical corpus spans 894 visits to the Children Epilepsy Unit which occurred in 2009 by 516 unique patients. The corpus contains 226K tokens / 12K unique tokens.

*Supported by the Lynn and William Frankel Center for Computer Sciences, Ben Gurion University

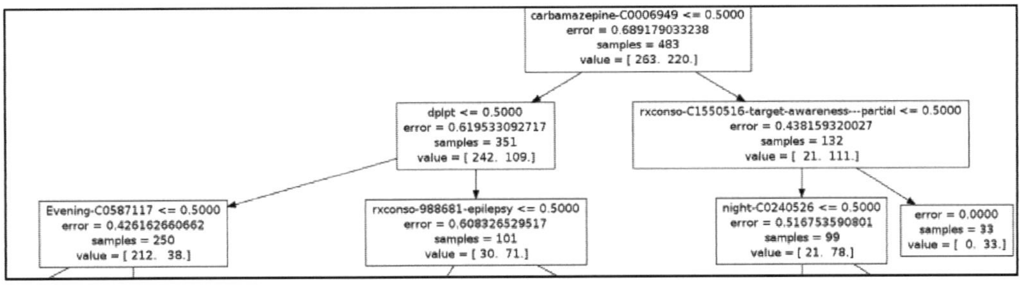

Figure 1 – Decision Tree for inclusion/exclusion. Sodium Valproate (dplpt) is a key term which is often segmented incorrectly.

The patients were marked by the attending physician as positive or negative for epilepsy. In the study year, 2009, 208 patients were marked as positive examples and 292 as negative. The inclusion criteria were defined as history of more than one convulsive episode excluding febrile seizures. In practice, the decision for inclusion was more complex as some types of febrile seizure syndromes are considered a type of epilepsy while some patients with convulsion were excluded from the study for various reasons.

3 Method

We developed a system to classify EHR notes in Hebrew into "epilepsy" / "non-epilepsy" classes, so that they can later be reviewed by a physician as eligible candidates into a cohort. The system analyzes the Hebrew text into relevant tokens by applying morphological analysis and word segmentations, Hebrew words are then semi-automatically aligned to the UMLS vocabulary. The most important tagged Hebrew words are then used as features fed to a statistical document classification system. We evaluate the performance of the system on our corpus, and measure the impact of Hebrew text analysis in improving the performance for patient classification.

4 Out-Of-Vocabulary Terms

The complex rules of Hebrew word formation make word segmentation the first challenge of any NLP pipeline in Hebrew. Agglutination of function words leads to high ambiguity in Hebrew (Adler and Elhadad 2006). To perform word segmentation, Adler and Elhadad (Adler and Elhadad 2006) combine segmentation and morpheme tagging using an HMM model over a lattice of possible segmentations. This learning method uses a lexicon to find all possible segmentations for all tokens and chooses the most likely one according to POS sequences. Unknown words, a class to which most borrowed medical terms belong, are segmented in all possible ways (there are over 150 possible prefixes and suffixes in Hebrew) and the most likely form is chosen using the context within the same sentence. Beyond word segmentation, the rich morphological nature of Hebrew makes POS tagging more complex with 2.4 possible tags per token on average, compared to 1.4 for English.

Out of 12K token types in the corpus 3.9K (30%) were not found in the lexicon used by the Morphological Disambiguator compared to only 7.5% in the Newswire domain. A sample of 2K unknown token was manually annotated as: transliteration, misspelling and Hebrew words missing in the lexicon. Transliterated terms made up most of the unknown tokens (71.5%) while the rest were misspelled words (16%) and words missing from the lexicon (13.5%).

Error analysis of the Morphological Disambiguator in the medical domain corpora shows that in the medical domain, Adler *et al*'s unknown model still performs well: 80% of the unknown tokens were still analyzed correctly. However, 88.5% of the segmentation errors were found in unknown tokens. Moreover, the transliterated words are mostly medical terms important for understanding the text.

5 Acquiring a Transliterations Lexicon

As transliterations account for a substantial amount of the errors and are usually medical terms, therefore of interest, we aim to automatically create a dictionary mapping transliterations in our target corpus to a terminology or vocabulary in the source language. In our case, the source language is medical English which is a mix of English and medical terms from Latin as represented by the UMLS vocabulary.

The dictionary construction algorithm is based on two methods: noisy transliteration of the medical English terms from the UMLS to Hebrew forms (producing all the forms an English terms may be written in Hebrew, see (Kirschenbaum and Wintner 2009)) and matching the generated transliterations to the unknown Hebrew forms found in our target corpus. After creating a list of candidate pairs (Hebrew form found in the corpus and transliterated UMLS concept), we filter the results to create an accurate dictionary using various heuristic measures.

The produced lexicon contained 2,507 transliterated lemmas with precision of 75%. The acquired lexicon reduced segmentation errors by 50%.

6 Experiments

6.1 Experimental Settings

An SVM classifier was trained using the 200 most common nouns as features. The noun lemmas were extracted with the morphological disambiguator in two settings: naïve setting using the newswire lexicon and an adapted setting using the acquired lexicon.

We divided the corpus into training and testing sets of equal size, we report on the average results or 10 different divisions of the data.

6.2 Results

The classifier using the baseline lexicon achieved an average F-Score of 83.6%. With the extended in-domain transliterations lexicon the classifier achieves F-Score of 87%, an error reduction of 20%.

We repeated the experiment with decision trees for visualization for error analysis. With decision trees we see an improvement from 76.8% to 82.6% F-score. In Figure 1, we see in the resulting decision tree the most commonly prescribed medication for epilepsy patients, Sodium Valproate "*depalept*" ("דפלפט"). This word appears in three forms: "*depalept*", "*b+deplapet*" and "*h+depalept*". The acquired lexicon allows better segmentation of this word thus removing noise for documents containing the agglutinated forms.

7 Conclusions

We presented the task of classifying patients' Hebrew free text EHR for inclusion/exclusion from a prospective study. Transliterated tokens are an important feature in medical texts. In languages with compound tokens this is likely to lead to segmentation errors.

Using a lexicon adapted for the domain impacts the number of segmentation errors, this error reduction translates into further improvements when using these data for down the line applications such as classification.

Creating domain adaptation methods for resource-poor languages can positively impact the use of clinical records in these languages.

Acknowledgments

Adler, M. and M. Elhadad (2006). An unsupervised morpheme-based hmm for hebrew morphological disambiguation. Proceedings of the 21st International Conference on Computational Linguistics and the 44th annual meeting of the Association for Computational Linguistics, Association for Computational Linguistics.

Albright, D., A. Lanfranchi, et al. (2013). "Towards comprehensive syntactic and semantic annotations of the clinical narrative." Journal of the American Medical Informatics Association.

Aronson, A. R. and F. M. Lang (2010). "An overview of MetaMap: historical perspective and recent advances." Journal of the American Medical Informatics Association 17(3): 229-236.

Bodenreider, O. (2004). "The unified medical language system (UMLS): integrating biomedical terminology." Nucleic Acids Research 32(Database Issue): D267.

Hirtz, D., D. Thurman, et al. (2007). "How common are the "common" neurologic disorders?" Neurology 68(5): 326-337.

Kirschenbaum, A. and S. Wintner (2009). Lightly supervised transliteration for machine translation. Proceedings of the 12th Conference of the European Chapter of the Association for Computational Linguistics, Association for Computational Linguistics.

Restificar, A., I. Korkontzelos, et al. (2013). "A method for discovering and inferring appropriate eligibility criteria in clinical trial protocols without labeled data." BMC Medical Informatics and Decision Making 13(Suppl 1): S6.

Savova, G. K., J. J. Masanz, et al. (2010). "Mayo clinical Text Analysis and Knowledge Extraction System (cTAKES): architecture, component evaluation and applications." Journal of the American Medical Informatics Association 17(5): 507-513.

Tateisi, Y., Y. Tsuruoka, et al. (2006). Subdomain adaptation of a POS tagger with a small corpus. Proceedings of the Workshop on

Linking Natural Language Processing and Biology: Towards Deeper Biological Literature Analysis, Association for Computational Linguistics.

Tsuruoka, Y., Y. Tateishi, et al. (2005). "Developing a robust part-of-speech tagger for biomedical text." Advances in informatics: 382-392.

Parallels between Linguistics and Biology

Ashish Vijay Tendulkar
IIT Madras
Chennai-600 036. India.
ashishvt@gmail.com

Sutanu Chakraborti
IIT Madras
Chennai-600 036. India.
sutanu@cse.iitm.ac.in

Abstract

In this paper we take a fresh look at parallels between linguistics and biology. We expect that this new line of thinking will propel cross fertilization of two disciplines and open up new research avenues.

1 Introduction

Protein structure prediction problem is a long standing open problem in Biology. The computational methods for structure prediction can be broadly classified into the following two types: (i) Ab-initio or de-novo methods seek to model physics and chemistry of protein folding from first principles. (ii) Knowledge based methods make use of existing protein structure and sequence information to predict the structure of the new protein. While protein folding takes place at a scale of millisecond in nature, the computer programs for the task take a large amount of time. Ab-initio methods take several hours to days and knowledge based methods takes several minutes to hours depending upon the complexity. We feel that the protein structure prediction methods struggle due to lack of understanding of the folding code from protein sequence. In larger context, we are interested in the following question: Can we treat biological sequences as strings generated from a specific but unknown language and find the rules of these languages? This is a deep question and hence we start with baby-steps by drawing parallels between Natural Language and Biological systems. David Searls has done interesting work in this direction and have written a number of articles about role of language in understanding Biological sequences(Searls, 2002). We intend to build on top of that work and explore further analogies between the two fields.

This is intended to be an idea paper that explores parallels between linguistics and biology that have the potential to cross fertilization two disciplines and open up new research avenues. The paper is intentionally made speculative at places to inspire out-of-the-box deliberations from researchers in both areas.

2 Analogies

In this section, we explore some pivotal ideas in linguistics (with a specific focus on Computational Linguistics) and systematically uncover analogous ideas in Biology.

2.1 Letters

The alphabet in a natural language is well specified. English language has 26 letters. The genes are made up of 4 basic elements called as nucleotide: adenine (A), thymine (T), cytosine (C) and guanine (G). During protein synthesis, genes are transcribed into messenger RNA (mRNA), which is made up of 4 basic elements: adenine (A), uracil (U), cytosine (C) and guanine (G). mRNA is translated to proteins that are made up of 20 amino acids denotes by the following letters: {A, C, D, E, F, G, H, I, K, L, M, N, P, Q, R, S, T, V, W, Y}.

2.2 Words

A word is an atomic unit of meaning in a language. When it comes to biological sequences, a fundamental problem is to identify words. Like English, the biological language seems to have a fixed alphabet when it comes to letters. However, unless we have a mechanism to identify atomic "functional" units, we cannot construct a vocabulary of biological words.

The first property of a word in NL is that it has a meaning; a word is a surrogate for something in the material or the abstract world. One central question is: how do we make machines understand meanings of words? Humans use dictionaries which explain meanings of complex words in terms of simple ones. For machines to use dictionaries, we have two problems. The first is, how do we communicate the meaning of simple words (like "red" or "sad")? The second is, to understand meanings of complex words out of simple ones, we would need the machine to understand English in the first place. The first problem has no easy solution; there are words whose meanings are expressed better in the form of images or when contrasted with other words ("orange" versus "yellow"). The second problem of defining words in terms of others can be addressed using a knowledge representation formalism like a semantic network. Some biological words have functions that cannot be easily expressed in terms of functions of other words. For the other words, we can define the function (semantics) of a biological word in terms of other biological words, leading to a dictionary or ontology of such words.

The second property of a word is its Part of Speech which dictates the suitability of words to tie up with each other to give rise to grammatical sentences. An analogy can be drawn to valency of atoms, which is primarily responsible in dictating which molecules are possible and which are not. Biological words may have Parts of speech that dictate their ability to group together to form higher level units like sentences, using the composition of functions which has its analog in compositional semantics. The third property of a word is its morphology, which is its structure or form. This refers to the sequence of letters in the words. There are systematic ways in which the form of a root word (like sing) can be changed to give birth to new words (like singing). Two primary processes are inflection and derivation. This can be related to mutations in Biology, where we obtain a new sequence or structure by mutating the existing sequences/structures.

3 Concepts

Effective Dimensionality: The Vector Space Model (VSM) is used frequently as a formalism in Information Retrieval. When used over a large collection of documents as in the web, VSM pictures the webpages as vectors in a high dimensional vector space, where each dimension corresponds to a word. Interestingly, thanks to strong clustering properties exhibited by documents, this high dimensional space is only sparsely populated by real world documents. As an example to illustrate this, we would not expect a webpage to simultaneously talk about Margaret Thatcher, Diego Maradona and Machine Learning. Thus, more often than not, the space defined by intersection of two or more words is empty. The webspace is like the night sky: mostly dark and few clusters sprinkled in between. In IR parlance, we say that the effective dimensionality of the space is much less than the true dimensionality, and this fact can be exploited cleverly to overcome "curse of dimensionality" and to speed up retrieval. It is worth noting that the world of biological sequences is not very different. Of all the sequences that can be potentially generated, only a few correspond to stable configurations.

Ramachandran plot is used to understand constraints in protein conformations (Ramachandran, 1963). It plots possible $\phi - \psi$ angle pairs in protein structures based on the van der Waal radii of amino acids. It demonstrates that the protein conformational space is sparse and is concentrated in clusters of a few $\phi - \psi$ regions.

3.1 Machine Translation

Genes and mRNAs can be viewed as strings generated from four letters (A,T,C,G for genes and A,U,C,G for mRNAs). Proteins can be viewed as strings generated from twenty amino acids. In addition proteins and mRNAs have corresponding structures for which we do not even know the alphabets. The genes are storing a blue-print for synthesizing proteins. Whenever the cell requires a specific protein, the protein synthesis takes place, in which first the genes encoding that protein are read and are transcribed into mRNA which are then translated to make proteins with relevant amino acids. This is similar to writing the same document in multiple languages so that it can be consumed by the people familiar to different languages. Here the protein sequence is encoded in genes and is communicated in form of mRNA during the synthesis process. Another example is sequence and structure representations of protein: Both of them carry the same information specified in different forms.

3.2 Evolution of Languages

Language evolves over time to cater to evolution in our communication goals. New concepts originate which warrant revisions to our vocabulary. The language of mathematics has evolved to make communication more precise. Sentence structures evolve, often to address the bottlenecks faced by native speakers and second language learners. English, for example, has gone out of fashion. Thus there is a survival goal very closely coupled to the environment in which a language thrives that dictates its evolution. The situation is not very different in biology.

Scientific community believes that the life on the Earth started with prokaryotes[1] and evolved into eukaryotes. Prokaryotes inhibited earth from approximately 3-4 Billion years ago. About 500 million years ago, plant and fungi colonized the Earth. The modern human came into existence since 250,000 years. At a genetic level, new genes were formed by means of insertion, deletion and mutation of certain nucleotide with other nucleotides.

3.3 Garden Path Sentences

English is replete with examples where a small change in a sentence leads to a significant change in its meaning. A case in point is the sentence "He eats shoots and leaves", whose meaning changes drastically when a comma is inserted between "eats" and "shoots". This leads to situations where the meaning of a sentence cannot be composed by a linear composition of the meanings of words. The situation is not very different in biology, where the function of a sequence can change when any one element in the sequence changed.

3.4 Text and background knowledge needed to understand it

Interaction between the "book" and the reader is essential to comprehension; so language understanding is not just sophisticated modeling of interaction between words, sentences and discourse. Similarly the book of life (the gene sequence) does not have everything that is needed to determine function; it needs to be read by the reader (played by the CD player). This phenomenon is similar to protein/ gene interaction. Proteins/genes possess binding sites, that is used to bind other proteins/genes to form a complex, which carry out the desired function in the biological process.

3.5 Complexity of Dataset

Several measures have been proposed in the context of Information Retrieval and Text Classification which aim at capturing the complexity of a dataset. In unsupervised domains, a high clustering tendency indicates a low complexity and a low clustering tendency corresponds to a situation where the objects are spread out more or less uniformly in space. The latter situation corresponds to high complexity. In supervised domains, a dataset is said to be complex if objects that are similar to each other have same category labels. Interestingly, these ideas may apply in arriving at estimates of structure complexity. In particular, weak structure function correspondences would correspond to high complexity.

3.6 Stop words (function words) and their role in syntax

Function words such as articles, prepositions play an important role in understanding natural languages. On the same note, function words exist in Biology and they play various important roles depending on the context. For example, Protein structures are made up of secondary structures. Around 70% of these structures are α-helix and β-strands which repeat in functionally unrelated proteins. Based on this criterion, α-helix and β-strands can be categorized as functional words. These secondary structures are important in forming protein structural frame on which functional sites can be mounted. At genomic level, as much as 97% of human genome does not code for proteins and hence termed as junk DNA. This is another instance of function word in Biology. Scientists are realizing off late some important functions of these junk DNA such as their role in alternative splicing.

3.7 Natural Language Generation

Natural Language Generation (NLG) is complementary to Natural Language Understanding (NLU), in that it aims at constructing natural language text from a variety of non-textual representations like maps, graphs, tables and temporal data. NLG can be used to automate routine tasks like generation of memos, letters or simulation reports. At the creative end of the spectrum, an ambitious goal of NLG would be to compose jokes, advertisements, stories and poetry. NLG is carried out in four steps: (i) macroplanning; (ii)microplanning; (iii) surface realization and (iv) presentation. Macroplanning step uses Rhetorical Structure Theory (RST), which defines relations between units of text. For example, the relation cause connects the two sentences: "The hotel was

[1] http://www.wikipedia.org

costly." and "We started looking for a cheaper option". Other such relations are purpose, motivation and enablement. The text is organized into two segments; the first is called nucleus, which carries the most important information, and the second satellites, which provide a flesh around the nucleus. It seems interesting to look for a parallel of RST in the biological context.

Analogously protein design or artificial life design is a form of NLG in Biology. Such artificial organisms and genes/proteins can carry out specific tasks such as fuel production, making medicines and combating global warming. For example, Craig Venter and colleagues created synthetic genome in the lab and has filed a patent for the first life form created by humanity. These tasks are very similar to NLG in terms of scale and complexity.

3.8 Hyperlinks

Hyperlinks connect two or more documents through links. There is an analogy in Biology for hyperlinks. Proteins contain sites to bind with other molecules such as proteins, DNA, metals or any other chemical compound. The binding sites are similar to hyperlinks and enable protein-protein interaction and protein-DNA interaction.

3.9 Ambiguity and Context

An NLP system must be able to effectively handle ambiguities. The news headline "Stolen Painting Found by Tree" has two possible interpretations, though an average reader has no trouble favoring one over the other. In many situations, the context is useful in disambiguation. For example, protein function can be specified unambiguously with the help of biological process and cellular location. In other words, protein functions in the context of biological process and within a particular cellular location. In the context of protein structure, highly similar subsequences take different substructures such as α-helix or β-strand depending on their spatial neighborhood. Moonlighting proteins carry out multiple functions and their exact function can be determined only based on the context.

Let us consider the following example: "Mary ordered a pizza. She left a tip before leaving the restaurant." To understand the above sentences, the reader must have knowledge of what people typically do when they visit restaurants. Statistically mined associations and linguistic knowledge are both inadequate in capturing meaning when the background knowledge is absent. Background knowledge about function and interacting partners about a protein help in determining its structures.

4 Conclusion

In this paper, we presented a number of parallels between Linguistics and Biology. We believe that this line of thought process will lead to previously unexplored research directions and bring in new insights in our understanding of biological systems. Linguistics on other hand can also benefit from a deeper understanding of analogies with biological systems.

Acknowledgments

AVT is supported by Innovative Young Biotechnologist Award (IYBA) by Department of Biotechnology, Government of India.

References

David B. Searls. 2002. The language of genes *Nature*, 420:211–217.

G. N. Ramachandran, C. Ramakrishnan, and V. Sasisekharan. 1963. Stereochemistry of polypeptide chain configurations *Journal of Molecular Biology*, 7:95–99.

Author Index

Association for Computational Linguistics
209 N. Eighth Street
Stroudsburg, Pennsylvania 18360

CURRAN ASSOCIATES INC
proceedings.com

10th International Workshop on Finite State Methods and Natural Language Processing

(FSMNLP 2012)

Donostia, Spain
23-25 July 2012

ISBN: 978-1-62748-362-9